Paradox Lost

Free Will and

Political Liberty in

American Culture,

1630–1760

New Studies in American Intellectual
and Cultural History
Thomas Bender, Series Editor

Paradox
Lost

JON PAHL

The Johns Hopkins University Press
Baltimore and London

973.2
P14p

The Johns Hopkins University Press
701 West 40th Street
Baltimore, Maryland 21211-2190
The Johns Hopkins Press Ltd., London

LIBRARY OF CONGRESS CATALOGING-IN-PUBLICATION DATA

Pahl, Jon, 1958–
    Paradox lost : free will and political liberty in American culture, 1630–1760 / Jon Pahl.
        p.   cm.—(New studies in American intellectual and cultural history)
    Includes bibliographical references and index.
    ISBN 0-8018-4334-0 (alk. paper)
    1. United States—Intellectual life—17th century. 2. United States—Intellectual life—18th century. 3. Calvinism—United States—History.
4. Political culture—United States—History. 5. Free will and determinism—History. 6. Liberty—Religious aspects—Christianity. I. Title. II. Series.
E162.P135   1992
973.2—dc20   91-41849

For Barbara J. and Frederick C. Pahl,
My Parents

Contents

Preface

The World was all before them, where to choose
Thir place of rest, and Providence thir guide:
They hand in hand with wand'ring steps and slow,
Through Eden took thir solitary way.

MILTON

The first English writers to settle in North America knew their Bible. Like Milton, therefore, those early Americans were well schooled in a set of paradoxes. Creation was good, but fallen. Persons were pilgrims on a quest, but often wandered en route. Humans were free to choose, but were guided by providence. This book is the history of how this last paradox—of a free choice simultaneously guided by providence—was assumed, argued over, transformed, and lost in some surprising ways in early American culture.

Like Milton, in other words, the earliest intellectuals in America all had an inclusive dream of paradise regained in mind when they sent Adam and Eve, in their various incarnations, out into the "New World." And if the English writers and readers of North America quickly turned their time in paradise to selfish purposes not unlike those suggested by the original serpent, they also managed to remember and to remind themselves that the ideal was something other than what actually prevailed. The British colonizers used both "providence" and "choice" as excuses to dominate and subjugate women, Native Americans, or people of opposing creeds. But at the same time whenever the writers of early America saw someone else distorting or losing the paradox of choice guided by providence, they inevitably pointed it out.

Thus the conundrum of free will, of grace and works, of divine providence and human choice, dominated the intellectual production of early America. Are we, the colonists asked themselves and one another, beings whose destiny is wholly determined by an extrinsic Being or forces? Are we somehow responsible for our own choices and works? Are we free to live at random? I have studied nearly two hundred separate colonial publications on this question, written by clerics, lay people, philosophers, and theologians, and I know I have missed some. Why, aside from geographical confusion about Eden, were the British colonizers of North America so fascinated with this question? In the course of my study I have become convinced that the debates over *freedom* and *providence* and other such terms defined the boundaries of thought and action in early America as fully as military conflicts defined geographical boundaries. In other words, the primary reason free will was debated so vigorously in early America was because the settlers had to define for themselves whether their own wills were free, and how far that freedom could extend, in the process of building new communities, if not a "New World."

I have written for a broad audience, fully realizing that eighteenth-century theology and metaphysics will inevitably have a difficult time against MTV. Arcane arguments that might be clear enough to scholars I have also tried to make accessible to undergraduates and general readers with an interest in American history. Anyone who seeks to understand what is distinctive about the culture of the United States, and how that culture developed, should find my argument interesting. I was astonished to discover that English intellectuals in America almost universally asserted simultaneously that human beings had free choice and that this choice was guided by providence. This paradoxical conception of freedom is, it seems to me, perhaps our most noble and dangerous cultural artifact, if in fact *we* have not lost it too. So if this book stimulates debate over the ways in which language created American culture, ideologies legitimated violence, and freedom both expanded and became limited in the eighteenth century and remains so in the United States today, I shall consider it a success.

Two remaining problems suitable for attention in a preface call for some comment. The easy problem has to do with spelling and capitalization. Early American manuscripts are highly erratic and idiosyncratic in the matter of style. I have followed the Yale University Press edition of the *Works of Jonathan Edwards* in modernizing all of the spelling, capitalization, and punctuation in my primary sources (aside from the actual titles of early writings). What this loses in authenticity and nuance of meaning—and there is admittedly a loss—is compensated for in ease of reading.

The more difficult problem has to do with the apparent regional and national biases of my study. Although I do examine sources from places other than Massachusetts and Connecticut, the majority of my sources are from New England, most of them were published in Boston, and many of them were written by members of the religious elite. Such an apparently narrow sample for my evidence would seem to preclude the sweeping generalizations to which I am prone, and might appear to warrant a more modest subtitle: "Free Will and the Boston Soul," perhaps. Regionalism and pluralism have replaced cultural unity and consensus as the prevailing assumptions among historians of early America.

But I have resisted the temptation to temper my rhetoric because I believe my full argument will bear out my conclusions. Historical contexts are as much the product of the historian's perspectives, choices, and language as is the meaning of any text. Obviously, we have no direct access to any place in the colonies in 1742. The circumstances that shaped human life in eighteenth-century Boston, or Richmond, or Baltimore, or New York must be as carefully reconstructed by historians as the meaning of any historical document. Hence, I call my "Boston" sources "American" because I believe they may be representative, but I also recognize that this usage will ring more or less true to a reader's experience. I expect that the implications of my study would be refined from different perspectives. And in any event, I hope others will be inspired or provoked to test my hypotheses in different venues. I shall welcome verifications, consider falsifications, and entertain qualifications or improvements from other contexts.

Similarly, even if drawn only from Boston, the idea of a cultural consensus—also currently out of favor among historians—does not need to be imperialistic. It may well be that a lack of cultural identity and integrity promotes greater violence than consensus. Even the most localized sampling from colonial American history reveals an inherently fluid and pluralistic culture, and my study confirms this. The consensus I find concerning free will in early America is a consensus in conflict. So if I do seem to write a lot about New England Calvinists, I take their relations to their environment and their interactions and debates with Anglicans, Quakers, Indians, blacks, and Enlightenment *philosophes* as the key to understanding the process of American cultural formation.

In short, the story I tell is by no means only or even primarily the story of Puritan New England. It is a story of debate, of the power of language, of the use and misuse of words. Historians of early America need not be, as one critic put it, "by Puritanism possessed." But the Puritans were part of the story. What I claim is that the debates of these seventeenth- and eighteenth-century men and women over the fundamental human question of free will reveal a part of what living in American culture has unavoidably come to mean. Even today, no thoughtful observer of life in the United States can avoid wondering about the meaning and uses of liberty.

Acknowledgments

The support I have received in writing this book over the past nine years has made my scholarship delightful. Without Lisa, my wife, and her many gifts, I would not have begun to write this, much less completed it. To Martin E. Marty goes the credit for whatever humane irony found its way into these pages, and whatever historical grace. From Jerald Brauer and Robin Lovin I learned how freedom can work, and from James Gustafson I learned how work can be free when done before God.

The Charlotte W. Newcombe Foundation, the University of Chicago Divinity School Fellowship Program, the Valparaiso University Faculty Fellowship Program, and the Religion Indexes of the American Theological Library Association helped to keep me economically solvent. To Jerry D. Weber, Craig Forney, Ellen Babinsky, Ken Sawyer, Bernard McGinn, and the Fellows of the Institute for the Advanced Study of Religion at the University of Chicago, 1987–88, I owe many thanks for good conversation.

The librarians at the American Antiquarian Society in Worcester, Massachusetts, the Joseph Regenstein Library and the Jesuit-Krauss-McCormick Library in Chicago, and the Moellering Library in Valparaiso have saved me many wasted steps, as have my research assistants at Valparaiso University, Celeste Duder and Jaclyn Jesse. My editors at the Johns Hopkins University Press—notably Henry Tom, Peter Dreyer, Anne Whitmore, Tom Bender, and Barbara Lamb—have made many helpful suggestions. And finally, to my colleagues at Valparaiso University, and especially the "Young Turks"—Betty DeBerg, Rick DeMaris, and Julian Kunnie—I give thanks for their friendship and solidarity. And to Justin and Nathan Pahl, I hope you find your Eden someday, too.

Paradox Lost

Introduction

*Those whom he predestined he also called; and
those whom he called he also justified; and those
whom he justified he also glorified.* ROM. 8:30

*I call heaven and earth to witness against you this
day, that I have set before you life and death,
blessing and curse; therefore choose life, that you
and your descendants may live.* DEUT. 30:19

*The wind blows where it wills, and you hear the
sound of it, but you do not know whence it comes
or whither it goes; so it is with every one who is
born of the spirit.* JOHN 3:8

When human beings first began to record in writing what they saw
and did, around the third millennium B.C.E., they quickly discovered
a problem. On the one hand, it seemed obvious from everything
ordinary going on around them—the alternation from day to night,
the change of the seasons, the orderly motion of the stars, the course
of birth, aging, and death—that there was an order to the universe
that was not humanly created or controlled. On the other hand,
there were anomalies, opportunities, tears in the fabric of the established order. Some things could be changed and improved, like shel-
ter, cultivation, actions, and associations. And some things were
strange, sudden, unexplainable deviations from the ordinary order,
like storms or wars or sudden death. In other words, humans observed both order and chaos, limit and license. And out of observations like these develops the problem of free will.[1]

The Babylonians were among the first to notice the problem,
although like most people they preferred to do something about it

rather than to reflect upon it. Thus they took to star-watching, writing, and reading animal entrails, and while we may wonder about the truth value of ox intestines, the Babylonians had little doubt that there was a connection between them and historic events. So the scribes recorded the diviner's findings in omen texts, and these texts were in turn used to determine the portents for an individual action, usually by the king, but sometimes for the nation as a whole. The underlying assumption, captured by the Akkadian word *shimtu,* was that all was "fated," determined, or predestined.[2]

But disasters kept happening. So specialists tried to discern and to control *shimtu.* And if the Babylonians wasted a lot of time on astrology and entrail-reading, they also wrote treaties, covenants, literary works, and law codes.[3] If *shimtu* could not be completely controlled, perhaps at least it could be tamed or predicted. Thus fate was linked to good or evil behavior, or to maintaining a proper relation to the god who controlled the tablets of fate.[4] By all accounts, court astrologers and diviners exercised an extraordinary degree of influence over Babylonian public affairs.[5] The problem was becoming sharper. If there was this inexorable order, what good were treaties, or covenants, or law codes? What power did human beings have if all was fated?[6] Which was the truer conception—predetermined fate or personal justice?

The ancient Greeks took over this problem, wrote epics and tragedies about it, and began arguing over it. Fate, or moira, is perhaps the dominant theme in the Homeric literature. Often, even Zeus cannot undo what destiny decrees; at other times fate is linked with the will of the gods.[7] Thales of Miletus (ca. 625?–?547 B.C.E.), Anaximander (ca. 610–ca. 547 B.C.E.), and their pupils took over the ideas of order and destiny from the Homeric legends and left behind talk of the Moirai and the gods as anthropomorphic superstition. Geometry and philosophy were born in this ancient process of secularization, and astronomy (as opposed to astrology) was reborn.[8] And of course Plato and Aristotle searched the depths of physics, metaphysics, ethics, and politics for answers to the question of where voluntary human action fit into the cosmic order.[9]

But it was Epicurus (341–270 B.C.E.) who dramatically changed the course of the problem. He explicitly denied the doctrine of fate, and, drawing upon the teachings of Democritus (460–370 B.C.E.), argued that "it would be better to subscribe to the popular mythology than to become a slave by accepting the determinism of the natural philosophers."[10] For Epicurus and thinkers like him, the entire cosmos was made up of constantly moving atoms that could spontaneously and capriciously change direction.[11] Consequently, what was truly real was flux, or, as Democritus had designated it, *automaton*, the whirl, indeterminism, chance, or chaos. A refuge could be found in choosing good friends and by appreciating momentary pleasures. This seems sensible enough, but in fact for the next seven centuries the Stoics and Epicureans had a running argument over fate and freedom, with the Stoics and their doctrine of resignation usually winning.[12]

Meanwhile, a small, subjugated nation was beginning to record its own traditions in writing. For the compilers of the books of the Hebrew Bible, and for later Jewish thinkers such as Philo of Alexandria, the problem of free will was usually subsumed under the problem of evil.[13] The redactors of the Hebrew Bible left the sacrificial animals with their intestines and concentrated on the struggle between good and its opposite. They simply assumed, giving Yahweh the credit where the Babylonians were due, that there would be laws, treaties, and covenants. Did this not imply human freedom to choose whether to obey or to break the covenant, as the Deuteronomist suggested? From another angle, if God decreed everything, was God not also responsible for evil? Among Hebrew Scriptures, the book of Job raised this issue explicitly, but gave at best an equivocal answer, while Habakkuk presented the opinion of the moralistic majority.

In the Hellenistic age, around the time of Jesus, these various approaches to the problem of free will coalesced. Jesus had nothing to do with this, but Paul, and later, Augustine, preserved the question of free will while also again altering its form.[14] Paul juxtaposed grace and works in a way that seemed reminiscent of Stoic resignation, but in fact his thought was indebted to the Hebrew theological and ethical paradigm. Romans put it well: God's predestination also justifies and glorifies human beings; grace does not abolish the law but fulfills it. For Paul, Christ neither freed humans to evade the categories of good and evil nor forced resignation to them; rather, the cross made human action possible again for people who ordinarily could "will what is right, but could not do it."[15]

Augustine (354–430 C.E.) was among the first thinkers to discuss a discrete human "will."[16] After Paul, Christian thinkers had generally stressed human freedom to choose between good and evil, largely because they hated the astrologers.[17] Augustine in contrast emphasized original sin, or an inherited human propensity to evil; predestination, or the predetermination by God of individuals to heaven or hell; and grace, or the doctrine that salvation was wholly a gift to human beings. He emphasized these doctrines because he hated Pelagius (d. 419 C.E.), a Briton who had emigrated to Rome preaching, of all things, a legalistic version of Pauline grace that stressed human free will. Augustine never denied humans free choice, but his characteristic emphases limited the range of human freedom by emphasizing the human tendency to choose evil. For Augustine, questions of cosmology and ethics—cosmic order and the nature of good and evil—were subordinate to theology and anthropology. The problem of free will was now almost entirely about God and human nature rather than about fate, chance, and justice.[18]

Thus, by the fourth century of the common era in the West a variety of forms of the problem of free will, not to mention solutions, had been posed. Astrologers, Stoics, Epicureans, Augustinian Christians, Pelagian Christians, and Jewish rabbis all contended for their particular point of view concerning order and spontaneity in the cosmos. Teachers advocated fatalism, freedom, chance, and many combinations in between. On through the Middle Ages and down to the early modern period, these basic paradigms prevailed. There were a few notable shake-ups. In the wake of the Arab rediscovery of Democritus, Epicurus, and, above all, Aristotle, Thomas Aquinas (1225–74) clarified the relation between nature and grace in a way that Augustine had not. His solution posited a significant degree of liberty for human beings, not unlike the Johannine emphasis on the freedom of the spirit.[19] Grace fulfilled and completed nature without obliterating it.

Partly in reaction to extreme interpretations of Aquinas, Martin Luther (1483–1546) reemphasized Augustine's immediate connection of grace and salvation. In his famous debate over free will with the Catholic humanist Desiderius Erasmus, Luther stressed the hiddenness, foreknowledge, and power of God over free will because he believed this was the only way humans could be saved.[20] Left to themselves, people turned in on themselves, and even the best works of free will were tainted with evil self-interest and led nowhere but to hell. Consequently, for Luther, the study of nature, ethics, and even human nature was at best a secondary concern to trust in God. Free will was a problem with no solution but faith.

Unfortunately, Luther and Erasmus never resolved their debate, and everyone lost as a result. They had agreed that God's grace and human works were paradoxically related, but they could not agree on the specific formulation of their relationship.[21] Following the Reformation and into the early modern period (to 1800), debates over fate and freedom, free will, and necessity raged almost endlessly, often with civil and political ramifications.[22] Every serious thinker felt obligated to wrestle with the problem. The most influential among them somehow persuaded (or paid) a publisher to print their reflections, and princes and rulers picked their favorite publications and went to war. Germany was rocked throughout the late sixteenth and early seventeenth centuries by religious wars that were as much over free will, nature and grace, and faith and works as anything else.[23]

But the problem was not just the Teutonic mind. A little later, Catholic France was torn by conflict between "fatalist" Jansenists and "free will" Jesuits.[24] In the early seventeenth century, the Dutch all but had a civil war over whether High Calvinists who advocated "necessity" or Arminian Calvinists who advocated "free will" possessed the truth.[25] And in mid-seventeenth-century England, a civil war did break out between Calvinistic Puritans and Anti-Calvinist Arminians.[26] It was during the unrest leading up to this last war that many English Calvinists sought to escape the conflict by settling in the "New World." And so they did.

In the culture those European colonists brought with them to North America, then, theological doctrine intermingled with political ideology. No colonist to North America could avoid knowing something about the paradoxes of the Christian story, and most knew them well. For many colonists, praying was a part of politics, and myth was a form of reason.[27] And, according to the myth they knew best, the ideal life, and the ideal "kingdom," embraced the most diverse and contradictory extremes—such as God and "man"—in an inclusive whole.[28] How these contradictions related and were to be applied was always the problem.[29]

Most broadly, the colonists of North America were agents in that experiment, common to the early modern world and still continuing, to define the proper relationship between spiritual and political power. Because there were openly competing political formulations of the right relation between the theory and practice of freedom, Christians often came to understand freedom less as an inclusive spiritual gift than as a private or tribal possession.[30] In other words, between 1630 and 1760, the American colonists transformed the Christian myth into political ideologies that legitimated *particular* locations of power and party positions, and that at best promoted debate, at worst physical violence, between the various parties.[31]

It is this process of distorting myth that I call the loss of paradox. The human will became an object to itself, first in churches, and eventually in nations, and was therefore exploited increasingly in violence against both nature and other people, all in the name of God. Most often in the colonies, at least between the Europeans themselves, debate prevailed over physical violence. The paradox was not completely lost. But although, in their debates to define freedom, the European settlers of North America struggled honestly to establish political order and to preserve the life of the spirit, they also defined the life of the spirit narrowly. In so doing, they created some tragic, and lasting, exclusions.

In short, I have written a history of the debates over free will in the colonies from 1630 to 1760 that explores the contours, causes, and consequences of those debates. I utilize a fivefold typology, best conceived of as a continuum of positions, to sort out the debates and to identify the parties.[32] "Determinism," called "necessity," "fate," or, imprecisely, "Stoicism" in the eighteenth century, is at one extreme of the continuum. Advocates of fatalism argued that everything that happened had to happen, and that everything originated or was predetermined outside of human action. Human agency was, in fact, a fiction. Moral accountability was ruled out by advocates of this position, and freedom of the will denied, since there was, strictly speaking, neither an act to be judged moral or immoral nor a will to be free. Benjamin Franklin expressed such a position in print on his first trip to Europe in 1725, only to drop it upon his permanent return to the colonies.[33] In fact, none of the leading intellectuals in early America advocated the concept of pure necessity. This avoidance of the fatalist extreme was an enduring contribution of this theological debate over freedom to American thought and culture.

"Indeterminism," "chance," or, as the Calvinist theologian Jonathan Edwards described it in 1754, "absolute blind contingence," was on the opposite end of the continuum from determinism. Also called "Epicureanism" and "enthusiasm" in the colonies, indeterminism stressed the intrinsic causes of events, where every atom or at the least every human individual was its own agent and thus free to act more or less at random. Anne Hutchinson was among those tagged with the Epicurean label. She hardly deserved this, but aspects of her thought—and that of other spiritualist and mystical groups in America, such as the Quakers—were indeterministic. The leading colonial intellectuals, however, were both antifatalist and anti-Epicurean. In the seventeenth and eighteenth centuries, enthusiasm was a vice, often violently repressed. Together, opposition to the extremes of fatalism and enthusiasm combined in the colonies with constructive, but also devastating, consequences.

In between the two extremes were the three positions typically favored by the leading colonial writers. All three attempted to mediate between fatalism and chance, but in doing so favored one side or the other, or dimmed the extremes, of the paradox. The position closest to fatalism, but allowing that humans had a limited degree of liberty of action was called variously "inclining necessity," "moral necessity," or "regular necessity," and has more recently been identified as "soft determinism."[34] Advocates of this position stressed that the word *freedom* meant primarily, if not solely, freedom from physical coercion. Causes operated for the most part independently and from outside human beings, most notably by the agency of God, so that humans were driven by necessity, with some few exceptions. American Calvinists especially advocated this position. In fact, they developed it into an ideology of providence I call the "predestinarian ideology" or the public theology of the "aristocracy of grace."[35]

Opposed to Calvinists and their doctrine of predestination, but like them advocating a mediating position on free will, were the advocates of "innate liberty." This position was close to chance, but it held to enough of a doctrine of providence to fall short of complete indeterminism. Colonial Anglicans and Enlightenment *philosophes* often argued that humans were free to achieve pretty much whatever they chose, even to a degree to contradict God or fate, and this freedom mirrored a similarly limited indeterminism in the cosmos.[36] God gave human beings liberty to effect change through their various innate or developed abilities. In the eighteenth-century colonies, this anti-Calvinism flourished—the mature Franklin is a good example—and developed into an ideology of providence of its own, which as a public theology I designate the "democracy of law."

Finally, between regular necessity and limited indeterminism was free choice. Advocates of this position held that people chose, but that their choices were also free gifts. By 1760 many Calvinists and Anglicans—representing the two largest theological parties in the colonies—supported this position. Human beings were neither compelled nor capricious, but were susceptible to reason, grace, persuasion, affection, providence, motives, and a whole host of other "gifts." In the eighteenth century, in other words, to assert "free choice" meant to recognize that life was both a gift and a task, something given and something to be developed. If advocates of this position thus came closest to embodying in language the paradoxical ideal that brought together God's order and human spontaneity, they also limited liberty in accord with the political situation of their time. Only certain groups or individuals were free to choose—essentially those identified with the other two predominant public theologies in the colonies—the "aristocracy of grace" and the "democracy of law." Nevertheless, by 1760 "free choice" was the predominant ideology of providence in the colonies. I call the public theology of its advocates the "republic of virtue," and I believe it forms the most distinctive theological contribution to American culture.

In short, my argument is that in the interplay between myth and politics in early America, politics prevailed in a way that limited liberty to advocates of the three mediating positions on the question of free will, and "free choice" above all. And, if it seems obvious that this eighteenth-century conception of free choice preserved a considerable range of the Christian myth, at the same time it did so in a way that ruled out or dimmed, rather than included, the extremes. The single greatest legacy of the colonial debates over free will, in other words, was the assumption that *particular* human beings or communities—namely, those gathered around the three ideologies of providence—mediated the very work of God through their own acts of free choice. Consequently, people who were thought to represent the extremes, most notably Indians, women, enthusiasts, and Africans, were excluded from participation in political life. I call this anti-extremism—as expressed by the advocates of the three competing, but compatible, ideologies of providence—the "establishment of mediation." It also seems to me that to understand how this "establishment of mediation" developed and functioned is to understand even today the source of both the greatest virtues and vices of American culture, both the expansive openness and the provincial idolatry of the American understanding of liberty.

Such modesty behind me, I had best begin to back this claim up. The story has four parts. Part 1, "The Trial of the Center, 1630–1700," highlights the mythic dimension of Puritan covenant theology and how this was distorted in colonial New England into an ideology of predestination. The Puritans encountered a flourishing natural environment and plural Indian civilizations upon landing in New England; an environment and civilizations, furthermore, they felt called to rule. Chapter 1 analyzes the civil and ecclesiastical trials of Anne Hutchinson in early Boston as a paradigmatic struggle between myth and politics. Hutchinson was banished from Massachusetts by John Winthrop and John Cotton because she represented an extreme of piety that seemed dangerous to political control. Chapter 2 demonstrates the same process at work in the self-definition of a Puritan clergyman, Thomas Shepard, and in the treatment of the Indian cultures by the colonists. The "Saints," as the Calvinists called themselves, felt called to rule by ruling out anything in themselves or others—most notably the Pequots, Wampanoags, Narragansetts, and Mohegans—that reminded them of chance or chaos. Chapter 3 describes the first real debate over free will in the colonies—between Samuel Willard, president of Harvard, and George Keith, a Quaker who converted to Anglicanism. In that debate, Willard had to defend the claims of the Calvinist aristocracy of grace to be "the true middle." Part 1 thus traces the way the Puritans, rebels in England, became rulers in America.

Part 2, "Anti-Calvinism, 1700–1730" follows what happened after the Puritans established control over New England. In brief, the limits of the predestinarian ideology were exposed by a range of anti-Calvinist critics, all of them laymen, which suggests at the least a possible tension between lay and clerical theology in the early eighteenth-century colonies. Chapter 4 sketches how the earliest Quaker antislavery writings in America were linked to a critique of the doctrine of predestination. Chapter 5 traces the growth of the Anglican church in the colonies, and especially looks at a tract by the Boston Arminian John Checkley challenging predestinarian ideology. And chapter 6 describes "Enlightenment thought" in America, as exemplified by the writings of Benjamin Franklin, as an anti-Calvinist critique. This chapter also hints that the "innate liberty" and "democracy of law" so dear to Franklin, who himself invented the term *public theology,* was as anti-extremist, as compatible with a notion of providence, and as susceptible to ideological distortion as predestination.

Part 3, "The Prelude to Debate, 1721–1743," traces the creative and divergent ways Calvinists responded to the anti-Calvinist challenges. Chapter 7 describes Cotton Mather's various attempts to support predestinarian ideology, most notably his tract *The Christian Philosopher* (1715), in which he attempted to use Newtonian science to support the providence of God. If Mather's work indicated one direction Calvinist elites might develop their ideology, the widespread conversions to Christianity of the 1730s and 1740s, since known as the "Great Awakening," indicated another direction for popular thought. Chapter 8 describes the way some Calvinists— most notably Jonathan Edwards, James Davenport, and Sarah Parsons Moorhead—developed a "rhetoric of fortune" to encourage conversions. In the process, some of the inclusive features of myth were restored to the predestinarian ideology, with lasting political consequences. Chapter 9 sketches how the revivals produced a "strange revolution" in colonial thought by simultaneously legitimating a mythic quest for inclusion and ideological contention between two parties—the revivalistic "aristocracy of grace" and the opposing "democracy of law." Perhaps the most enduring contribution of revivalism to American culture was this increased public debate about theology.

Part 4, "Harmony in Discord, 1734–1760," thus explores the debate over free will that took place both before and after the revivals. Chapter 10 argues that the Great Awakening was in many ways a failed strategy to revive predestinarian ideology and thereby produce Calvinist hegemony. Chapter 11 sketches how this failure promoted debate—an American Arminian controversy, largely between the Calvinist Jonathan Dickinson, Presbyterian minister at Elizabethtown, New Jersey, and first president of the College of New Jersey (Princeton), and the Anglican Samuel Johnson, first president of King's College (Columbia). Through their debate, the participants exemplified and legitimated the peculiar eighteenth-century American understanding of "free choice." Chapter 12 identifies how Jonathan Edwards's *Freedom of the Will* (1754) synthesized the competing discourses and, in fact, supported the "establishment of mediation." Ever after in American culture, within a pluralistic consensus, advocates of the distinct ideologies would contest as equals, in a society where some people at least would be free to choose between them.

In a lengthy epilogue that doubles as conclusion to my argument and (through the notes) as a bibliographic essay, I consider how this pluralistic consensus and the contest between the "aristocracy of grace" and the "democracy of law" may well have been a charter for an American "republic of virtue." In the most general terms, this debate over free will seems to have produced a distinctive ethos, sanctioned by all of the weight of eighteenth-century science, in the colonies. Free will had become a guiding problem in American culture, and the mediating positions became a guiding pattern—a tradition.[37] As the colonists struggled in the wilderness to gain legitimacy in all of their enterprises, the reflective among them invariably turned to the issue upon which all legitimate striving was founded— the question of free will. And the answers these colonial thinkers gave not surprisingly led them to positions that encouraged the virtu-

*Eighteenth-Century Positions Regarding Freedom of the Will and
American Public Theologies*

| | | Ideologies of Providence | | | |
	Necessity	Predesti-nation	Free Choice	Innate Liberty	Chance
Grace	Transcendent, imputed	Inclining, irresistible	Cooperating	Innate merit	Immanent, spiritual
Causality	Extrinsic	Mixed	Mixed	Mixed	Intrinsic
Definition of liberty	None	Liberty from coercion (to act)	Liberty to choose (from reason)	Liberty to effect (from ability)	Random (absolute)
Public theology	Tyranny	Aristocracy of grace	Republic of virtue	Democracy of law	Anarchy

NOTE: The distinctions between types of causality follow Aristotle. Advocates of predestination generally ascribed the material cause of the will's motion to human beings; advocates of free choice generally held out for both material and formal causes within the human will; natural libertarians attributed material, formal, and final causality to the human will, regarding only First Cause as extrinsic.

ous efforts of human freedom as oriented by the grace and order of God. Tragically, they increasingly interpreted this freedom to mean subordinating women, slaughtering Indians, or enslaving Africans.

Over time, in other words, the colonists began to perceive freedom as their own; as something that they had earned. Liberty was their "right," and to be deprived of it meant nothing less than to submit to "arbitrary tyranny."[38] Thus by 1775 King George could be described as a fatal "tyrant" and the slogan of the American revolution could become "liberty," and everyone would know the difference. In short, the rhetoric of the American revolution may have had theological roots in the debate over free will. Human beings are inescapably verbal. We have always been defined by our words more than we have defined them ourselves. This was especially the case in the eighteenth century, when words were nothing less than the medium through which the divine became manifest.

In short, the debates over free will from 1630 to 1760 did not merely produce quaint theological and metaphysical rhetoric. Put positively, there may have been a fundamental congruity between the anti-extremist ideologies early American intellectuals adopted when thinking about free will and the revolt against "tyranny," on the one hand, and the "ordering" of liberty into a republic, on the other, that these same thinkers, or their heirs and students, undertook when they had the chance. The American republic may have had theological roots.

In the end, my argument suggests the need for a theologically sophisticated rereading of the documents from 1760 to 1800 that are the charter of the republic. I believe such a rereading would provide some interesting insights into the origins of American culture. It may well be that what the founders established in the structure of U.S. political theory was a contest between a more or less Calvinistic and aristocratic public theology and a more or less Arminian and democratic one in a vision of an American "republic of virtue." This accomplishment, if that is what it was, may well have been foreshadowed, if not foreordained, by the religious factions present in the colonies and the typical positions their leaders took on the question of free will.

I

The Trial
of the
Center,
1630–1700

When the soul loves its own power, it slips from the common whole to its own particular part. Had it followed God as its ruler in the universal creature, it could have been most excellently governed by His laws. But in that apostatizing pride, which is called "the beginning of sin," it sought for something more than the whole; and while it struggled to govern it by its own laws, it was thrust into caring for a part, since there is nothing more than the whole; and so by desiring something more, it becomes less.

SAINT AUGUSTINE

Like Augustine, the Puritans who settled New England believed in, talked about, and practiced rituals designed to uphold the common whole. In other words, the Puritans understood myth. And the particular cosmic story they told themselves depicted a series of compacts or covenants between the Trinitarian God and himself, and between God and humanity, by means of which the entire course of history had begun, continued, and would eventually end. This "covenant theology" functioned to establish the symbolic center of the Puritan world.[1] It was their totem, their maypole, a constant source of orient.[2] God had a plan for the whole cosmos and an agreement with humanity to carry it out.

So even if we can hardly imagine New England's first settlers dancing around the doctrine that established the compatibility of God's grace and human action, they often and explicitly expressed an ideal that centered the whole. Puritans pledged allegiance to the federal or covenant theology clear through the mid eighteenth century.[3] Furthermore, this inclusive ideal of a center between the necessity of the Father and the freedom of the spirit was not an aberrancy in Puritan doctrine; it was not a way to evade "the shadow and tyranny of the doctrine of divine coercion,"[4] but a foundation—an *axis mundi* or pillar of the universe—of the Puritan mythos.[5]

But this inclusive center did not hold. Founded as it was in abstractions, rather than in, say, a cosmic tree, it was liable to move.[6] And in the midst of the wilderness, in their transition from rebels to rulers, the Puritans preserved their center by distorting it; by choosing a part rather than the whole. When outspoken women seemed to threaten the social order, when impulses in the self were deemed uncontrollable, when alienated Indians seemed to threaten Puritan civilization, or even when competing interpretations of the Christian myth began to contest with their own, the Puritans shifted toward and solidified their center in the direction of necessity. Far from fleeing coercion, they embraced it.

In other words, as Augustine said it, the Puritans chose their own part—their own laws. Today we would say that they framed an ideology. And if by framing this ideology, the Puritans kept the peace in New England, they also lost the whole. Through their answer to the problem of free will, the Puritan settlers of New England defined and legitimated a particular locus of power in a human community. By doing so, they left many out. But they also contributed to the American ethos one answer to the problem of free will that was, for better or worse, to be of lasting import in the development of a new nation.

1 "It Overthrows All"

Anne Hutchinson, John Wheelwright, and a band of other colonists were banished from Massachusetts in 1637 after a series of civil and ecclesiastical trials. Remembering these "antinomians" or "law-opposers" from the comfortable vantage of five years and several score miles, Governor John Winthrop still recalled that "it was a wonder of mercy that they had not set our Common-wealth and Churches on fire, and consumed us all therein."[1] Or, as Winthrop put it in the midst of the trial of Anne Hutchinson, just after she claimed to have experienced an "immediate revelation" from God, "It overthrows all."[2]

Now this antinomian controversy was "about" many things (almost simultaneously with it, the Puritans undertook the massacre of the Pequot Indians), but it was above all about the question of free will—about myth, ideology, and political control.[3] Three parties were central. To his peers, John Cotton, New England's most famous preacher, represented High Calvinism, or a position of fatalistic necessity. At the other extreme was Anne Hutchinson, who came to represent the opposite of Cotton's doctrine, or Epicurean chance. And in between, in what would pass for the center, was Winthrop, the foremost advocate of the covenant.[4] But the covenant being developed by Winthrop and the Puritan establishment threatened to abandon the full range of grace for political control. For having the audacity to point this out, Anne Hutchinson was banished to Rhode Island. The Puritans had chosen a part, rather than the whole, and if in the process they kept their society together, in the long run their choices also brought destruction.

I

John Cotton arrived in Boston, Massachusetts, in 1633, having fled Boston, Lincolnshire, after being summoned as a Puritan to appear before the Court of High Commission. And while there can be little doubt that Cotton's religious practice at St. Botolph's in Lincolnshire had been "Puritan," his theology had drawn accusations of "Arminianism," among Puritans the most dreaded of heretical deviations on the matter of free will.[5] For instance, Cotton had written that "nothing did put upon Adam any necessity of breaking" the law, thus conceivably denying God's control over the course of events prior to the Fall and giving more room to human liberty.[6] This was a characteristic move of Arminians. Cotton's theology was so suspect that it drew a detailed critique from William Twisse, one of the most zealous defenders of anti-Arminian "High Calvinism" in England.[7]

Cotton was duly repentant after this inquisition, but throughout his career in England, his theology remained moderate. Even after this inquiry, Cotton could argue on the question of the will that "the Holy Ghost in every good action, doth not turn the course of my faculty and affection against their proper and voluntary bent: For then we should not do good actions voluntarily . . . and then we should lose our reward."[8] Arminians emphasized the same points. Indeed, the predominance of such statements in Cotton's early writings led his modern biographer Larzer Ziff to conclude that the young minister preached a "gentle species of Calvinism."[9]

In contrast, Cotton clearly became the representative of "High

Calvinism" in New England. He preached absolute grace and human passivity before God, which was as close as a Puritan came to what would later be called determinism.[10] Especially on the topic of causality, Cotton stressed the priority of God's decree in the chain of events leading to salvation. There was no active role for human agency, reason, or will in this process. Grace originated completely apart from human action, in the extrinsic decrees of God. When it came to salvation, human beings were nothing but "living stones" rolled about by the will of God.[11] The reason for this shift in Cotton's thinking from "gentle" Calvinism to High Calvinism is the key to understanding his role in the antinomian controversy.

The course of the controversy is well known.[12] Anne Hutchinson, who had worshipped at Cotton's parish in England, followed him to New England in 1634. Married to a successful merchant, Hutchinson began to hold weekly meetings at her home for those women unable to attend public sermons. Beginning in the summer of 1635, and continuing through 1636, Hutchinson's meetings became increasingly popular, drawing men as well as women, including three deputies to the General Court—William Aspinwall, William Coddington, and John Coggeshall. Cotton apparently knew of the meetings, in which Hutchinson explained sermons and Scripture, and did not disapprove.

In October 1635, after John Wilson, Cotton's senior pastor in the Boston church, returned from overseas, the tone of the meetings became increasingly critical. Wilson especially was a target of Hutchinson's critiques, but apparently most of the other New England ministers also failed to meet her standards. This criticism led to a move by what was now clearly a faction in the church to "censure" Wilson in January 1637. The censure failed, obstructed primarily by John Winthrop, who had recently been demoted from the governorship.

As the elections for the year 1637 approached, Winthrop, in his role as deputy governor, managed to shift the site of the voting to Cambridge, away from Boston and the Hutchinson faction. Given this maneuvering, he was restored to the governorship, and he acted immediately to deal with Hutchinson. Winthrop alerted those clergy who had not already perceived things his way that they had a problem on their hands. A series of letters had been exchanged earlier between representatives of the clergy and John Cotton, who was being claimed as their legitimate leader by the Hutchinsonians. And it was in this exchange, and in the civil and ecclesiastical "trials" of Hutchinson that followed, that the transformation in the thought of John Cotton from a mild to a High Calvinist became apparent.

The first sign of change was in mid 1636, when Peter Bulkeley, minister at Concord, questioned Cotton on the matter of causality. Both Bulkeley and Cotton worked with ease the four Aristotelian causes—efficient, material, formal, and final.[13] For Bulkeley, the process of salvation included the *anima rationalis*, or rational soul, as the formal cause of salvation. "*Forma dat esse*," form gives being, stated Bulkeley; and "*Anima rationalis* gives the being to the human, and is not merely passive."[14] In other words, human reason contributed somehow in the process of salvation. This was a characteristic postulate of moderate Calvinists.

For Cotton, however, this postulate was no longer tenable. His response to Bulkeley summarized the four causes as follows: "The spirit of God is the principal and next efficient cause. . . . The humbled sinner, the material cause. The grace (or habit) of faith the formal cause. The glory of grace, and the salvation of the sinner, the final cause."[15] For Cotton, even the formal cause of salvation needed to be clearly grounded in the gift of God's grace in faith. "*Anima rationalis* makes a man to be what he is, a man," argued Cotton, "and so united to Adam" and his sin.[16] The gentle Calvinist had turned into the most rigorous defender of orthodoxy. No means, apart from God's order of causes, could contribute to salvation. Reason needed to be humbled for salvation to occur, not used.

Shortly after this exchange with Bulkeley, Cotton was again questioned on the matter of causality, among other things, in a list of sixteen "serious and necessary" questions compiled by a group of prominent New England ministers. Cotton responded as fully as was befitting his status as "the most learned of the New England preachers."[17] A critical area of inquiry was the relation between the doctrine of sanctification—literally, how humans become "holy" or do good works—and justification, or how humans are "made right" before God. Bulkeley and most of the rest of the ministers asserted that sanctification was a "ground" or "evidence" of justification.

Cotton objected, or rather, qualified: "To give my Sanctification for an evident ground, [and] cause, or matter of my justification, is to build my justification upon my sanctification, and to go on in a covenant of works."[18] This latter accusation raised the Protestant taboo against works-righteousness. Cotton was adamant that no human contribution could cause even assurance of salvation, much less its reality. He was removing, in short, what Max Weber much later identified as the major bulwark against fatalism, namely, "the doctrine of proof."[19] Salvation was God's work, and God was jealous when his prerogatives were infringed on.

The combined New England clergy understandably bristled at being accused of the doctrinal equivalent of adultery by Cotton. They issued a lengthy response to the Boston teacher, going over the sixteen questions in more detail and peppering their responses with phrases such as "We much want satisfaction."[20] Cotton just as quickly issued a rejoinder, which has been aptly described as "the most important exposition of [his] theology at the time of the Controversy."[21] In this piece, Cotton repeatedly stated his intention to reduce belief in intrinsic causality and to advance the creed of God's causative role in all affairs. He sought to establish himself as a defender of the strictest interpretation of the faith.

It will not "stand with the glory of grace," Cotton objected, "to bring us to rest or assurance of peace in Christ, in the mediation of our Works."[22] Anything other than pure divine causality smacked of Catholicism. "If we will speak as Protestants, we must not speak of good works as causes or ways of our first assurance."[23] The point could be made positively as well: "The way to find the God of Israel declaring himself a merciful God unto our Souls in the pardon of our Sins, is rather to come with halters about our necks . . . than with golden chains of righteousness and holiness."[24] The image was unmistakable.

So Cotton apparently went from gentle to rigorous Calvinism overnight. Even human action fell under the sway of necessity. Bulkeley again raised the point. In his understanding of the process of salvation, there had to be "a mutual giving/taking each other" between the individual and Christ. As Cotton presented it, however, "here is a meer taking on God's part, no giving or act on man's part."[25] This was the least a person could ask for. Even machines or tools actually moved in use. Could a human being not even do that much?

Cotton was intransigent, if subtle. There is indeed a "giving" in the process of salvation, he said, but it is only that "God giveth us his Son and his Spirit in a Promise of Grace." This was not what Bulkeley had in mind. Neither was what followed: there is a role for the believer in salvation, said Cotton, but it is only a role "of an emptying nature, emptying the soul of all confidence in itself and in the creature, and so leaving the soul as an empty vessel."[26] This notion that the human being became an "empty vessel" was a venerable mystical idea, but not all that common in Reformed thought.[27]

Whatever Cotton's source was for the idea, it did unmistakably raise the issue of free will. When empty, Cotton argued, the soul can be said to be dead, and this is in fact the believer's final aim as far as the self is concerned. For "how much a greater work it is to get life in Christ when we are dead, than to keep it, when we are alive. I dare not acknowledge any *liberum arbitrius* [free choice] to close with Christ, till *arbitrius* be liberated. And *liberatum arbitrius* is not, but by Christ and in Christ."[28]

Just as causality was purely extrinsic, so human action was finally void: "All we are, or have, or can do, is of God and not of ourselves."[29] The elders, according to Cotton, claimed that "we ourselves produce the acts of sanctification" that follow from grace, thus establishing a degree of independent human activity in the order of salvation.[30] And Cotton called this as he saw it; idolatry at worst, heresy at best: "Your judgment in this point jumpeth with Grevinchovino," accused Cotton, thus throwing his fellow New Englanders in with a notorious Arminian heretic.[31]

Bulkeley and the other ministers were willing to grant that God initiated human action, but they held out for a degree of independence by asserting that God caused "habits" in human beings, and that these habits as developed became more or less self-determining. This was conceivably a ground for compromise. Cotton, it will be recalled, said that the "grace (or habit) of faith" was the formal cause of salvation. But by the time of the rejoinder, he was unyielding. "You may not put me off with a distinction between material and formal," Cotton stressed:

The truth is, the Holy Ghost doth not work in us gifts and habits of sanctification to act and work by their own strength. . . . But he himself setteth faith awork and stirreth it up. . . . Whence that which our Saviour saith of his apostles is true concerning all his disciples (though not in like measure). It is not you that speak (and consequently not you that think or do) but the Spirit of your Father that speaketh in you.[32]

More succinctly, "without me you can do nothing" were words that Cotton took literally.[33]

Thus, in the course of his controversy with the other New England ministers, Cotton's commitment to a purely extrinsic causal system, and to denying any role for the free human agent in gaining salvation, grew stronger.[34] At the same time, when Hutchinson came to trial, Cotton participated in her banishment.[35] How could he have done so? He shared her abhorrence of works-righteousness and her commitment to the covenant of grace. To begin to understand the differences between Hutchinson and Cotton, we must be introduced more fully to the theology of Anne Hutchinson as it can be reconstructed from the historical documents.

I I

If we have ample documentary evidence regarding the historical theology of John Cotton, identifying the historical Anne Hutchinson is more than a little like identifying the historical Jesus; the sources are not transparent.[36] We do know nearly for certain that like Cotton, Hutchinson preached grace. We also have reason to suspect that she directly or indirectly accused the New England clergy of preaching works-righteousness. But this was unclear then and is unclear now.[37] Perhaps the most critical thing we know about Hutchinson is that from the moment she landed in Boston, John Winthrop disliked her.[38]

The only documents from which we can extract Hutchinson's views are the transcripts from her "trials," and since they were recorded by the authorities, they deserve to be read with suspicion. They may tell us more about how the authorities perceived Hutchinson—than what she actually thought. And it is from this point of view that we can see Hutchinson as a mystical indeterminist.[39] In contrast to Cotton's High Calvinism, Hutchinson preached "immediacy"—that is, that she received truth directly from God. And, also in contrast to Cotton's scholastic dialectic, which grounded every assertion in impersonal or second-person address, Hutchinson presented her thought in language that was dominated by the first person.

In other words, although there was a superficial similarity between Cotton's and Hutchinson's mysticism, in fact the two came to represent opposites on a continuum to their peers. To be sure, Cotton preached against works-righteousness too, but he did so in a way that stressed the extrinsic causal necessity of God's action in human affairs. Hutchinson preached against works-righteousness in a way that stressed the intrinsic location of grace, to the point where God's action seemed to be equated with her own insights. To the Puritans, Cotton was a High Calvinist—a preacher of predestination—Hutchinson an Epicurean—a preacher of chance.

Hutchinson's doctrine of immediacy was the central issue in her civil trial. After carefully justifying her position as a lay leader in the church against sexist charges by Winthrop, and after being shielded by Cotton from the charge of condemning ministerial authority, Hutchinson, apparently without prompting, broke into a monologue. "If you please to give me leave I shall give you the ground of what I know to be true," she said. This was followed by a long autobiographical narration of her spiritual development. Being "much troubled" by affairs in the Church of England, she had considered becoming a separatist, but private study of Scripture convinced her otherwise. Further study of Scripture led her to

see which was the clear ministry and which the wrong. Since that time I confess I have been more choice and [God] hath let me to distinguish between the voice of my beloved and the voice of Moses, the voice of John the Baptist and the voice of antichrist. . . . Now if you do condemn me for speaking what in my conscience I know to be the truth I must commit myself unto the Lord.[40]

To this point, Hutchinson's development could still be read as grounded in Scripture—always the surest of media for Puritans when it came to instruction of the conscience.

But Increase Nowell of Charlestown asked what was to be the pivotal question:

MR. NOWELL: How do you know that that was the spirit?
MRS. H.: How did Abraham know that it was God that bid him offer his son, being a breach of the sixth commandment?
DEP. GOV. [Thomas Dudley]: By an immediate revelation.
MRS. H.: So to me by an immediate revelation.
DEP. GOV.: How! an immediate revelation.[41]

It is worth pointing out that the actual phrasing "immediate revelation" was not unprompted. But whether intentional or not, Hutchinson had stated a doctrine of immediacy different from anything Cotton's system of causality could encompass.

The difference between Hutchinson and Cotton came down to a manner of speaking. As we have seen, Cotton held forth against the ordinary Puritan statement of mediation by stressing the extrinsic and causal order of salvation. His carefully crafted, scholastic distinctions constantly shifted the locus of power away from the self and to God. Hutchinson explicitly wanted to encourage the same shift; from attention to works to attention to grace, but her language just as insistently located the power of grace intrinsically.[42] First-person address, highlighting the intrinsic location of grace, rather than its objective operation, is characteristic of her speeches before the court. "I shall give you the ground of what *I* know to be true," Hutchinson addressed the elders as she began, significantly, her spiritual autobiography. And as she concluded her monologue: "*I* desire you to look to" your decisions, Hutchinson warned the court, for "if you go on in this course you begin you will bring a curse upon you and your posterity, and *the mouth of the Lord hath spoken it.* . . . Having seen him which is invisible I fear not what man can do to me."[43] To the Puritan leaders, this was blasphemy: God's mouth had long ago stopped speaking.

III

Now when Anne Hutchinson spoke those words in 1637, John Cotton was at her side, facing John Winthrop.[44] As they waited in that courtroom, both Hutchinson and Cotton were participants in a ritual drama.[45] They were both being acted upon as much as they were agents. They both had been prompted—one through a debate, the other through a trial dialogue, to play the role of theological extremist—Cotton as a High Calvinist, Hutchinson as an enthusiast.[46] They adopted—or were forced into—these roles for the sake of their society; to remake the range of ideas the Puritans in New England knew to be the world.[47]

In other words, by representing the extremes of potential worlds in which the New Englanders could live, Cotton and Hutchinson enabled the Puritans to clarify the character of the actual world in which they would live. By setting up an equilibrium between a more or less determined and a more or less indetermined universe, the "center" of the world was defined for the Puritans. Father and spirit, male and female, order and caprice—these were associations familiar to every Puritan mind. In the center of that courtroom in 1637, by having the opposites before them in the flesh of Cotton and Hutchinson, the Puritans were enabled to embrace them both or to choose between them.

They chose.[48] In that courtroom, Cotton had been called to Hutchinson's side by one of her supporters, and his position next to her eventually led the questions to be addressed to him. Shortly after her autobiographical discourse, Hutchinson became all but silent, and Cotton became the focus of the accusations.[49] He had joined Hutchinson in being on trial. But only one party was convicted. It was Winthrop who brought it to a close: "Mr. Cotton is not called to answer to anything," he said, aborting the questioning, "but we are to deal with the party here standing before us."[50] The trial of the center was over. Hutchinson, not Cotton, became the scapegoat.[51]

So the opposites had been together; as Hutchinson and Cotton waited before the court, the Puritans had recreated the original state of the cosmos. As Cotton and Hutchinson waited, order and chaos stood in the balance; the full range of myth—the whole of fate and chance—was together and waited upon the decision of the court. And it was Winthrop who acted as creator and concluded the case, who chose the part and lost the whole. As he later explained his motive for banishing Anne Hutchinson:

She walked by such a rule as cannot stand with the peace of any State; for such bottomless revelations, as either came without a word, or without the sense of the word (which was framed to humane capacity), if they be allowed in one thing, must be admitted a rule in all things; for they being above reason and Scripture, they are not subject to control.[52]

Indeed, control was the key word. The Puritans were moving from rebels to rulers, and they had to have control.[53] Chance, the spirit, the person herself, could not coexist, so they came to believe, with that control that was coming to be the state.

In the religious trial of Hutchinson, four months after her civil trial, the issue for which she became famous, antinomianism, was more prominent than in the civil trial. And, in that trial it became even clearer that the elders considered Hutchinson to represent a world with no bounds, governed only by chance. They arrived at this conclusion through the seemingly unlikely means of testing Hutchinson on the doctrine of the resurrection of the body after death. Was Christ united to the body through grace, and did the body, along with the soul, then pass on into glory? Hutchinson was of the opinion that not only the body, but also "the soul dies," and that whereas Christ is united by grace to a new soul, the body itself is not part of this union. John Wilson, Cotton's beleaguered colleague at First Church, and the most frequent object of Hutchinson's apparent attacks on works-righteous ministers, drew out the supposed implications: "If we deny the resurrection of the body then let us turn Epicures. Let us eat and drink and do any thing, tomorrow we shall die." And for Puritans, "Epicureanism" meant in part an indetermined universe and its moral, or rather supposedly amoral, consequences.[54] It was "an Argument of the *Epicureans*," Urian Oakes, a later commentator, pointed out, that "all things in the world are rolled up and down, tumbled and toss'd about by mere chance, and fall out as it may happen, uncertainly and fortuitously."[55] And it was as an Epicurean, then, that Hutchinson was banished. Cotton himself read this judgment. The "things that you hold," Cotton announced to her, "of the mortality of the soul by nature, and that Christ is not united to our bodies are of dangerous consequence and set an open door to all Epicurism and libertinism; if this be so, let us eat and drink for tomorrow we shall die. . . .

What need we care what we speak, or do, [or] hear if our souls perish and die like beasts."[56]

The center had moved. By banishing Hutchinson, by choosing their own part, by leaving Cotton's predestination intact and banishing Hutchinson's indeterminism, the Puritan authorities lost the whole, and paradoxically, lost themselves. The antinomian controversy "overthrew all" in ways that Winthrop could not have foreseen. By choosing to rule by the control of an ideology of predestination, the New England Puritans had lost the very spirit of their rebellion.[57]

2 "There Is Chance, There Is Not"

In the years following the antinomian controversy, the Puritan leaders worked hard to support their emerging state. They were encouraged by the emergence of the Commonwealth in England, where
true believers showed signs of ushering in the millennium. For a
moment, the Puritans in the old country seemed to be following
their New England counterparts on the road from rebellion to ruling.
Consequently, a jeremiad from one of the colonial experts on control, Rev. Thomas Shepard, was published to warn Calvinists on
both sides of the Atlantic about the perils of a "time of liberty."

Apparently, Shepard's warning did little good. The Commonwealth quickly spun into anarchy, and shortly after King Charles II
regained the throne, the Puritans in New England were threatened
by a king of a different sort. King Philip's War (1675–76) between
the English and Native Americans was as challenging to the ideology
of predestination in the colonies as the Restoration was to the Commonwealthmen in England. Both struggles were depicted in theolog-

ical and metaphysical terms by Puritan authors; as challenges to control. The passage from rebels to rulers demanded a clear sense of destiny, and a resolute, if not ruthless, will to realize it.[1]

I

Thomas Shepard, minister at Cambridge, witness against Anne Hutchinson in both her civil and ecclesiastical trials, and one who was convinced to his death that "Mr. Cotton repents not, but is hid only," explained the connection between theology and politics.[2] In his diary, while reporting on the synod meeting at Cambridge in August 1637, Shepard interspersed commentary on the banishment of Anne Hutchinson with commentary on the New England massacre of the Pequots of the same year. Both the banishment and the massacre, Shepard thought, were providential victories:

The Pequot Indians were fully discomfited, for as the opinions [of the antinomians] arose, wars did arise, and when these [opinions] began to be crushed by the ministry of the elders and by opposing Mr. Vane and casting him and others from being magistrates, the enemies [i.e., the Pequots] began to be crushed and were perfectly subdued by the end of the synod. . . . Thus the Lord . . . delivered the country from war with the Indians and Familists.[3]

Theology and politics merged; the center, whether challenged by heretics such as Hutchinson or by infidels like the Pequots, had to be controlled by the Saints.

In the eyes of his contemporaries, Shepard was an expert in the matter of control. Two colleagues who penned an introduction to some of his lecture sermons, "preached, most of them, in the year 1641," claimed simply that in them Shepard defined the "right understanding and sober use of liberty."[4] In other words, these sermons displayed the proper control of liberty, by making it clear how

men run into extremes, either stretching and paring every one to the giant's bed, and thereby denying liberty to the saints to serve him, according to the measure of their stature in Christ, or else, on the other hand, opening the door so wide as to plead for liberty to all the disguised enemies and sins against Christ, thereby, instead of uniting the saints in one, endeavoring, through a dreadful mistake, to unite Christ and Belial![5]

Shepard, whose sermons, of course, avoided these twin errors, neither wore people down with necessity nor left them hanging without any order. His "right understanding" of liberty was in need of hearing in both Cromwellian England and the "New World."

Although he always retained vestiges of adherence to the mythic center, then, Shepard made it clear that the two extremes were not equal evils. Anarchy, "opening the door so wide as to plead for liberty to all the disguised enemies of Christ," was clearly the less acceptable, more Belial-like of the two extremes. On this point, Shepard was both an exemplary New England Puritan and a perfect example for the Commonwealthmen. In New England, the Puritans had already had to rule, and if Shepard at all represented the way in which they had gone about doing so, old England needed to hear what he had to say. Shepard effectively shaped mythic paradox into an ideology of predestination in his *Subjection to Christ . . . The Best Means To Preserve Our Liberty.*[6] He promoted the rule of the Saints.

Shepard and John Cotton were different in many ways, but the most notable of their differences was in their attitude toward the self.[7] Cotton, at least when he spoke as a High Calvinist, emphasized the self's emptying, becoming void, or ceasing to act at all in face of the extrinsic process of salvation. Shepard, in contrast, spoke in more characteristically moderate Puritan discourse of the self's subjection. The difference was as great in the end as that between zero and one. Hence, when Shepard spoke of liberty, it was not to emphasize its absence in human beings without God, but rather the need to subject liberty to the pattern of grace.[8]

"How sweet it is," Shepard exclaimed, that "the greatest liberty and sweetest liberty is to be under the government of Christ Jesus, although men do not think so."[9] Implicitly, Shepard was admitting that humans had a liberty of their own. "Make use of liberties," Shepard exhorted. "He that hath them, but sees not so much glory in them, or gets not much good from them, he will be no more thankful than one that hath large grounds may walk at liberty, but the trees, for want of manuring, bear no fruit, nor ground corn, through sloth; such a man will starve there."[10] The practical wisdom of this was to encourage worldly activity, sanctified or not, insofar as manuring probably fell under the latter. Thus, whereas Cotton preached the cessation of willing, Shepard merely preached its subjugation. Humans possessed liberty; they were agents, albeit agents who needed to be subjects to avoid abusing what liberty they had: "When the will is in captivity, [i.e., to other than Christ] no captivity like it, no galley slave like it."[11] The problem was not to stop willing; it was to control it.

Shepard consequently described the will as a substance, rather than as "nothing." His metaphors all stressed the caprice of the will; it was "unruly," "wild," "like dried leaves in the wind." Cotton had conceived of the will as an agent potentially rivaling God. It needed to be obliterated, or remade, in unity with God.[12] For Shepard, the problem with the will was its unruliness. It needed to be tamed. Shepard's view was the less paradoxical of the two and the more psychological. The struggle between order and chaos was a struggle within the continuous self rather than in the cosmos.[13] The paradox was contained. As Shepard explained to one interested inquirer: "It is no small piece of a Christian's skill and work to put a difference between himself and himself, himself as he is in Christ . . . and himself as he is growing on his first root."[14]

There were, of course, historical reasons why Shepard thought this way. He had, his introducers found it useful to inform the reader, "when he was first awakened to look after religion," been "moved and tempted to the ways of Familism," or the exact heresy he had charged to Hutchinson.[15] Shepard himself recalled the period as one in which "I did question whether that glorious state of perfection might not be the truth" and whether Puritan divines were "not all legal men and their books so."[16] Fortunately, Shepard recalled, "the Lord delivered me at last" from these errors, but one can at least wonder today whether the deliverance was as complete as the Cambridge minister had thought.[17]

For Shepard continued to struggle to control the "wild" and "unruly" will. For instance, describing the labor of a typical Christian to submit to Christ, Shepard found that there are some who conclude that "I can not pray, I can not believe, I can not break this vile and unruly will."[18] Closer to home, describing himself, Shepard lamented: "I had a wild heart which was as hard to stand and abide before the presence of God in an ordinance as a bird [before] any man." The caprice of children at play was another of Shepard's

images for the fickle, untamed will: "There is an abundance of wildness in our hearts, which naturally seek to have their liberty abroad,
and can not endure to be pent in the narrow room of holy performances, extraordinary duties, etc., no more than children can be
pent up from their play."[19] The will was naturally indetermined; only
grace could properly hem liberty in.

Shepard's work was thus the perfect gospel for Cromwell's England. The Commonwealth was "a day of rest from persecution,
which should be a time of liberty to the saints to serve God." But
in such a time of liberty, people were "apt to be not only somewhat
fond of their liberties, but to wax giddy and wanton with liberty,
and instead of shaking off the bloody yokes of men, to cast off, at
least in part, the government and blessed yoke of Christ also."[20]
And Shepard's work was designed to make clear, across the Atlantic,
how useless and even destructive giddiness and wantonness was. His
personal struggle was a type of the struggle then going on to contain
the aberrancies breaking out among the New Model Army.

But his work was also about life in the New World. The whole of
Shepard's treatise was, as the subtitle had it, "A Wholesome Caveat
for a Time of Liberty." By banishing Epicureanism to Rhode Island,
the Puritans had hardly gotten rid of the libertine impulse. It had
simply gone underground, been internalized, characteristic of an
entire time and part of the Puritan self. The Puritans in England,
like their more experienced counterparts such as Shepard in New
England, were willful children when it came to ruling, and were
growing wanton and giddy with their liberty. And as a result, the
ideological reaction first manifested against Hutchinson became embedded in the Puritan understanding of the self.[21] To curb it Shepard,
like Winthrop, embraced control, order, and coercion.

"This is certain: when the soul will not subject itself to God, [it]
goes about to subject God to [it], nay, to [its] lusts." "The Lord hath
a kingdom in this world most glorious; hence, when men will not
be under it, if they will not be ruled by him, they must be ruled by
the whip; and if Christ's laws can not bind, Christ's chains must."
Indeed, the "main and first original of all" insubordination, whether
to Christ, the church, the ministers, or the magistrates, is when a
person "does profess . . . that not the will of Christ, but his own

will, shall rule him."[22] Ruling was proving more difficult for the Puritans than rebellion had been, for:

These cast off the Lord's government over them, who will have no rulers or governors in churches . . . but leave all to themselves and their liberty. . . . This generation of men, sons of Korah, are risen up in these latter times; especially amongst Anabaptists, Familists, and rigid Separatists, and who are privily crept into New England churches; whose condemnation sleeps not, Satan carrying them to extremes, and pride lifting them up above themselves, above men, above officers, above ordinances, above God. . . . As commonwealths are under greatest bondage where there is an anarchy, where everyone must be a slave, because everyone must be a master, so, in the churches, no greater bondage can come than this.[23]

Shepard ably perpetuated the Puritan bias against indeterminism and vividly developed its violent implications.

And yet, although contained, the paradox remained alive. Like most of the Puritan divines, Shepard explicitly preserved at least a shred of faith in intrinsic human liberty. He could declare that "every act is determined by God," and that God "worketh all in all things," but what this meant was that

If God did work upon believers as upon blocks or brute creatures, they might then have some color to cast off all attendance to the directive power of the law, and to leave all to the Spirit's omnipotent and immediate acts. . . . But believers are rational creatures, and therefore capable of acting by rule . . . [they] have some inherent power so to act . . . according to the rule of life: the image of God, renewed in them, is (in part) like to the same image which they had in the first creation, which gave man some liberty and power to act, according to the will of Him that created him.[24]

With this statement Shepard expressed the heart of New England orthodoxy; an ideal of a center, balancing order and caprice, but with a strong undertow toward necessity. In trying to govern the wilderness—of the Commonwealth, or the forest, or the self—the Puritans typically reacted against chance in favor of coercion whenever the opportunity arose. And nowhere did opportunity seem greater, and their myth seem more vulnerable, than when the Puritans encountered the Native Americans.

11

It was by no means inevitable that Puritans would massacre Indians. Both Puritan and native cultures were extraordinarily religious, sharing the logic of myth. The Indians, furthermore, were disposed to treat the white settlers with respect, and the whites were initially unsure whether the Indians were types of Adam and Eve or of the serpent.[25] If Anne Hutchinson had somehow succeeded in keeping her dissenting voice in Boston, and if Puritans like Winthrop and Shephard had been more secure with their own mythology, perhaps the cultural encounter between English and Native Americans would have been more of a conversation, and less of a confrontation. This was, to a degree, what happened with the French.[26]

But bolstered by their ideology of predestination, the English quickly established a mission for themselves in the New World, and so Shepard and Winthrop and the other Puritans could create in the Indians an enemy: the "Indian menace," a "ferocious, wild creature, possessed of an alternately demonic and bestial nature, that had to be exterminated to make humanity safe."[27] That this "wild enemy" essentially signified the projection and distortion of a rejected aspect of their own mythology did not, of course, dawn on the Puritans. Too much was at stake; so much, in fact, that in the end the Puritans had physically to sacrifice some of their own.

And indeed, by the time Urian Oakes, who had succeeded Shepard as pastor at Cambridge, stood before the assembled Massachusetts Artillery Company on September 10, 1677, he had to work hard to explain why things had gone wrong. Anne Hutchinson was all but forgotten, but Rhode Island continued to be a cesspool of heresy. Oliver Cromwell was long since dead, and the hopes for a millennial beginning in England shattered. A new special agent of the Crown, Edmund Randolph, seemed to threaten to reinstitute persecution of Nonconformists in Massachusetts. And worst of all, almost unthinkable, in fact, the colonies had just suffered through a war with Indians, King Philip's War, in which half the towns in New England had been damaged and twelve completely destroyed.[28] It was not at all clear that the control of the Saints was winning over chaos.

Like his predecessor, Oakes was probably considered something of an expert at handling chaos by his peers. After spending his youth in Massachusetts, Oakes had been called back to England during the Commonwealth, where he held a prestigious preaching appointment. In 1662, following the Restoration, the position was stripped from him. He had experienced personally the consequences of the New Model Army's disordered dalliance with liberty. His call to Thomas Shepard's former pastorate at Cambridge, Massachusetts, in 1671 undoubtedly came none too soon.[29]

But on that day in September 1677, all of his resources were demanded. Battles of King Philip's War were still being fought in Maine and New Hampshire. Across the colonies, fully 6 percent of the adult male members of a total population of about thirty thousand had been killed.[30] Memories of losses had to be vivid to Oakes's audience.[31] New England was facing a massive reconstruction, and as Oakes stood before the artillerymen, he wanted to let them know that the preachers were going to do their part. The sermon Oakes preached on that day, *The Soveraign Efficacy of Divine Providence*, was perhaps the most striking exposition of the predestinarian ideology in the seventeenth century.[32]

Oakes was a skilled craftsman. His chosen text was Eccles. 9:11: "the race is not to the swift, nor the battle to the strong . . . but time and chance happeneth to them all." What "determined my thoughts to this text," Oakes "confessed" to his audience, was that "we have seen that a despised and despicable enemy, that is not acquainted with books of military discipline, that observe no regular order, that understand not the soldier's postures, and motions, and firings, and forms of battle; that fight in a base, cowardly, contemptible way, have been able to rout, and put to flight, and destroy our valiant and good soldiers."[33] Time and chance may have happened to them all. But it seemed to be happening especially to the Puritans.

So Oakes had to strain. His text would at first seem to have affirmed indeterminism. "Time and chance happeneth to them all" does not directly lead to a doctrine of providence or predestination. But Oakes noted in the first section of his sermon that "expositors are not at perfect agreement among themselves" about the meaning of the text. And having opened this door to equivocation, Oakes could proceed to rule out "Epicurean" expositors who "make I know not what imaginary blind fortune the predominant deity in the world." Indeed, Oakes asserted, "there seems to be no necessity of fixing upon such an [Epicurean] exposition, considering that [the passage] may well admit of a better, and more savory construction."[34] And of course the most notable feature of the "better" exposition was that it was not Epicurean: "time and chance happeneth to them all" did *not* mean "that the determination of events is reduced and referred to mere chance and fortune, as the Epicurean philosophers imagined: but that the counsel and providence of God disposes and orders out all successes, or frustrations of second causes."[35] Order and providence happeneth to them all.

Oakes had hit his theme. The human is "a poor dependent nothing," and God "works all in all." "Impediments and obstructions" may "seem wholly casual and fortuitous emergencies . . . yet they are governed by the secret counsel and effectual Providence of God." "The sovereign counsel and the providence of God *orders* time and chance." "The great God hath the absolute and infallible determination of the successes and events of all."[36] The list went on, but the point was no doubt clear. God's predestining providence was sovereign for Urian Oakes.

Yet there was a counterpoint to the theme of order. Humans had "a kind of sufficiency . . . to the putting forth of this and that act," proclaimed Oakes. The counterpoint was even clearer when he informed the artillerymen that they could "act or effect this or that in a way of counsel, and with freedom of will." Even God did not complicate the matter: "Though God is able to give being to things in an immediate way, yet it is his pleasure in the course of his Providence to use means, and to produce many things by the mediation and agency of second causes."[37] Not just God, but the Saints had to shape whatever order was going to happen.

And when Oakes linked the theology and politics together in a military metaphor, the artillery company had to be persuaded that "God who is the Lord of Hosts, the great leader, commander and ruler of nature, not only permits, but also effectually commands and causes his whole militia, ordinarily, to move and act according to their natures and natural properties respectively, without countermanding them, or turning them out of their way."[38] Grace "counseled" nature and did not coerce it, at least for the artillerymen, if not for the Indians.

But this emphasis by Oakes on liberty of human action was, again, only a counterpoint. Although Oakes could indeed make a truly paradoxical statement, such as "there is chance, there is not," there was little question which side of the paradox he finally favored. For by the time he addressed the company, the biggest battles of King Philip's War had already been won by the English. Much of the sermon was thus akin to a jeremiad—the ritualistic Puritan denunciations of pride and vice. Oakes's words were an attempt to encourage military endeavors and stir up hatred against heathenish chaos, while simultaneously preventing any artilleryman from getting an exalted opinion of himself.[39] Oakes had chosen his text well.

So the most basic theme of Oakes's reflection upon the war, and indeed the most basic reality about the war itself as represented in the Puritan mind, was the need to assert order in the face of a frighteningly indetermined cosmos.[40] "We see that there is, and there is not chance in the world," Oakes concluded, "chance there is, in respect of second causes . . . but no chance as to the first cause. That piece of atheism, and heathenism ascribing things to fortune and chance, is hardly rooted out of the minds of men, that are or should be better instructed and informed."[41] It is not unfair to point out that the term *heathen* here probably did not bring to mind the Greeks for Oakes's audience.

In other words, the very presence of Native American cultures had turned into a threat to the Puritans, and when the cultural contact broke into a life-and-death conflict, theologians and preachers such as Oakes committed their pens and voices to the attempt to impose order.[42] "The Lord is a man of war," Oakes quoted Exodus, and while God "gives military skill, and other accomplishments, and successes," it is also true that "we have met with many disappointments in the late war, and in other respects. We should see God in all. When he blasts our corn, defeats our soldiers, frowns upon our merchants, and we are disappointed; now acknowledge the hand of God, ordering time, and chance according to his good pleasure."[43] This sentence was that much easier to utter now that the Wampanoags were largely subdued.

But the predestinarian ideology was not intentionally ruthless, and on the personal level it was no doubt comforting. Puritans died in the tragedy of King Philip's War too. The cultural clash produced real chaos, as well as imagined. The Puritan poet Benjamin Tompson captured the *kairos* exactly, if less than eloquently, in a piece penned just after the fall of Providence, Rhode Island, in 1674:

> Why muse we thus to see the wheels run cross
> Since Providence itself sustains a loss:
> And yet should Providence forget to watch
> I fear the enemy would all dispatch;
> Celestial lights would soon forget their line,
> The wandering planets would forget to shine,
> The stars run all out of their common spheres,
> And quickly fall together by the ears:
> Kingdoms would jostle out their kings and set
> The poor mechanic up whom next they met,
> Or rather would whole kingdoms with the world
> Into a chaos their first egg be hurled.[44]

The New England Puritans developed their predestinarian ideology as a bulwark against whatever they perceived as chaos. The Puritans needed to tame the Native Americans, Anne Hutchinson, the wilderness itself, and finally, something in their own souls, for fear of, quite literally to them, all hell breaking loose.[45] If then it was a tragedy that the Puritans failed to preserve an inclusive center, and to perceive the integrity of the Native American centers, it was also a wonder that they survived at all.

3 "The True Middle"

As the turn of the century approached, at least two other confrontations—with the first Quakers in New England and with the growing presence of the established Church of England—were to challenge the rule of the Puritans. And, conveniently for historians, in one remarkable career George Keith spoke for both Quakers and Anglicans against the Calvinists. Examining these two clashes over the question of free will further illumines the characteristic seventeenth-century Calvinist answer to that question, which also foreshadows a different type of answer that was to become increasingly popular in the century to follow.

I

George Keith was born Presbyterian in the region near Aberdeen, Scotland, in 1638.[1] He developed an interest in theology through his schooling, and upon graduation he served as tutor and chaplain in Edinburgh. There he encountered Gilbert Burnet, later bishop of Salisbury, and these two made a gradual intellectual pilgrimage away from Presbyterianism. The writings of the French philosopher Descartes and the Cambridge Platonist Henry More were apparently the two greatest influences leading both Keith and Burnet away from their childhood faith.[2] But whereas Burnet converted to the established church, Keith first went to Quaker meeting houses. In 1663 he openly professed his belief in the inner light, and he quickly thereafter became one of the most articulate advocates for the Society of Friends, publishing no fewer than fifteen defenses of the Quaker way in the 1670s alone.[3]

In 1685 Keith emigrated to New England. He settled at first in East Jersey, where he was appointed as surveyor-general and served as a "traveling friend" or itinerant Quaker leader throughout New Jersey and Pennsylvania. In the course of his travels, Keith came to feel that in contrast to his own studied English Quakerism, many of his new American neighbors were "airy notionists," or, as his biographer E. W. Kirby puts it, "lacked that check which dogma and logical thinking gave."[4] At the same time, Keith was fiercely loyal to the cause of the inner light, and on a trip to Boston in June of 1688 he challenged the collected Calvinist clergy of the city to a debate. Not surprisingly, they refused, calling the paper Keith posted with his challenge "blasphemous and heretical" and issuing a challenge of their own to Keith: "If he would have a public audience, let him print."[5]

So print Keith did, in a volume the Puritan authors of the challenge—James Allen, Joshua Moody, Cotton Mather, and Samuel Willard—could hardly have expected. Keith's ten-chapter indictment, *The Presbyterian and Independent Visible Churches in New England Brought to the Test*, arraigned Calvinism along the entire spectrum of systematic theology, but focused especially on the doctrines of election and reprobation and the question of free will. Keith began by noting that Quakers had been persecuted by Puritans. In 1656 Ann Austin and Mary Fisher had been imprisoned in Boston and eventually exiled, and around the turn of the decade, four Quakers had been executed on Massachusetts's gallows.[6] But this persecution was not, Keith asserted, because Puritans had truer answers to questions of doctrine. Rather, the Puritans had been able to do violence to the Quakers because most members of the Society of Friends had "not freedom to use the words" of human wisdom to defend themselves.[7] Keith intended to correct the imbalance in articulation.

Keith directed his critique precisely at the ideology of predestination. His Presbyterian upbringing had made him familiar enough with the Westminster Confession to quote it verbatim: "God hath unchangeably ordained whatsoever comes to pass, yet so as neither is God the author of sin, nor is violence offered to the will of creatures."[8] This orthodox Puritan statement Keith found incredible. "So say many of the worst sort of Ranters," Keith satirized, "but how they clear their doctrine" of charging God with evil and with coercing the will, "they have not told the world."[9] By thus identifying the Puritans and the Ranters, Keith sought in one stroke to invert the authorized assumption. Now the Puritans were the extremists, linked with a subversive and even blasphemous ideology that had emerged during the Civil War in England. And if the Puritans were Ranters, and destroyers of public morals, then Keith's own sect, the Quakers, were the true advocates of freedom and responsibility.

The doctrine of reprobation, or absolute predestined damnation, was especially vulnerable to charges of extremism. The Bible does not say, Keith claimed, "that men hate God because He first hated them," but rather that God considers the reprobate, or damned, as having had "a day of visitation, and a call to repent, and a tender of grace, love and mercy . . . and as having resisted and rejected the same."[10] Keith was especially eloquent when he argued that it was unjust to consider infants being damned by God. "All are put under a capacity or possibility of salvation," asserted Keith; and

this without any violence done to their rational faculties or free-will; for God doth well know how to gain and prevail upon the understanding, and will, and inclinations of his people, by such gentle and yet prevalent and overcoming persuasions and allurements, and motions of his holy Spirit of grace, of light and life, as shall infallibly gather them unto himself.[11]

Each person had within his or her own self the God-given power to choose life or death. As things stood, the Puritans were choosing death. Therefore, "turn your minds to that light of Christ within you," Keith urged Mather, Allen, Moody, and Willard, for "if you tinarian ideology was before him. He consequently labeled it uncontrollable, as had every other New England Puritan before him when faced with the enemy.

But Willard also struggled to answer Keith. The topic was whether God caused sin. Willard first tried to distinguish between a "physical cause" and a "moral cause." "When we say, a sinful action, we consider it in a complex sense, viz. physically as an action, and morally as sinful; and in this complex sense, divines do call the former the substrate matter of the action . . . and the other the formality of it." In other words, God did not physically determine a sinful act, only that some acts freely done by physical beings were good and some evil. "The form of an action, as an action, is not the moral goodness or evil of it, but that which individuates it from all other actions whatsoever." Even more to the point: "no action, *qua action,* is sin; sin being the anomy that cleaves to it." In short, "there is a rational distinction," Willard asserted, "between the action itself, and the sinfulness of it, for the one belongs to physics, the other to morals."[24] Physically, humans were free; morally, they were not.

But did this mean that God caused sin? Willard was left with assertions: "It is far from God to do any unjust thing; if therefore we cannot, by our reason reconcile all his doings to our rules, we ought to adore him." But this did not mean, Willard wanted to be careful to note, that the human had not liberty. "Liberty is primarily and formally rooted in the lubency or readiness of the will to act; and this is generally interpreted by *spontaneity,* i.e., it acts of its own accord, and is under no compulsion." And this liberty to act was as full a liberty as a human needed: "it is therefore to be observed, that not the understanding, nor the will . . . , but the whole man is a free cause." "Necessity of compulsion would destroy this liberty of will. . . . [God's] providence determines" human beings "to act according to their own nature; i.e., not only that they shall act thus, but act spontaneously."[25]

The language of spontaneity was somewhat new in Puritanism, but the overall answer to the question of free will was not. The distinction between physics and morals was essentially the Aristotelian one Keith had predicted. Willard had the mind of a codifier,

believe in Christ the light, the life, the wisdom and power of God in you . . . He will anoint the eyes of your understanding . . . and then your eyes shall be opened." The immediacy of the light made its reception not a violent act but as natural as opening one's eyes. "It is the nature and property of all light, to reveal itself immediately to everyone, or else not at all."[12] Puritan predestination implied that God did violence to humans; Keith saw salvation in gentler terms.

When the Puritan ministers responded, they confirmed the worst of Keith's accusations. "In Quakerism," rhapsodized Boston's elite, "we see the vomit cast forth in the by-past ages of whole kennels of those creatures, for whom the Apostle to the Philippians has found a name, licked up again for new digestion."[13] Somewhat more moderately, the ministers simply labeled Keith one of those "heretics . . . who with fraud would persuade the people of the saints of the most high to unchurch themselves by parting with all means of communion between them and their God." And, in a passage that speaks volumes about the Puritan mind, they concluded: "Quakerism is the peculiar plague of this age."[14]

The real Ranters, in other words, were the Quakers, with their dangerously unsettling enthusiasm. Thus, regarding Keith's quoting of the Westminster Confession, the ministers (and here Willard was probably the author) suggested that Keith study more thoroughly "the doctrine of divine concurse." "If he were more familiar with it," Willard claimed, Keith "would realize that it does not follow that if God decrees all things, He must needs be the doer of them." Positively, this meant that although humans "depend absolutely upon God, as in respect of their being, so of all their actions," nevertheless "notwithstanding this influence upon the creature, in respect of its action, the creature hath its action of its own, subordinate to, and assisted by this influence."[15] Calvinism, asserted Boston's elite, was not an extreme.

Keith had asked for a public debate. The ministers (perhaps wisely) refused. In an appendix to their diatribe, they explained why. "We knew," they said, "that there would be no holding of him to any law or rule of disputation, but he would bring all to his revelations, and therefore the whole must needs issue in a tumultuous brangle."[16] The "inner light," no matter how gently stated, seemed to the Puritans to promise nothing but chaos. And by now, when the Puritans anticipated a "brangle," they would seek to stomp it out.

With Keith, they tried to do so by calling his thought vomit, and failed. Within a year the Quaker had published a rejoinder, *The Pretended Antidote Proved Poyson*. Predestination, even if tempered with the doctrine of "concurse," was the poison. Again, Keith accused the Boston clergy of blindness, deadliness, and violence. Keith had answered the challenge of the Puritans to print, and apparently the "brangle" had become tumultuous enough to silence the ministers, for they published no further reply.

II

For his part, the itinerant Friend was increasingly occupied with matters within the Quaker fold. He had moved to Philadelphia in 1689, and by 1691 was embroiled in a controversy that led to his expulsion from the Society of Friends in 1695. His effort at fitting the inner light to words of human wisdom went unappreciated. During the controversy, Keith returned to London, where he eventually converted to the Church of England. He had few other options at this point.[17] And by the time he returned to New England in 1702, it was as one of the first missionaries of the Society for the Propagation of the Gospel. He was charged especially with converting the Quakers.

But he could hardly avoid his old Puritan foes, especially since he was now living in Boston. In July 1703, Keith attended the Harvard commencement, where he heard the candidates for degrees discuss the following theses:

1. That the immutability of God's decree doth not take away the liberty of the creature.
2. That the fall of Adam, by virtue of God's decree, was necessary.
3. That every free act of the reasonable creature is determined by God, so that whatever the reasonable creature acteth freely, it acteth the same necessarily.[18]

Samuel Willard was the presider at the commencement, and within days he received a letter from Keith questioning both his

students' and his own doctrines of free will. Willard did not im[m]ediately reply, since the letter was in Latin, but when Keith pub[lished] the paper in an English translation, and when rumors that p[...] opinion considered the letter unanswerable began to filter [to] Willard, he acted.[19] His *A Brief Reply to Mr. George Keith* was [proba]bly the best New England work on the question" of free wi[ll].

Keith may have converted from Quaker to Anglican, but [...] saw similar flaws with the Puritans. He nearly ignored the [first and] third Puritan theses—both of which indirectly affirmed hu[man lib]erty, in order to reiterate his charge that absolute election a[nd repro]bation made God the author of sin. The issue of causality v[... the] center of his critique: "If the cause of a cause is the cau[se of the] caused thing, [then] the determination of man's will by [God to a] sinful action, being the next cause of that sinful action, ma[y be said] to be the author of that sin." Less obtusely, Keith was ar[guing that] if God causes all human action, and if that human actio[n is a] sin, then God causes sin. "But the latter is absurd," if n[ot blasphe]mous, argued Keith, and "therefore so is the first."[21] Cal[vinism was] absurd.

Keith knew enough Aristotle to reinforce his compla[int. He an]ticipated that Willard might attempt to qualify predesti[nation with] a distinction such as "God determines the will . . . to [the matter] of the action" of sin only, "but not to the formal thereo[f." Keith] had imbibed enough of Descartes and the Cambridge [Platonists to] distrust the distinction. "In many sinful actions there [is no distinc]tion betwixt the material and the formal of the actio[n. . . . He] who is the cause of [a] sinful action according to the [matter . . .] is also the cause . . . according to its formal."[22] As [a path]way to Descartes, one characteristic Puritan solution [to the problem] of free will also came into question.

It was not, however, as if Willard had nothing left [to say, and] his reply to Keith was a line-by-line commentary full[y three times as] long as the Anglican's letter. It began by asserting [that Keith's po]lemical intent was "to overthrow the doctrine of an a[bsolute decree."] In language just as telling, Willard claimed that [Keith's larger] purpose was to "establish an uncontrollable sovere[ignty . . . in the will] of man."[23] Willard clearly recognized that a challe[nge . . .]

not of an innovator.[26] But now Willard had to take Keith seriously. The old days when heretics could simply be banished or hanged were coming to an end.[27] The predestinarian ideology had come under fire, and therefore Willard increasingly saw his task as preservative rather than assertive. As presider at commencement and de facto president of Harvard, he pledged to "prevent [students] from imbibing the precious doctrines of Pelagianism, Jesuitism and Arminianism" as much as in him lay.[28]

But Keith and his type simply would not go away. Even worse, they were claiming with alarming consistency that the Puritans were extremists. In the final argument of his letter to Willard, Keith told the story of his life in the terms of the ideology of predestination:

[So] that I may ingeneously declare my sense in this point, the aforementioned doctrine of God's determining men to sinful actions, did some years ago drive me from the society of many (of those called Presbyterians) who held it, and taught it, and prepared the way for my turning to Quakerism, whilest by a preposterous zeal I wandered from one extreme to another. . . . I fear that what of this sort has happened to me, has also happened to many others.[29]

The center may not have been Quakerism, but it surely was not predestination.

Willard responded predictably, and with more than a touch of malice: "This gentleman [Keith] is by custom, naturalized to live in the fire."[30] "And here let me," Willard concluded,

make a short reflection upon a passage . . . viz., that he wandered from one extreme to another; and it appears, that either he hath not found the true middle as yet, or that he envies the world the experiment. Certainly the doctrine that ascribes to God his glorious perfections, and allows to the free will of man its due boundaries, is unworthily called *an extreme*.[31]

Keith feared, Willard concluded, "that what happened to him on this account, hath happened to others. What argument there is in this, I cannot see."[32] But the members of the society developing around Willard were able to see the argument with increasing clarity. The true middle was in dispute once again, and no amount of simple assertion of the Puritan claim to it was likely to persuade "Americans" as the new century dawned.

The seventeenth century thus saw the trial of the center take place in several forums, with various defendants and prosecutors. The first trial was that of the covenant theology, where Puritans represented for themselves the inclusive ideal of a center balancing determinism and indeterminism, order and caprice, the Creator and the spirit, in the figures of John Cotton and Anne Hutchinson. In the trial of Hutchinson, the verdict was stated in such a way that the center was distorted into an ideology of predestination. Her banishment from Massachusetts symbolized a broader rejection by the Puritans of any approach to life that did not stress causal order or a limited, politically controllable definition of liberty for the aristocracy of grace. By ejecting those they thought sought to "overthrow all," the Puritans sought to establish and control all.

While this ideology was forming, however, there were some who sensed that the problem was not simply "out there" in the heretics of the colonies. Thomas Shepard best articulated how the indeterminist impulse was in fact part of the Puritan soul. His *A Wholesome Caveat for a Time of Liberty* reflected the sense of chaos that dwelt within Puritan piety and at the same time reacted against it. Shepard rejected anarchy and endorsed coercion, while still trying to preserve some human freedom. As an articulate advocate of this "right use" of freedom, Shepard was represented by his peers as a model against whom to judge both personal and public life.

Why such judgments seemed necessary had become manifest to the Puritans in King Philip's War. Native Americans were regularly depicted as uncontrollable heathen by the Puritans, and when massacres led to open military conflict, the predestinarian ideology was called upon to bolster the Puritan claim to the center. Urian Oakes's speech before the Massachusetts Artillery Company was designed to assure his listeners that the Puritan "center" would in fact be preserved, and that the verdict of the earliest trial of the center was still in force.

Finally, as the seventeenth century waned, a role reversal in the trial took place. George Keith, as both Quaker and Anglican, was nothing if not a prosecutor of the ideology of predestination. Samuel

Willard, correspondingly, represented an individual committed to defending Puritanism as "the true middle." His task was easy when Keith was a Quaker. But by the time Keith wrote as an Anglican, the challenge could not be dismissed as simply the raving of a mystic. Keith spoke now with the authority of the established church. His portrait of Puritanism as a system of extreme doctrines that constricted human freedom was a charge to be heard again, with some new and startling nuances, as the next century began.

II Anti-Calvinism
in America,
1700–1735

*Nothing brings more pain than too much pleasure;
nothing more bondage than too much liberty.*

POOR RICHARD

Calvinism and its predestinarian ideology provided many of the seventeenth-century colonists to North America with a complete worldview. In the first decades of the eighteenth century, however, a number of colonists published critiques that questioned the Calvinists' claim to represent the "center." Typically, these "anti-Calvinists" portrayed the Congregationalist Puritans or their Presbyterian colleagues as Stoical, fatal antinomians.[1] In other words, a variety of lay writers—antislavery Quakers, an Anglican Arminian, and one enlightenment-inspired philosopher—all tried to depict Calvinism as an extreme that led to violations of moral law.[2] The answer of the Calvinist aristocracy of grace to the problem of free will remained the predominant public theology of the colonies, at least in New England, but, especially in the thought of Benjamin Franklin, a different ideology of providence was emerging.

4 "Little Love and Charity to God or Man"

In common with other colonists, the Puritan Calvinists kept slaves. "Slavery," in the words of Stanley Elkins, "was created in America—fashioned on the spot by Englishmen in whose traditions such an institution had no part. American slavery was unique."[1] Now of course chattel slavery had been practiced elsewhere in the world, but the uniqueness of American slavery resided especially in the intellectual justifications that built the practice into a self-perpetuating, almost unquestioned institution in the New World.[2] According to some members of the Society of Friends, writing against slavery as early as 1714, the central justification for human bondage could be found in the Puritan doctrine of predestination. These early anti-Calvinists implied that the fatal necessity of predestination helped to close the shackles of slavery.

Had the Quakers read the Puritan arguments for keeping slaves, they would have found plenty of evidence to confirm their suspicions about predestination and providence. The leading Calvinist argu-

ments justifying slavery almost invariably invoked one or the other
doctrine. Samuel Willard, for instance, treated the topic of slavery
under the fifth commandment, to "honor thy Father and Mother,"
the same commandment John Winthrop had used to banish Anne
Hutchinson. The conjunction was not coincidental. Slaves shared
with women and children a responsibility to submit to providential,
and paternal, authority. Predestination bred, or fed upon, paternalism.

Willard had the logic all worked out. "Dominion and servitude
were brought in by the apostacy," or the Fall of humanity into sin,
he argued. And since the Fall was predestined by God, then it
followed that "[slavery] is so ordered in the providence of God, [that]
it becomes beneficial to mankind. And such is the condition of some
that they do fall unavoidably under this state, and are made servants
of others."[3] Thus slaves and servants, like women and children, had
an obligation to obey their masters, "and are to adore the providence
of God, in disposing them to a better or worse condition in this
regard."[4] A few years later, Cotton Mather virtually echoed Willard's
argument. He advised slave owners that "it is come to pass by the
Providence of God, without which there comes nothing to pass, that
poor NEGROES are cast under your government and protection."[5]
Slavery was part of the scheme whereby God ordered the cosmos.

Paternalism, then, connected the rule of God the Father with the
rule of human masters over their slaves.[6] The Puritans, and later
slaveholders as well, confused God's predestination with human dominion. Of course, Mather and Willard attempted to locate slavery
within the scheme of providence not only, and perhaps not even
primarily, to justify keeping slaves. They also wanted to inspire slave
owners to exercise benevolent care of their property. And yet the
Puritans perceived both the relationship between God and humans
and the relationship between white and black in hierarchical terms.[7]
Grace in early American theology promoted a coercive aristocracy.

It did not need to be this way. In fact, Samuel Sewall, a Boston
layman, merchant, and judge, applied grace in a dramatically different fashion.[8] In his *The Selling of Joseph: A Memorial*, published in
1700, Sewall used Puritan theology to question human bondage. "It
is most certain, that all humans, as they are the offspring of Adam,

are coheirs; and have equal right unto liberty, and all other outward comforts of life," argued Sewall, a Puritan who had listened to and read the sermons of Willard, but who applied the lessons of providence in a strikingly different way.[9]

As his title suggests, Sewall considered the biblical figure of Joseph—sold into slavery by his brothers, to be a "type" of African slave. Just as it had been unjust for Joseph's brothers to sell him into slavery, so too it was unjust for English colonists to buy and sell black human beings. "There is no proportion between twenty pieces of silver, and liberty," wrote the Puritan judge. And this argument had a practical import. "It might not be unseasonable," Sewall advised his fellow Puritans, "to inquire whether we are not culpable in forcing the Africans to become slaves amongst ourselves."[10] Confidence in God's grace did not need to legitimate coercion.

But Sewall's call for an inquiry into culpability was not taken up by many of his co-believers. In fact, John Saffin, another Puritan judge, who happened to trade in slaves, thought Sewall's suggestion highly unseasonable. To assert as Sewall did that all humans deserved liberty,

seems to invert the order that God hath set in the world, who hath ordained different degrees and orders of men, some to be high and honorable, some to be low and despicable; some to be monarchs . . . others to be subjects; . . . yea, some to be born slaves, and so to remain during their lives. . . . Otherwise there would be a mere parity . . . and it would then follow that the ordinary course of divine providence of God in the world should be wrong and unjust, (which we must not dare to think, much less to affirm).[11]

Well, Sewall was both thinking it and affirming it. Providence could not justify anything and everything. If the golden chain of election was being translated into the iron shackles of slavery, then maybe the whole idea of the chain needed to be done away with.

Of course, there were slaveholders and traders who cared not at all about predestination or providence, and there were critics of slavery who did not bother to use the Bible to justify their critique. Slavery was far too complex a social phenomenon to be simply the outgrowth of a theological position.[12] And yet the doctrine of predes-

tination clearly lent itself to a hierarchical, and paternalistic, interpretation. A doctrine that bound the human will to God could be
used to bind one human will to another. If from one perspective,
then, providence and predestination seemed to be the only way to
guarantee a peaceable social order, from another perspective the
doctrine of predestination could also be blamed for an unjust one.

A few early Quaker writers took the latter approach. In 1688 the
Friends of Germantown, Pennsylvania, described the obvious fact
that "the most part of such [blacks] are brought hither against their
will and consent."[13] Slavery coerced wills. George Keith reiterated
the point in 1693. Africans were "brought from their own country
against their wills," wrote Keith, and this fact was directly contrary
to Christ's "gospel of peace, liberty and redemption from sin, bondage and all oppression." Blacks "are a real part" of humanity, Keith
argued, and "Christ the light of the world hath (in measure) enlightened them . . . and [they] are made conformable unto him in love."[14]
Like Sewall (who was hardly a Quaker), Keith believed that all
humans possessed a wide range of liberty through Christ, and that
blacks had a share in this. "Therefore," ran the conclusion, "we
earnestly recommend it to all our Friends and Brethren, not to buy
any negroes, unless it were on purpose to set them free."[15]

This recommendation, like Keith's Quakerism generally, was not
well received. Many Quakers continued to hold slaves until late in
the eighteenth century.[16] But Keith's argument may have had an
impact upon John Hepburn, an obscure tailor from New Jersey, who
put together a book that provides the clearest and earliest link between antislavery and anti-Calvinism. Hepburn's book, *The American Defense of the Golden Rule, Or an Essay to Prove the Unlawfulness
of Making Slaves of Men*, not only included a number of tracts against
the practice of slavery, it also contained a treatise attacking Puritan
predestination as a doctrine showing "little love and charity either
to God or man."[17]

Hepburn had apparently met Keith on one of the latter's trips
through New Jersey.[18] This may explain in part why Hepburn assumed throughout his writings a doctrine of free will. Given Keith's
antislavery interest, the contact between the two men may also
explain why Hepburn drew out the social consequences of such a
doctrine more explicitly than previous colonial writers:

God hath given to man a free-will, so that he is master of his own choice (whether it be good or evil) and will in no way force and compel the will . . . yea, not unto that part which is good, far less unto evil. . . . And seeing then, it is thus with God and His creatures, we ought also to do so by our fellow mortals, and therefore we ought not to force and compel our fellow creatures, the Negroes . . . for when we force their will, this is a manifest robbery of that noble gift their bountiful Creator hath given them.[19]

Theology and society were inextricably connected. Slavery in theory promoted it in practice.

Throughout Hepburn's writing, he described slavery as a system of necessity. Slavery was "bondage"; it was "tyrannizing"; it laid "all manner of unavoidable necessities upon" slaves in order to break them. God had created human beings with free will, but slavery made it seem "that God did miss the matter . . . when he gave the Negroes (his creatures) the freedom of their wills." Hepburn had a shrewd eye for the economics as well as the theology of the case. Indeed, he charged, "our negro-masters have found out, by their ingenuity, how to mend this seeming defect" in God's creation, "and highly enrich themselves by the bargain."[20] No colonial satire was more pointed.

Admittedly, however, the satire was not specifically addressed to either Puritans or Calvinism. Hepburn hinted at the connection between the necessity of predestinarian ideology and the bondage of the social practice, but he did not draw the noose tightly. Published along with his treatise, however, was a little tract, specifically addressed to the Presbyterians, entitled "A Short Answer to that Part of Predestination, which asserts that Christ died for None but the Elect." The piece was written by Hepburn's father-in-law, Thomas Lowry, and it clearly identified Calvinism with an extreme position against free will.[21] In the literary context the point of this piece was obvious: Calvinism enslaved.

Lowry's central assumption was that Christ died for "every person," and therefore that "God wills the salvation of all." "These two put together," Lowry continued, "makes salvation possible to all . . . and puts everyone in a capacity of life, so that not so much as one need[s] to be lost." A doctrine of free will followed closely upon this universalistic assumption. "Everyone that will," Lowry wrote, "is welcome to eat of the bread of life, and drink of the water of life, freely."[22] The consequence of these assumptions was that Puritan doctrines such as predestination, election, and reprobation seemed to be "harsh thoughts" that rendered "the God of all love and mercy to be more cruel than the savages of the desert."[23] Puritan doctrine was extreme, resting wholly upon "the decree of an omnipotent power," so that "all other means" of salvation, including the humane treatment of other human beings, were "superfluous and unnecessary."[24] In no way a doctrine of the center, predestination was a rigid system of necessity that bound human beings spiritually, just as slavery bound them physically.

Both Lowry and Hepburn, in short, were anti-Calvinists; Lowry directly on the theological level, Hepburn indirectly on the social. The combination was admittedly precocious and inchoate, and it had little impact upon the surrounding culture. Apparently, even Quakers did not read the book. But the elements were in place.[25] And as the eighteenth century advanced, members of the Anglican Communion in the colonies joined the Quakers in opposing both the ideology of predestination and the Puritan aristocracy of grace which upheld it.[26]

5 "The Armies of the Philistines"

Prior to 1700, the colonial Church of England was, in the words of its modern historian J. F. Woolverton, "simply part of the scenery."[1] Even in Virginia, where the church possessed a virtual monopoly on the religious life of the populace, it remained marginal, and this was all the more the case in Massachusetts, Connecticut, and other strongholds of the Dissenters. But after 1700, Woolverton observes, "the church expanded significantly." Between 1701 and 1725, forty-five new Anglican churches were constructed in the colonies, and along with the buildings came clergy, missionaries of the Society for the Propagation of the Gospel, and theological polemicists willing to contend with Calvinists on matters such as the will.[2]

I

Without question the most notorious such polemicist was John Checkley. Checkley was a Boston native who as a youth had traveled widely in Europe, where he had developed an aesthetic sensibility and a preference for High Church liturgy. His return to Boston in 1717 as the proprietor of a bookstore and an apothecary positioned him strategically to disseminate Church of England propaganda. He published and sold a number of Anglican treatises, most in support of apostolic succession and the episcopacy, and was tried and convicted of seditious libel (fine of £50) after one such broadside, in 1723.[3]

But Checkley was also an author himself, and his 1720 *Choice Dialogues Between A Godly Minister, and an Honest Country-Man, Concerning Election and Predestination* were a summary of everything Anglicans from Maine to Georgia found wrong with Calvinism. Checkley advertised his dialogues as written "in a very easy and familiar manner, so that the meanest plough-man . . . may understand them." Indeed, he framed his dialogue as a conversation between an Anglican cleric and a remarkably literate farmer. The Boston pharmacist reasoned that a popular approach was necessary to counter the prevalence of "many pernicious (and I fear alas! soul-destroying) books . . . that debauch men's minds." There was simply "too, too great occasion for" the publication of his work, and Checkley thus offered his dialogues as an antidote to Calvinist "poison" and to "rightly instruct" his fellow laymen "concerning the true Scripture doctrines of election and predestination."[4] Apparently, at least a few ploughmen read the dialogues, for they were reprinted as late as the 1740s.[5]

But if popular motives were foremost in Checkley's mind, the better part of his narrative was devoted to theological reasoning designed to show that "Presbyterian notions concerning election and predestination" were "rigid doctrines . . . [that] will take away our free-will, and transform us into something worse than brutes, for the brutes plainly discover a freedom of election in their actions."[6] To hold to doctrines like predestination was not only injurious to humanity, however, for it also derogated from God, and seemed "all blasphemy." Indeed, Checkley noted, "therefore the Lutherans have charged the Calvinists with worshipping the Devil." Puritan clerical shepherds and their sheep in the pew were "servile and abject slaves"; or, in more spiritual parlance, they were possessed, not only because their doctrines inplied as much, but because the Calvinists in power refused even to allow the preaching of an alternative to the aristocracy of grace.[7]

Having been arrested and fined by the established church leaders in Boston for nothing more heinous than publishing a tract, Checkley had plenty of reason to resort to *ad hominem* attack. But more often he trusted in the ability of ploughmen to follow logic. The Calvinist doctrine of reprobation, the idea that God predestined the majority of human beings to hell, called forth some strong arguments from the Boston bookseller. If God "made creatures on purpose to damn them, this has all the notion we can have of cruelty." In fact, reprobation made God appear unjust: "If [God] left [persons] no free will to choose whether they would sin or not, I see not how this can be reconciled to justice."

Checkley's most imaginative argument used an extended analogy—here drawn from experience, to support his case against Calvinism. Imagine that the "Calvinist" God was a jailer and the writer his prisoner:

Suppose you should tie me hand and foot, throw me into a prison, bolt and fetter me down to the floor, lock the doors fast upon me, and then set-fire to it,—then preach to me in at the window, and use the most pathetical exhortations to me to come out, and why would I stay there to be burned? . . . Yet this is the notion those rigid Calvinists would have us entertain of the goodness of God.[8]

What was the use of preaching to people God had imprisoned in flesh only to burn? Checkley articulated the standard Arminian critique of Calvinist doctrine. Reprobation was the "abhorrent" and "detestable" climax of a web of "Stoical and fatal schemes."

Between them, the arguments of the ploughman and the godly minister touched upon the most important matters of social life. "More of these [predestinarians] die in despair," the ploughman observed, "than of any other sort of people. I have seen them cry out on their death-beds for Assurance! Assurance! . . . [when] nothing but Election! Election! was in their minds. The condition of these poor people is lamentable."[9] In day-to-day life, the ideology of predestination made people careless: "Their heads being perpetually filled with the abstruse notions of predestination, election, reprobation . . . and that they have no free will or choice what to do. . . .

makes men careless (for why should they struggle when there is no remedy?)."[10] And finally the entire Calvinist system bred irrationality and chaos. "They can have no other assurance [of salvation] . . . but that of their own imagination. They cannot . . . render a reason of the hope that is in them. Nay, they speak against reason, and think it rather an hindrance to faith."[11]

Needless to say, between the ploughman and the godly minister, Checkley revealed himself to be a clever rhetorician. The facts of ordinary Puritan lives cut at least two ways: they were afraid of death, but faith in election no doubt comforted many; some were occasionally prone to antinomian excess, but more were scrupulous to a fault about moral endeavor; and the clergy may have occasionally spoken against "natural" reason, but they also used logic and persuasion to buttress their assumptions and the social order. But Checkley had personally perceived and persuasively pointed out a disparity between the inclusive claims of the Calvinists to represent the true Church of England and their attempts to enforce their claims with theoretical and political coercion. The ploughman had unearthed a problem: the facts did not meet the rhetoric of the "true middle" when it came to everyday life in Puritan Boston. The Puritans might have taken control, but they were not yet comfortable with it. Therefore the "Presbyterians" were, in an image no one could mistake, "the armies of the Philistines."[12]

In form as well as substance, Checkley's dialogues called the Calvinists Philistines because they had forgotten, in their attempt to control human life, that their doctrines were images and symbols. It was therefore the godly minister who pointed out that

the assurance of the predestinarians is all imagination, being built upon decrees which they confess to be secret and hidden from us. . . . Impressions upon the imagination may give great pleasure and even raptures of joy. And if these are built upon the true foundation, they are gold and precious stones; otherwise they are but hay and stubble, and will not endure the fire. They are often the delusions of Satan, who thus transforms himself into an angel of light, and deceives many an unstable soul. But they must be tried by the foundation. Upon which they are not built, if we can give no reason for them, but are flashes and meteors, and give a false light.[13]

Predestination had become a fantasy; a way for the Saints to deceive
and to coerce themselves and others.

Checkley thus concluded his pamphlet with what seems to the
modern mind to be a bizarre conclusion to a steady critique, namely,
that "reverently bowing in the public assemblies of Christians, at
the solemn mention of the sacred name" of Jesus ought to be restored
in the worship of New England's churches. But this made perfect
sense in the eighteenth century.[14] It was, in today's shorthand, a call
to the celebration of myth and ritual, in contrast to the struggle for
legitimation and control characteristic of the ideology of predestination. The "festivals and feasts of the church," as Checkley called
them, "are like the cask to the wine; the cask is no part of the wine,
but if thou breakest the cask, thou inevitably wilt lose the wine."[15]
The fact of the simile itself here, as much as its substance, was the
clue to the whole treatise. The Calvinists had become destructive
of the life of symbol-making spirits. Much wine had been lost.

II

The Calvinist response to Checkley came from the pen of the
twenty-four-year-old Thomas Walter, Harvard class of 1713, pastor
of the church at Roxbury, and at one time a friend of Checkley's.[16]
It is unlikely the friendship survived the exchange. Walter revealed
at least an implicit debt to the urbane bookseller by styling his
response also as a dialogue, *Between John Faustus A Conjurer, and
Jack Tory His Friend*. But the title had an edge. If Checkley had
wanted to present himself as a faithful member of the Anglican
Communion, and as a man of common sense, Walter reminded his
readers that the real author was a chemist and Tory. And just as
Walter's title dismissed any claim by Checkley to unearth spiritual
truth, so did the substance of his dialogue. As Perry Miller puts
it, "Walter tried to win by ridicule."[17] His response in kind to
Checkley's polemic reveals pointedly the political and spiritual limits
of the ideology of providence.

"Since you began with so much pomp and show," Walter began
his response to his former friend, "How is it man, the end's so vile
and low? Prithee, what wilt thou bring worth all this rout and touse,
the mountain groans in travail, and brings forth a mouse."[18] Neither

the style nor the substance of the piece improved. The ploughman's insights represented a "scurrilous work," "easy and shallow enough," and the godly minister was "a tinker," a "block-head," "a bastard . . . of the Church of England," and "if any people receive any impressions from thy pamphlet, they must be only such as have not so much brains as a mouse-squirrel in them."[19] "You are so far from doing any hurt . . . [to] the Calvinists," Walter derided the recently imprisoned Checkley, "that you only make sport for them."[20]

Walter's response suggests in a sinister way the accommodation of Calvinism to political power. Coercion and violence had become sport. For a few years yet, the heirs of the Puritans, at least in Boston, could get away with this. Eventually Checkley's argument needed to be answered. For underneath his exaggerations was a serious criticism of Calvinism that had been being aired in England at least since the time of Archbishop Laud (1633–45).[21] But Walter could even deny history at this point: "You have charged the Calvinists," he responded to Checkley, "with asserting that, which you and all the world knows they for ever abhor and disclaim."[22] However convinced this twenty-four-year-old Harvard graduate was that people in his world knew that Calvinism was not "Stoical," not "fatal," not a system that made "God the author of sin," nevertheless in other worlds, such as the one Checkley inhabited, these charges made increasing sense.

If the inclusive mythic ideal was still alive somewhere in the colonies, then, it was in places where people like Checkley struggled to point out the extremes Calvinism and its adherents were failing to hold together. By calling reprobation a "fatal" doctrine, Checkley called attention to necessity, and by calling predestination a fantasy, he highlighted the creative spontaneity of the human imagination. All in all, New Jersey Quakers and Boston Anglicans—and probably Indian children and African youth, if we only had records of their voices—could criticize Christians who had truncated their own story in the service of political control. The Calvinists had become the "armies of the Philistines." In the early eighteenth century, theology was anything but an arid intellectual exercise.

If the year 1720 was thus critical in the history of the question of free will in America, by virtue of seeing a direct critique of the ideology of predestination go to the public substantially unchallenged, the years immediately following were to be no less significant. In 1721, James Franklin published the first issue of the *New England Courant*, an anti-Calvinist newspaper if there ever was one. Significantly, Checkley was one of its regular contributors. A year later, at the Yale commencement of 1722, Samuel Johnson and Timothy Cutler, the tutor and rector of the school respectively, made public their conversion to Anglicanism, along with four other Calvinists. And in 1723 Benjamin Franklin, the brother of James, fled Puritan Boston for Philadelphia, and a year later for London, where he encountered a strain of thought regarding free will that led him not only to oppose Calvinism, but to develop an alternative public theology.

6 "The Doctrine of Devils"

I

Benjamin Franklin was the son of a Puritan.[1] He was selected by his father quite early for "service in the church," and although Franklin never came close to fulfilling his father's ambition, the Boston youth did attend Old South Church until his teens. Franklin could thus report in his *Autobiography* that he had been raised "piously in the Dissenting Way" and inculcated with the dogmas of "the eternal decrees of God, election, reprobation," and others. He also reported that "my Father's little library consisted chiefly of books in polemic Divinity, most of which I read, and have since often regretted."[2] Almost certainly, among these polemics were some concerning the problem of free will.

But although the mature Franklin often expressed disdain for Puritan theology, he also acknowledged a beneficial influence in his pious upbringing. Most notably, and oddly, Franklin recommended Cotton Mather—the same Mather who would write a work called *The Good*

Old Way in praise of predestination.[3] Mather's *Essays to Do Good*, Franklin claimed, "perhaps gave me a turn of thinking that had an influence on some of the principal future events of my life."[4] In another context, Franklin clarified the point: Mather's *Essays* had inspired "such a turn of thinking as to have an influence on my conduct through life; for I have always set a greater value on the character of a doer of good, than on any other kind of reputation; and if I have been . . . a useful citizen, the public owes the advantage of it to that book."[5] Franklin was the son of a Puritan.[6]

But his inheritance became mixed early on. By the time Franklin was sixteen, he had absented himself from Puritan sermonizing. Around the same time, he began to write for the *New England Courant*, the alternative Boston paper, which also printed the writings of the anti-Calvinist Checkley. Among these earliest writings of Franklin may be the comment of "Silence Dogood" (a delightfully ironic pseudonym given his later expressions of admiration for Mather's work) on the 1722 defections of the Yale tutor and students to Anglicanism.[7]

As "Silence Dogood," then, Franklin expressed sympathy with the converts. "I would not be suspected of uncharitableness to those clergymen at Connecticut," wrote Mrs. Dogood, for they "made their professions with a seriousness becoming their order."[8] Franklin also gave reasons for his judgment. One who "alters his opinion on a *religious account*," argued Mrs. Dogood, "must certainly go through much reading, hear many arguments on both sides, and undergo many struggles in his conscience, before he can come to a full resolution."[9] There is reason to suppose that Franklin himself, having decided to leave the community at Old South and having chosen to write for the anti-Calvinist *New England Courant*, was undergoing an alteration of religious opinion from Calvinism to Anglicanism.[10] If so, he was more likely than not hearing some arguments from his father. At the least, he was struggling in his own mind with the arguments from those "polemical books of divinity" about "election, reprobation," and the like.[11]

In any event, Silence Dogood wrote her letter, in the main, to counter the "suspicion . . . that those who are thus *given to change*, neither *fear God*, nor *honor the king*." Most of Puritan Boston no doubt thought the behavior of the converts scandalous, if not heretical and seditious, but the young Franklin, through Silence Dogood, was implying that they might in fact be worth emulating.[12] However, this little letter illumines much more than the changing opinion of an alienated Puritan youth. For the nascent theology Franklin expressed proposed a radically different ideology of providence from the Puritan doctrine of predestination. A change following the struggle of the free conscience was compatible with the fear of God and political order, and indeed, might be both pleasurable and beneficial. This precocious insight, expressed first in the voice of Silence Dogood, would eventually mandate a revolution.

II

But, of course, it took Franklin a few years to develop into the foremost advocate of "innate liberty" or "the democracy of law" in the colonies. In fact, Franklin's first published treatment of the problem of free will was frankly deterministic. Franklin's A Dissertation on Liberty and Necessity, Pleasure and Pain, written while he was in London in 1725, was a thoroughgoing statement of absolute fatalism, without a shade of Calvinist, or any other, mediation.

The thesis of the work, as Franklin explained it to Benjamin Vaughan more than a half century after its composition, was "to prove the doctrine of Fate, from the supposed attributes of God."[13] More accurately, in fact, the treatise assumed the doctrine of fate in both theological and materialist forms, and then set out to draw the moral (or rather amoral) consequences of such a doctrine. London probably did a lot of strange things to a lively and thoughtful youth in the eighteenth century. As Carl van Doren puts it, Franklin was "a young Bostonian trying to find reasons for doing as he liked in London," including initiating his notorious "foolish intrigues with low women."[14]

The eighteen-year-old Franklin prefaced his Dissertation as "my present thoughts of the general state of things in the universe." If it thus lacked something in specificity, it was nothing if not clear. The work was in two parts. Part 1 began with five propositions:

I. There is said to be a First Mover, who is called GOD, Maker of the Universe.

II. He is said to be all-wise, all-good, all powerful. . . .

III. If He is all-good, whatsoever He doth must be good.

IV. If He is all-wise, whatsoever He doth must be wise.

V. If He is all-powerful, there can be nothing either existing or acting in the Universe against or without His consent; and what He consents to must be good, because He is good; therefore evil doth not exist.[15]

This was, needless to say, predestination pushed to an extreme.

Franklin's sixth proposition, however, would have made a Calvinist wince:

If a creature is made by God, it must depend upon God, and receive all its power from Him; with which power the creature can do nothing contrary to the will of God, because God is Almighty; what is not contrary to His will, must be agreeable to it; what is agreeable to it, must be good, because He is good; therefore a creature can do nothing but what is good.[16]

Given his assumptions, Franklin's reasoning was ironclad. God controlled things not only generally, but, against the usual Puritan qualification, even the most particular actions. "If the creature is thus limited in his actions, being able to do only such things as God would have him to do . . . ; then he can have no such thing as liberty, free-will or power to do or refrain an action." And "if there is no such thing as free-will in creatures, there can be neither merit nor demerit. . . . And therefore every creature must be equally esteemed by the creator."[17] Franklin's Puritan father, no less than his brother's Tory friends, would have been appalled.

Part 2 of the treatise followed the same logical tack, but merely replaced the theology with physics and psychology. Human beings sense pleasure and pain. Pain or uneasiness produces a proportional desire to be freed from it. "The accomplishment of this desire produces an equal pleasure. Pleasure is consequently equal to pain." All action, Franklin was arguing, can be reduced to one motive, the desire to be free from pain, just as theologically all action proceeded from one cause, God's decree. The moral consequences, furthermore, were also identical when physics replaced theology: "Since every action is the effect of self-uneasiness, the distinction of virtue and vice is excluded." It would therefore be hard to argue with the author's conclusion: "Both parts of this argument agree with and confirm one another, and the demonstration is reciprocal."[18]

Indeed, Franklin's demonstration showed a considerable command of logic, and more than a little perverse creativity.[19] This was Puritanism gone to rot. While in London, Franklin had been reading the works of infidel freethinkers like Anthony Collins, Joseph Priestley, and David Hartley.[20] These *philosophes* had, apparently, become for him antinomian heroes. His chief antagonist was William Wollaston, a former Anglican priest and optimistic deist, for whose 1725 work *The Religion of Nature Delineated* Franklin had set the type.[21] When writing his *Dissertation*, Franklin was literally in a different world from that of Willard, Keith, Checkley, and the rest. It was only later, on his return to the colonies, that he arranged to have all but two copies of the *Dissertation* burned, and described its publication as one of the great "errata" of his life.[22]

III

While crossing the Atlantic after leaving London in 1726, Franklin composed a "Plan for Regulating My Future Conduct in Life." Most of the "Plan" is now lost, but in the preface, Franklin not surprisingly expressed the feeling that his life had hitherto been "a confused variety of scenes." The "Plan" itself was thus a practical program to "live in all respects like a rational creature."[23] This document was thus the direct antecedent of such famous Franklin productions as "The Way to Wealth" and the "Project of Arriving at Moral Perfection," and it is probably fair to say that it signified the end of young Benjamin's identity crisis.

Shortly after settling back into colonial life, Franklin's thoughts turned again to the problem of free will. His new understanding, consistent with the precocious insights he had expressed as Silence Dogood, was expressed in a short address to his discussion group, the Junto, probably in 1730.[24] This brief discourse has been published under the title "On the Providence of God in the Government of the World," and it clearly shows a change in the theology and metaphysics of the young printer.

In contrast to the fatalism of his *Dissertation on Liberty and Necessity*, Franklin's new position combined both providence and free choice.[25] There were, Franklin argued to the Junto, four possible solutions to the problem of free will:

1. Either [God] unchangeably decreed and appointed everything that comes to pass; and left nothing to the course [of] Nature, nor allowed any creature free agency. or
2. Without decreeing anything, he left all to general Nature and the events of free agency in his creatures, which he never alters or interrupts. or
3. He decreed some things unchangeably, and left others to general Nature and the events of free agency, which also he never alters or interrupts. or
4. He sometimes interferes by his particular Providence and sets aside the effects which would otherwise have been produced by any of the above causes.[26]

It was the fourth position above that Franklin took as his own, as "most agreeable" to "the common light of reason," and "most probably true."[27]

The first position above, that God "unchangeably decreed" everything, was fatalism. Its chief characteristic was absolute, extrinsic causality. Nothing was left to either immanent "general Nature" or human free agency. Franklin's reasons for rejecting this position were twofold. First, if God has from the beginning decreed everything, he "has no more to do . . . and has now no greater power than an idol of wood or stone; nor can there be any more reason for praying to him or worshipping of him."[28] Fatalism implied an otiose or absent deity. Second, Franklin rejected fatalism because it made worship worthless. He wrote to Benjamin Vaughan that "if all things are ordained, prayer must among the rest be ordained. But as prayer can produce no change in things that are ordained, praying must be useless and an absurdity. God would therefore not ordain praying if everything else was ordained. But praying exists, therefore all things are not ordained, etc."[29]

The second position of the four Franklin offered was chance. Franklin established the contrast between fate and chance clearly. In fatalism, God decreed "everything." In this second position, "without decreeing anything," God left all to whatever causes were stronger in "general Nature and the events of free agency." Suppose, he wrote, that God is "looking on and beholding the ways of his creatures." He sees some "heroes in virtue" who incessantly strive to do good, but are constantly meeting with obstacles, "incredible hardships," and "miseries" in their attempts to "please a good God." If God decrees nothing, however, "what answer can he make" to these virtuous heroes except, "take the reward Chance may give you, I do not intermeddle in these affairs"? Franklin thus rejected chance along with fate. If God saw some people "continually doing all manner of evil, and bringing by their actions misery and destruction among mankind, what can he say here but this, if Chance rewards you, I shall not punish you, I am not to be concerned."[30]

Franklin's first two possible positions, then, were the popular extremes expressed by the polarity fate-chance, or determinism-indeterminism. But by 1730 Franklin conceived of the question as a continuum, not a dichotomy. His third and fourth positions were unmistakably mediating. The third began, "[God] decrees *some things* unchangeably," and the fourth, "[God] *sometimes* interferes by his particular providence."[31] The difference between these two is subtle, and important. In the third position, the initial assumption is on the side of extrinsic order, with some concessions to free will.[32] God first determined some things, and continues to cause them, but he left a few things indifferent, to be determined by other causes, such as free agency.

In contrast, Franklin's fourth, and own, position, begins with the assumption of a plurality of causes, and limits it by an occasional providential intervention. Any number of causes can produce effects in the universe, including free agency, and "the general course of Nature." God's involvement is described as an "interference," or, as the title of the piece has it, "governance" of an otherwise self-determining, or at least intrinsically caused, universe. Needless to say, this was not quite the same thing Puritans meant by *providence*, but providence Franklin called it.

By 1730 the cosmos of Benjamin Franklin included a greater degree of freedom for the human than the average Puritan would have sanctioned. Franklin could affirm providence without predestination. For Franklin, God was able, not bound, to effect his will, and the Philadelphia printer also saw reflections of a similar freedom residing in the universe and in human beings. Thus, while "some may doubt whether 'tis possible there should be such a thing as free agency in creatures," Franklin admitted, it was easy to show how "the duties of religion necessar[ily] follow the belief of a providence," or how providence and moral responsibility could coexist.

"You acknowledge that God is infinitely powerful, wise and good, and also a free agent," Franklin began. And "you will not deny," he went on, "that he has communicated to us part of his wisdom, power and goodness; . . . and is it then impossible for him to communicate any part of his freedom, and make us also in some degree free? . . . I should be glad to hear what reason any man can give for thinking in that manner; 'tis sufficient for me to show 'tis not impossible."[33] If it were not impossible for God to be both just and free, then neither should it be impossible for humans to share in both a sense of duty and freedom. Humans mirrored the innate liberty of the divine.

In short, free agency and providence were compatible. And while Franklin could suggest that it was providence that was the more prominent notion, even the "foundation of all true religion," in fact it was free agency that assured the ability and power to act, to choose, and to live a virtuous life that was the more fundamental idea for him. For *providence* did not mean primarily an extrinsic system of causality to Franklin. *General* providence was the imma-nent working of nature, the innate abilities given to human beings as free agents, and *particular* providence was the occasional direct intervention from "outside" by God. Franklin had inverted the usual Puritan dialectic, without losing its substance.

I V

So, Franklin advocated "innate liberty." His support for a wide range of human free will was shaped further by a conflict in 1735 whose study should both clarify the issues distinguishing Franklin from the Calvinists and show the anti-Calvinist development of Franklin's ideology. The conflict centered around Samuel Hemphill, assistant minister at Philadelphia's first Presbyterian Church from 1732 to 1735. An Irish immigrant of limited ability (it was later discovered that he had plagiarized most of his sermons), Hemphill had satisfied Franklin's taste for rational, edifying sermons, no doubt because most of them were stolen from Anglican or Enlightenment sources.[34] Franklin was thus disappointed when Hemphill was accused of heresy, and his disappointment turned to outrage when Hemphill was convicted.[35] It was not long after the conclusion of the trial that Franklin's newspaper published the anonymous *Observations on the Proceedings against Mr. Hemphill.* There was little doubt that Franklin was the author.[36]

The Philadelphia Presbytery had accused Hemphill of preaching "nothing but morality," and that he had thereby departed from the teachings of the Westminster Confession. Six more specific charges had been brought against Hemphill by Jedediah Andrews, the senior pastor at the Presbyterian Church in Philadelphia, and Franklin's *Observations* took up the charges one by one. Among the most prominent of the accusations was that Hemphill had preached that "the Gospel is . . . implanted in our very nature and reason" rather than being an "imputed" gift of grace. Franklin did not deny the accusation, but argued rather that this account of Christianity is the only sensible one. "The opposite opinion," in fact, that God directly causes salvation from outside nature by "imputing" it to human beings, is "destructive both of the Gospel, and all the notions we have of the moral perfections of God." The gospel encourages duties that tend to both our temporal and eternal happiness, and, because they tend to give pleasure, are "agreeable to our nature."[37] Franklin's position on free will linked providence and pleasure.

In a second accusation, the Calvinist ministers had condemned a passage from a Hemphill sermon where the latter had urged his listeners to consider Christ "as a law-giver as well as a Saviour."[38] Franklin responded by suggesting that Mr. Hemphill was

here preaching against the Antinomians, who hold, that Christ's merits and satisfaction will save us, without our performing good works. . . . This is the most impious doctrine that ever was broached, and it is the duty of every christian minister to explode such errors, which have a natural tendency to make men act as if Christ came into the world to patronize vice, and allow men to live as they please.[39]

And a little later, Franklin made it clear that in fact the orthodox Calvinist ministers themselves were guilty of such impiety: "I am afraid," he wrote, "that it is the Antinomian doctrine of Christ's merits and satisfaction, which they call the true and proper one, with whose principles these gentlemen seem to be too much tinctured." By leveling this charge, Franklin joined other anti-Calvinists in relegating Puritans to the extreme on the question of free will. In the name of their doctrines, the Calvinists misused their political authority. Indeed, Franklin described Hemphill's trial as an American version of the Spanish Inquisition.[40]

A few months after these initial *Observations*, Franklin published yet another criticism of the trial, which stressed further what he saw as dangerous political implications of the Calvinist teachings. The treatment of Hemphill showed that the reigning orthodoxy was a denial of "the cause of liberty," and that the Calvinist ideology was full of "unrighteous claims." Franklin appealed to lay people especially to counter the dominance of such a clerically run system by "asserting our own natural rights and liberties." The Presbyterian ministers were "creed-imposers" who "get upon our backs, and ride us . . . where they please," and whose inquisitory tactics "tend to nothing less than utterly to subvert and destroy all."[41] Admittedly, this was as much anticlericalism as anti-Calvinism, but it was obviously the Calvinist ministers Franklin had in mind.

After the Calvinists responded with a detailed commentary justifying all six charges against Hemphill, Franklin wasted no time in issuing a third writing on the controversy, *A Defense of the Rev. Mr. Hemphill's Observations*. This was to be not only his last word on the trial, but also the most extensive comment on the topic of religion in his entire career. The piece was, furthermore, the most immoderate piece of writing he ever produced.

The tenor of the work was clear from the outset. Presbyterians, Franklin accused, held "slavish and arbitrary principles" inconsistent with "every thing that is real virtue, religion and Christian liberty." The ministers had prided themselves upon their unanimous vote against Hemphill, and had claimed that such unanimity was a sign of God's providence, to which Franklin retorted: "To make God the author of a palpable piece of injustice is little better than blasphemy, and I charge it on them as such." The largest part of the *Defense*, however, was taken up with showing how the supposedly "orthodox" doctrines in fact promoted "enthusiasm, demonism, and immorality in the world."[42] The doctrines of the Calvinists were "the doctrine of devils."

Franklin turned once again to the notion of "imputed righteousness," or the idea that Christ's good works merit salvation rather than the works of individual human beings. This notion "is abominably ridiculous and absurd in itself; . . . [and tends to nothing] less than the utter subversion of religion in general, and Christianity in particular." To help his case, Franklin turned to an expert, quoting at length from a book by Joseph Boyse, an Irish theologian who defended the compatibility of the gospel with a supposition that humans are "reasonable and free agents."[43] "Imputed righteousness" was nothing but "antinomianism."

A second focus for Franklin's anti-Calvinist argument was the doctrine of original sin. Hemphill had apparently preached that the Christian life could be a gradual progress in virtue. At least the ministers had accused him of denying the need for conversion, and denying universal human depravity. Regarding this latter conception of original sin, Franklin claimed it was

every whit as ridiculous as that of imputed righteousness. 'Tis a notion invented, a bugbear set up by priests . . . to fright and scare an unthinking populace out of their senses, and inspire them with terror, to answer the little selfish ends of the inventors and propagators. . . . Moral guilt is so personal a thing, that it cannot possibly in the nature of things be transferred from one man to myriads of others.

Again, Franklin sounded the antinomian critique: "If this be not Antinomianism, if it be not to preach the doctrine of devils, instead of the gospel of Jesus, I know not what is."[44] The Calvinists were extremists who terrified humans into giving up their innate liberties.

Throughout—and the treatise goes on through four more furious sections—Franklin's passion was proportionate to the degree to which he had also developed an alternative to the predestinarian ideology. Of course, the Philadelphia printer was neither metaphysician nor theologian. Hence his public theology was not worked out systematically. Ordinarily, throughout his long and vigorous life, Franklin expressed his religion in practical ways—through moral, scientific, and political programs that exemplified the assumptions of innate liberty, and that encouraged humans to exercise their abilities to will, to act, and to effect change.[45]

And yet the logic of "innate liberty" was present throughout Franklin's mature moral writings and in his political work. In the realm of morality, Franklin conceived of virtue as an art—something to be worked at—and indeed he assumed that all human beings had ability to achieve the good. He planned to write, although never completed, a book called "The Art of Virtue." He once argued that self denial was not the essence of virtue. And of course he framed his famous "Project for Arriving at Moral Perfection." God might have designed the palette, but human beings had to paint the picture. Franklin's conception of the moral life simply presupposed free will and the responsibility and initiative that went along with it.[46]

Similarly, in Franklin's social and political thought, free will and human ability were basic axioms. His *Proposals Relating to the Education of Youth in Pennsylvania,* for instance, stressed that while American pupils did not "want capacity," nevertheless "the best capacities require cultivation," just as "the best ground, which unless well tilled and sowed with profitable seed, produces only ranker weeds." The whole purpose of education must be to "fix in the minds of youth deep impressions of the beauty and usefulness of virtue of all kinds, public spirit, fortitude, etc. . . . and to strengthen the natural abilities."[47]

And in Franklin's most famous political writings, namely, the *Albany Plan of Union* of 1754 and the Articles of Confederation of 1775, a similar valuation of ability and assumption of free will are evident, albeit implicitly.[48] Having once defined his public theology of the democracy of law, Franklin never abandoned it. On the eve of the Revolution, for instance, Franklin could unfavorably compare colonial citizens under British rule to humans under the sway of a predestining God: "We are in your hands as clay in the hands of the Potter," Franklin echoed Romans 9 to an English correspondent.[49] The desirable and "natural" situation was of course the opposite state—to be free in a democracy of law. Similarly, Franklin's Articles of Confederation became the governing document of the former colonies precisely because of their decentralized character, and because of the autonomy they gave to the independent communities and their peoples. They failed for much the same reason.

It was, of course, a long way from Franklin's anti-Calvinism of 1735 to the founding of the Republic. But just as in the founding period Franklin would hardly be alone as a revolutionary advocate of the democracy of law, neither had he been alone in his earlier anti-Calvinism. The Philadelphia printer had been preceded by other writers who questioned the political control exercised by Calvinists in the name of the ideology of predestination. Even the most enlightened colonial *philosophe,* though, did not find it necessary to shed all ideas of providence. The extremes were quickly being ruled out, but whatever consensus early Americans were going to reach about the question of free will was going to be reached through conflict and debate. And in the middle years of the eighteenth century, as Newtonian science and the piety of revivalism captivated the minds and hearts of many colonists, both were quickly harmonized with the prevailing ideologies as tools to forge a new culture.

III The Prelude to Debate, 1721–1743

> To souls immersed in the black Gulph of Sin,
> Who [despairing] drink the deadly Poison in;
> Pleas'd with the fancy'd Freedom of their Will,
> They seek their crying Conscience to still;
> Nor can they bear dear Nature to deface,
> Pride will no Beggar be to Sov'reign Grace.
>
> SARAH PARSONS MOORHEAD, 1742

In the middle decades of the eighteenth century, Calvinists struggled to respond to the various anti-Calvinist challenges.[1] Cotton Mather, early America's most prolific author, made his career out of defending "the good old way."[2] But in one work, *The Christian Philosopher* (1721), Mather also sought to use the new Newtonian science to bolster the Calvinist ideology of predestination. Drawing on Newton and his popularizers, Mather recommended a "Holy Epicurism" that could, in principle, have revived the inclusive, mythic range of Calvinist theology. In the end, Mather's "Holy Epicurism" failed (it was more holy than Epicurean), but *The Christian Philosopher* did suggest one new direction for the "good old way."[3] Science and salvation could be compatible.

More successful than Mather's work, or at least more popular in revitalizing Calvinist claims to cultural authority, were the mid-eighteenth-century revivals and conversions that have come to be known as the Great Awakening. And although there were many players in this prelude to the emergence of a distinctive American culture, Jonathan Edwards was clearly the conductor. Edwards used a "rhetoric of fortune" to promote a popular indeterminism in association with the conversions of the era. As Edwards saw it, the revivals were a "surprising work of God." This popular emphasis on the unpredictability of the spirit, and hence of all of human reality as well, promised to serve as an effective apologetic counter to those who thought Calvinism a "fatal" scheme. As it began, then, the Great Awakening sanctioned extremes of piety that had been suppressed, at least within Calvinism, since the middle of the seventeenth century.[4]

But this balanced sort of extremism did not last, and in fact even Edwards pulled back over time. This retreat was in part because of the strong presence of opposers to the revivals, many of whom also took the name "Calvinist." Out of this opposition came a debate in which theology and politics merged. Edwards developed and deepened the public theology of the "aristocracy of grace,"[5] while the leading opposer, Charles Chauncy, picking up on many of the themes of enlightenment thought, paved the way for many Calvinists to support "the democracy of law."[6]

The Great Awakening, in other words, was an inconclusive, but pregnant, set of events in the intellectual life of the colonies. If it was a "revolution" in the American consciousness, as many scholars have claimed, it was at best a strange one. The causes and the contemporary explanations of the revivals were more significant than the revivals themselves, and both the causes and contemporary explanations of the revivals focused on the question of free will. The Great Awakening began, and ended, in doctrinal controversy; and in the very inability of Calvinists to agree we can perceive anticipations of the central dynamic of a new culture.

7 "Holy Epicurism"

It was always vital for New England's Calvinists to present a united front, but Cotton Mather must have sensed that he was stretching credulity when he claimed in 1726: "I cannot learn, that among all the pastors of two hundred churches [in New England], there is one Arminian."[1] Perhaps Mather's conclusion derived from a parochial focus; perhaps it was a creative bit of self-justification for a life spent fighting heresy, but in any event it was contrary to some of his own earlier perceptions. Mather knew plenty of anti-Calvinists, and on at least one occasion he had no difficulty at all in identifying them.

Indeed, as early as 1706, Mather was convinced that there was "a very numerous party" in New England who "hold no grace neces-sary," and who "very sinfully pervert" the doctrine of predestination. Predestination—the doctrine that God controlled the eternal des-tiny of each human being, "so plainly asserted by the Church of England"—was "every day," Mather believed, "unaccountably de-cried, and reproached, by many . . . who boast themselves the sons of the Church." There was a "snake in the grass" in New England. It was "high time," Mather thought, that his "country should be called upon to watch against the growth of these tares."[2]

Now we have already observed that the Anglican church was expanding throughout the colonies in the late seventeenth and early eighteenth centuries, and Mather certainly had no love for Episcopalians, but his 1706 treatise entitled *Free Grace Maintained and Improved* made it clear that not all of the vipers worshipped at Boston's King's Chapel, the most prestigious of New England's Anglican churches.[3] Indeed, more dangerous even than overt papists were the "numerous" unorthodox Calvinists who professed to believe in predestination but distorted the doctrine. Some of these heretics used predestination to emphasize the "security" of sinners, making them "presumptuous." Others taught predestination in such a way as to "discourage" natural virtue, and thus made people "desperate." Mather found both fatalism and antinomianism in New England, and he wanted to distance himself and his hearers from both.[4]

But the Arminian Anglicans were also among Mather's targets. These "sons of pride and profaneness" pointed to the predestinarian excesses of both the antinomian enthusiasts and the fatalists and simply "decried" the entire doctrine of predestination "as if it were useless, yea, and a hurtful doctrine." These were the "giants to be encountered with" who "hold no grace necessary . . . but only that which they call moral grace, or moral suasion; and which amounts to no more than a rational proposal of our duty." This position led to "no end" of doctrinal deviations. It denied the "fore-knowledge of God." It denied "infused habits." It denied "special grace." And above all, it denied "all sanctifying operations of the almighty Spirit on the will . . . as will or can certainly incline it to act. . . . All that [the Arminians] will allow grace to do, is to propose unto the will, and leave the will indifferent, and leave it wholly unto the determination of the free-will." Stated positively, Arminians "ascribe such a vast power unto the will of sinful man, that they expressly assert, the will of man cannot be determined unto its acts by any irresistible motion, no, not from the great God himself."[5]

And Mather left no doubt about what the appearance of such doctrinal deviation meant for his country.[6] To see such open profession of human willpower was to see "an idol set up, which has more people, and nations, and languages falling down before it" than ever before. Stated more rhetorically, Mather asked the members of his own congregation who found Arminianism plausible what they would think of themselves if "the disposition of a carnal mind, so generally, to dethrone the grace of God, and set up the will of man in the throne of God, should be found, but a refined idolatry after all?"[7]

To put it mildly, then, for Mather, the anti-Calvinist Arminian way exhibited a "dangerous tendency." Mather's *Free Grace* was a jeremiad in a venerable tradition of Puritan denunciation of idolatry. And while his catalog of doctrinal deviations may well have prevented some sheep from straying, such a litany could just as easily lead directly to the jaws of the wolf.[8] Warnings inevitably breed curiosity, and the likelihood that Mather's rhetoric backfired is heightened when it is perceived that the alternative he was offering to Arminianism in 1706 was not only nothing new but rested upon little more than an appeal to "mystery" and "incomprehensibility." This was not likely to persuade many budding rationalists.

Essentially, to answer the anti-Calvinists, Mather stripped Puritan covenant theology of most of the doctrine of reprobation. God decided who was saved and damned, and hence election was "indeed absolute," Mather asserted, but at the same time "salvation is tendered unto every one of us all; and none of us will miss of [it] . . . but such as wilfully refuse it."[9] Following the same logic, Mather could assert that "God will determine the wills" of humans infallibly, "without destroying the nature, the freedom of them."[10] The Puritan ideology of providence was alive, if not well.

For when it came to explaining, amplifying, and supporting the truth of his paradox, Mather stumbled. "The doctrine of predestination hath its mysteries, its abstruse difficulties," he admitted. Indeed, "it is no little part of the homage, which we owe unto the glorious God . . . [to] acknowledge [predestination] incomprehensible."[11] Plato, Aristotle, even Augustine was gone. What remained was simply an appeal to the Calvinist theologian William Perkins's "golden chain" of election "that shall never be broken:"

[Election] lies not at the arbitrary determination of a sinner's free-will, whether it shall be broken or no. God will so move by his powerful grace upon the will . . . that it shall not be broken. Though we do not know the way of the Spirit, in this illustrious part of divine providence, . . . [so that God moves his people] and yet [does] not extinguish or overwhelm the free-will of the rational creature: Yet this we know, the determination of this point, who will, and who will not, be brought unto the faith of God's elect, is not left unto such a contingency, as what the free will of a fallen and corrupt man . . . shall please to do concerning it.[12]

Appeal to tradition was nothing new for Cotton Mather—his *Magnalia Christi Americana* virtually enshrined the practice as a hermeneutic.[13] But when the opposition was posing a problem to be solved by reason, one may wonder how much weight tradition and mystery were likely to carry.

In *Free Grace*, then, Cotton Mather was aware of the problem posed by anti-Calvinism, but uncertain, apart from an appeal to piety and the tradition of anti-indeterminism, how to respond. However, *Free Grace* was hardly the prolific Bostonian's only word on the problem.[14] Indeed, in his most popular work, *Bonifacius, or Essays to Do Good,* Mather had coined the paradox "Holy Epicurism" to describe the joy resulting from a life lived in useful harmony with true doctrine and piety.[15] in *The Christian Philosopher,* almost without knowing it, Mather suggested the philosophical basis for a holy Epicurism that was to point the way to the regrounding of Calvinism that had escaped him in *Free Grace*.

The Christian Philosopher was written in 1715, but not published until 1721. The broad thesis of the work, drawn directly from the pages of Newton and his popularizers, was that the new philosophy was not only not antagonistic to Calvinist Christianity, but was a direct support for it. This argument had more than an oblique bearing on the question of free will. Some European interpreters of Newton, such as John Toland, Julien LaMettrie, and the abbé d'Condillac, tried to replace mystery with mechanism, and thereby rule out free will; others, such as Samuel Clarke, found in the human *discovery* of mechanism a strong argument for the innate liberty of reasonable humans.[16] Mather, in opposition to both the determinists and the Arminians, declared that the "paradisaic regularities" of nature were unaccountable except as reflections of the purposeful providence of God.[17]

On the question of the will, then, Mather shaped the argument from design to give the greater weight to God's determination, while allowing a "secondary" freedom of action to rational human beings. In other words, he tailored the new philosophy to reinforce the ideology, if not the doctrine, of predestination.[18] This was no small intellectual achievement, and it had two key facets. First, Mather criticized interpretations of Newton that stressed the materialistic contingency—call it unholy Epicureanism—that the mathematicians' theories might seem to support. Second, after clearing nature's deck of atheistic chance, Mather directly connected the observable uniformities in nature with the providence of God.

The two moves often coincided. For instance, in Essay I, on the nature of light, Mather began by citing Newton's law of motion. "Would it not be proper," Mather inquired, "to lay down those laws of nature, by which the material world is governed, and which, when we come to consider, we have in the rank of second causes, no further to go?" The qualifications were important. Newton's laws described the "secondary causes" of harmony. First Cause, of course, was God. At some point beyond Newton's laws, "all mechanical accounts are at an end; we step into the glorious God immediately."[19]

For an example, Mather took the word of Newton's popularizer Samuel Molyneux regarding the movement of the planets. The coordination of the planets in their orbits was immediately resolvable into the will of God. "Chance, or dull matter," Mather quotes the British astronomer and politician as saying, "could never produce such an harmonious regularity in the motion of bodies so vastly distant: this shows a design and intention in the First Mover."[20] Newton himself was probably in sympathy with Molyneux's hypothesis, but early in his career he had at least considered the ether as the means by which motion across distances was conveyed.[21]

But fidelity to the legacy of Newton was hardly Mather's primary aim. The point was to make it clear that the axioms of the new philosophy, including notions such as that of gravity, were completely consistent with Calvinism. Gravity especially was "a most notable contrivance" by God, "to keep the several globes of the universe from shattering to pieces." Indeed, without gravity, "our globe in particular . . . would . . . be soon dissipated, and spirtled [sic] into the circumambient space, were it not kept well together by this wondrous contrivance of the Creator." And this axiom, said Mather, quoting Edmond Halley, was "insolvable by any philosophi-

cal hypothesis; it must be religiously resolved into the immediate
will of our most wise Creator, who, by appointing the law . . . keeps
all bodies in their proper places and stations, without it would soon
fall to pieces, and be utterly destroyed." Gravity provided indeed "a
very noble idea of providence."[22]

Mather's celebration of regularity occasionally went so far as to
seem to capitulate to those materialists who proposed a thorough
determinism.[23] He thus began Essay XXXII on the human being by
observing that "the body of man being most obvious to our view, is
that which we will first begin with; a machine of a most astonishing
workmanship and contrivance!"[24] For Mather, however, the doctrine
of the human machine did not lead to materialistic determinism.[25]
Mechanism controlled only the body, not the human being as a
whole. Mather's use of the "machine" image served primarily as a
contrast to Epicurean chance. "No sign of chance in the whole
structure of our body," Mather thereby concluded, making clear that
it was design and purpose he was interested in highlighting, not the
autonomous working of the mechanism itself.[26]

For when describing "voluntary motion," Mather clearly implied
that the will played some role in the process. The passage is admittedly cryptic to anyone not familiar with the jargon of early modern
medicine:

Voluntary motion should not be left unconsidered; whereof Dr. Cheyne
observes, the only conception we can form, is, that the mind, like a skilful
musician, strikes on that nerve which conveys animal spirits to the muscle
that is to be contracted, and adds a greater force than the natural to the
nervous juice, whereby it opens its passage into the vesicles, of which the
muscular fibres consist; but this action of the mind or will on these animal
spirits, is altogether unaccountable from the laws of motion. My God, in
thee I move! The astonishing power of spontaneous motion is what thou
hast given me! Oh! may I never employ it in any acts of rebellion against
Him that gave it.[27]

The foundations of the predestinarian ideology were changing. The
form was not.

Throughout *The Christian Philosopher*, then, Cotton Mather sought
to enlist "the more modern and certain philosophy" in the service
of Calvinist faith. The laws of motion, the regular orbits of the

planets, the working of gravity, the frame of the human body, all were clear evidence of the providence of God, ruling out any simple Epicurean chance.[28] At the same time, a small region of liberty was reserved for the human being in the area of voluntary motion, where the will was given spontaneous power by God to act. This correspondence between the "new philosophy" and the ideology of predestination was no coincidence. Mather's reconstruction of the way of the Fathers in his other writings was too thorough.

The conclusion of *The Christian Philosopher* was thus a celebration of the downfall of unholy Epicureanism:

Atheism is now forever chased and hissed out of the world, every thing in the world concurs to a sentence of banishment upon it. Fly, thou monster, and hide . . . ; never dare to show thyself in a world where every thing stands ready to overwhelm thee! A BEING that must be superior to matter, even the Creator and Governor of all matter, is every where so conspicuous, that there can be nothing more monstrous than to deny the God that is above.[29]

Mather was simply repulsed at the indetermined, or hyperdetermined, world of the "raving atheist."

Atheism was a system of "inconsistencies," it was "a bundle of contradictions," "a delerious phrenzy." "There would be no integrity left in the world," without God's governance; "men would soon be cannibals to one another." Human beings would be "as the fishes of the sea," and "worse than the creeping things, having no ruler over them." In the face of this frighteningly anarchic prospect, mechanism had to be sanctified. " 'Tis not from your fortuitous concourse of atoms" that matter had order, Mather chided "ye foolish Epicureans." Indeed, as holy Epicureans knew, order emerged from chaos through the immediate presence of the Triune God.[30]

If, then, Cotton Mather had predicted one way Calvinist elites could respond to any and all anti-Calvinists, his effort to harmonize Newtonian science with the ideology of predestination always remained more holy than Epicurean. But in the outbreak of pious emotion in the 1730s and 1740s in New England, another attempt to reconcile the opposites of necessity and chance, spontaneity and order, would have an even more profound impact on the cultural life of the New World.

8 "God Gone Out of His Ordinary Way"

Cotton Mather's dabbling with Newtonian physics made little direct impact on the debate over the question of free will in the New World.[1] But the events known as the Great Awakening, starting with the revivals in Northampton, Massachusetts, in 1734, touched every level of life in the colonies. The philosophy of science most colonists could take or leave. Salvation was, for many of them, another matter.

I

Throughout his early reports on the mid-eighteenth-century revivals in which many colonists claimed to be saved, Northampton's pastor, Jonathan Edwards, employed a "rhetoric of fortune" to highlight just how unpredictably the spirit worked.[2] Predestination was compatible with surprising changes, even chaos. The rhetoric simply rolled off the pages of Edwards's *A Faithful Narrative of the Surprising Work of*

God. In December of 1734, Edwards reported, "the Spirit of God began extraordinarily to set in" at Northampton, and "there were, very suddenly," five or six converts. The news spread throughout the Connecticut Valley, and converts—"some of them wrought upon in a very remarkable manner," were reported at Northfield, Deerfield, Windsor, Groton, and at least twenty-five other towns.[3]

As Edwards's title pointed out, the revivals were a surprise, both in that they had happened and in the ways that they had happened. "The work was glorious, . . . [it] was carried on in a most astonishing manner." The conversions multiplied "like a flash of lightning," with an "endless variety" of forms.[4] "A glorious alteration" was produced in Northampton; the town was "never so full of love, nor so full of joy," as when these "remarkable tokens of God's presence," such as sorrow for sin and joy in grace, were manifest in tears and holy conversation. The outbreak of conversions was "wonderful," "very remarkable," a "shower of divine blessing," a time when "those that were wont to be the vainest and loosest . . . were now generally subject to great awakenings." Overall, the revival was "a very extraordinary dispensation of Providence: God has in many respects gone out of, and much beyond his usual and ordinary way."[5]

If the revivals themselves had been a surprise, Edwards's report on them was a careful rhetorical experiment. Edwards used the striking images of caprice, fortune, and change to balance the usual Calvinist emphasis on the order of predestination.[6] This experiment was especially evident when Edwards described the conversion of Abigail Hutchinson. A young, single woman, "long infirm of body," Hutchinson was from "a rational understanding family: there could be nothing in her education that tended to enthusiasm," Edwards tellingly reported.[7] Hutchinson was awakened in the winter of 1734, after learning of the first wave of conversions in Northampton. She began to read Scripture in earnest, and her reading produced a "great increase" in "the sense of her own sinfulness," which in turn led to increased study. Her sense of her unworthiness grew so strong, and so exaggerated her physical illness, that she could not attend worship one Sunday. Then:

As she awaked on Monday morning, a little before day, she *wondered within herself* at the easiness and calmness she *felt in her mind,* which was of that kind which she never felt before; as she thought of this, such words as these were *in her mind*: "The words of the Lord are pure words, health to the soul and marrow to the bones." And then these words *came to her mind,* "The blood of Christ cleanses [us] from all sin;" which were accompanied with a lively sense of the excellency of Christ. . . . By these things *her mind was led* into such contemplations and views of Christ, as filled her exceeding full of joy. She told her brother that she had *seen (i.e., in realizing views of faith)* Christ last night. . . . On Monday she felt all day a constant sweetness in her soul.[8]

The pivotal movement in this passage, from a rhetorical point of view, is the way Edwards describes Abigail's own role in her conversion. At the outset of the narrative, it is simply reported that she "wondered within herself" and felt calmness "in her mind." But in the course of the narration, Edwards shifts to the passive voice. Scripture "came" to her mind, and then "her mind was led" into views of Christ. By the end of the narration, the purpose of this shift is explicit. The visions Hutchinson saw were not physical manifestations of the deity, much less spiritual apparitions, but were seen "by faith," to which Abigail's mind had been "led." In other words, Edwards's report gave a joyous intrinsic experience the sanction of extrinsic authority; not only the implicit authority of God's first motion, but the extrinsic authority of the Protestant teaching of salvation by grace through "faith."[9] The unpredictable inner working of the spirit was compatible with the orderly ways ordinarily imposed by God. It mattered little, then, that Abigail's illness increased and her physical body passed away. She had been given a greater gift than life on earth.[10]

And whatever one makes of such theology, the linguistic move contained within Jonathan Edwards's description became paradigmatic for revivalism ever after. During the revivals of 1734 and 1735, and on into the 1740s, Edwards radically destabilized the usual Calvinist theology of grace by rhetorically stressing its extraordinary, "surprise" elements. He made salvation by grace through faith appear to be as much a matter of fortune as of fate. The Holy Spirit was unpredictable. In other words, Edwards's reconstruction of the Puritan center was thoroughly mythopoeic, and for this reason, it was the perfect counterpoint to the anti-Calvinist charge of fatalism. At the outset of the Great Awakening, Edwards appeared to be as much an indeterminist—an enthusiast—as a determinist.

So when the revivals moved beyond Northampton, Edwards welcomed them as continuing surprising works of God. The itinerant revivalist George Whitefield first visited New England in September 1740, and before then other traveling Calvinist preachers, such as Gilbert Tennent, Eleazer Wheelock, Samuel Davies, and James Davenport, had advanced their own versions of the rhetoric of fortune.[11] The continuity with the revivals of 1734 and 1735 was widely recognized. It was precisely that continuity that made the Awakening appear "great" to later historians, rather than just an episode.[12] But as the rhetoric of fortune began to take flesh, most notably in the person of James Davenport, it began to meet with resistance.

II

Davenport was the Yale-educated minister of the church in Southold, Long Island, who heard Whitefield preach in 1740 and who took to itineracy in the spring of 1741.[13] He visited first Connecticut, then Rhode Island, and finally made another sweep down the coastline as the summer drew to a close, including a stop at New Haven. Throughout his visits, Davenport preached in a manner designed to effect conversions. He used the rhetoric of fortune. Along with preaching to the congregations, however, Davenport interrogated the established clergy of the cities he visited concerning their spiritual well-being and denounced those he considered unconverted (most of them) as complacent blind guides, Pharisees, and unfit ministers.[14] And, to make matters worse, Davenport endorsed hymn-singing in the streets.

One of these street hymns was printed, and even in this form it provides a telling glimpse of the rhetorical relocation of grace under way in the most extreme expressions of revivalist theology. "Me," "my," "home," "into my breast," and similar images of intrinsic grace dominate the song:

> My soul doth magnify the Lord,
>   My Spirit doth rejoice
> In God my Saviour, and my God;

I hear his joyful voice.
I need not go abroad for Joy,
    Who have a Feast at home;
My sighs are turned into Songs,
    The Comforter is come.

Down from above the blessed Dove
    Is come into my Breast,
To witness God's eternal Love;
    This is my heavenly Feast.
This makes me Abba Father cry,
    With Confidence of Soul;
It makes me cry, My Lord, my God,
    And that without controul.[15]

Such a personal and "uncontroulled" apprehension of grace was bound to make some heirs of the Puritans uneasy.

It did. Objections to Davenport's first tour through Connecticut had been aired by residents of Stonington, New London, and New Haven. When Davenport made a return visit in the spring of 1742, he was almost immediately arrested, and "after a riotous trial" in June, the General Assembly of Connecticut declared its verdict:

This assembly is of the opinion, that the things alleged, and the behaviour, conduct and doctrine advanced and taught by the said James Davenport, do and have a natural tendency to disturb and destroy the peace and order of this government: Yet it further appears to this assembly, that the said Davenport is under the influence of enthusiastical impressions and impulses, and thereby disturbed in the rational faculties of his mind.[16]

Hence Davenport was banished, sent back to Long Island, "the place from which he came, and wherein he is settled." Or at least so the assembly hoped.

But the peace was not so easily decided by a General Assembly of Connecticut, and in fact Davenport was in Boston by June 28. An observer penned the following report:

He has preached every day . . . upon the Common, to pretty large assemblies. . . . When he first ascends the rostrum, he appears with a remarkable settled countenance, but soon gets into the most extravagant gesture and behaviour both in prayer and preaching.—His expressions in prayer are often indecently familiar; he frequently appeals to God, that such and such impressions are immediately from his holy Spirit, but especially his sermons are full of his impressions and impulses, from God. . . . He has no knack at raising the passions, but by a violent straining of the lungs, and the most extravagant wreathings [sic] of his body, which at the same time that it creates laughter and indignation in the most, occasions great meltings, screamings, crying, swooning, and fits in some others. . . . Were you to see him in his most violent agitations, you would be apt to think, that he was a madman just broke from his chains: but especially had you seen him returning from the Common after his first preaching, with a large mob at his heels, singing all the way thro' the streets, he with his hands extended, his head thrown back, and his eyes staring up to heaven, attended with so much disorder, that they looked more like a company of Bacchanalians after a mad frolick, than sober Christians who had been worshipping God."[17]

So Davenport had somehow turned the staid New England laity into Bacchanalians. To make matters worse, he had also once again denounced the established clergy as complacent, blind guides who imperiled souls.

Purely by chance, the associated pastors of Charlestown and Boston were gathered during Davenport's visit. With nothing whatsoever of chance in mind, these ministers took the occasion to invite Davenport to a meeting the day after one of his "Bacchanalian" sermons. The effect of the meeting was predictable. The ministers first accused Davenport of abandoning his flock on Long Island and then got around to the meat of the issue: It "appears to us that he is a gentleman acted much by sudden impulses . . . as we can by no means approve of or justify, but must needs think very dangerous and hurtful to the interests of religion." The majority of the Boston clergy apparently did not have Edwards's ability to justify sudden impulses with faithful order:

We judge also that the Reverend Mr. Davenport has not acted prudently, but to the disservice of religion, by going with his friends singing thro' the streets and high-ways . . . and by encouraging private brethren to pray and exhort in larger or smaller assemblies . . . ; a practice which we fear may be found big with errors, irregularities, and mischief.[18]

By August, Davenport was in jail, and by October, he had been judged once again *non compos mentis*, and shipped back across the Sound.

III

But even then the real trial was barely under way. Sarah Parsons Moorhead, probably the wife of John, the first pastor of the Arlington Street Church, published a poetic letter *To the Rev. James Davenport, on his Departure from Boston, by Way of a Dream*.[19] The letter concludes *With a Line to the Scoffers at Religion* suggesting that the judgment against Davenport was less than unanimous. "I love the zeal that fires good Davenport's breast," reports Moorhead, "but his harsh censures give my soul no rest."

> Our worthy Guides whom GOD has much inflam'd,
> As unexperienced Souls, alas, he nam'd;
> Hence giddy youth a woeful licence take,
> A [strike] at reverend hoary heads they make.

In the main, Moorhead supported Davenport's goals. But his "unguarded sad imprudence" in criticizing "reverend hoary heads" had led conversion to be labeled "the drunkard's song," with the result that "contention spread her harpy claws around."[20]

The bulk of Moorhead's subversive poem is a vision of Davenport transported alive to heaven. There he is robed in "roses, honeysuckles, and Jessamine" and reclines on "sheets of white lilies." In paradise, Davenport is attended by "pretty birds" in a place where "gilded clouds ambrosia drops distill." He is guarded by "shining warriors" and "singing angels," while a voice whispers "gentle checks"—basically, judge not that ye be not judged—in his ear.

Perhaps not surprisingly, the result of this advice is that Davenport repents: "In his breast a holy shame there springs," as Moorhead puts it; or, as she later has Davenport himself exclaim: "The very End my Zeal pursu'd the most, the glorious End untemper'd Zeal has lost." After eliciting this confession, Moorhead returns Davenport to Earth, where he apologizes to the Boston clergy he had condemned and vows to cooperate with them in spreading true religion.[21] Ironically, this is not far from the actual course of Davenport's career. After one last "Bacchanal" and book-burning fling at New London, Davenport settled down to preach respectably for fourteen more years on Long Island, even publishing in 1744 a "Retraction" emphasizing his "misguided zeal."[22]

But Moorhead in 1742 also saw another outcome. Once checked of a few misapplications, Davenport's message could be driven home

> To souls immersed in the black Gulph of Sin,
> Who [despairing] drink the deadly Poison in;
> Pleas'd with the fancy'd Freedom of their Will,
> They seek their crying Conscience to still;
> Nor can they bear dear Nature to deface,
> Pride will no Beggar be to Sov'reign Grace;
> Array'd in moral Duties, gaudy shew,
> They for a Saviour little have to do;
> They wonder any such Complaints should make,
> In Reformation they a Shelter take:
> Dare you appear before th' eternal Throne
> In this vile Cob-webb Garment of your own! . . .
> While at the worthy Man you railing stand,
> Say, should such Truths as these your Minds offend?[23]

Moorhead was a supporter of conversions, but she was saddened by the overt political turn that the revivals were taking. Her nuanced and subtle critique of both revivalistic excesses and those elites enamored with "the fancy'd freedom of their will" made her a perceptive observer of eighteenth-century New England. If her husband was indeed one of New England's "reverend hoary heads," the subversive public theology recommended by her poem is all the more remarkable.

IV

In his *The Distinguishing Marks of a Work of the Spirit of God*, delivered at Yale commencement in the aftermath of Davenport's 1741 visit, Jonathan Edwards joined Sarah Parsons Moorhead in seeking to subvert religious deadness while still preserving Calvinist orthodoxy. Edwards's thesis was: "That extraordinary influence that has lately appeared on the minds of the people abroad in his land . . . is undoubtedly, in the general, from the Spirit of God."[24] The caprice of the revivals was in fact grounded by an orderer, God.

Again, Edwards showed himself a rhetorical master. He repeated, like a chorus: "*'Tis no sign* that a work is not the work of the Spirit of God, that it is carried on in such a way as the same Spirit of God heretofore has not been wont to carry on his work." God could do new things. "*'Tis no argument* that an operation that appears on the minds of a people, is not the work of the Spirit of God, that it occasions a great ado." God could cause confusion. "*'Tis no argument* . . . that many . . . have great impressions on their imaginations." God could work through images. "*'Tis no sign* that a work that is wrought amongst a people is not from the Spirit of God, that many that seem to be the subjects of it, are guilty of great imprudences and irregularities in their conduct."[25] God's people made mistakes.

The repetitive "*'Tis no sign*" beginning provided a stable rhetorical base upon which Edwards sanctioned the unusual and the "extraordinary." By not condemning, Edwards approved remarkable "effects on the bodies . . . such as tears, tremblings, groans, loud outcries, agonies of body," "a kind of ecstacy."[26] And indeed, Edwards juxtaposed order and disorder, ordinary and extraordinary, in a way that went beyond rhetorical devices. The myth was stated directly. God's order was not the same as that of human prudence, and a holy confusion might, in fact, be as much God's way of saving people as a thunderstorm was his means of watering plants.

Some objected that the chaos attending the conversions was a sure sign that they were false, since God "is the God of order, not of confusion. But let it be considered," Edwards said:

What is the proper notion of confusion, but the breaking [of] that order of things whereby they are properly disposed, and duly directed to their end, so that the order and due connection of means being broken they fail of their end; but conviction and conversion of sinners is the obtaining the end of religious means. . . . [Therefore] if God it pleases to convince the consciences of persons, so that they can't avoid great outward manifestations, even to the interrupting and breaking off those public means they were attending, I don't think this is confusion . . . any more than if a company should meet on the field to pray for rain, and should be broken off from their exercise by a plentiful shower. Would to God that all the

public assemblies in the land were broken off from their public exercises
with such confusion as this the next Sabbath day![27]

God could not be limited, and if He chose to work beyond the
ordinary means, humans were to praise Him for the variety.

The myth Edwards had in mind in fact went back to creation.
After all, he pointed out: "In the first creation God did not make a
complete world at once; but there was a great deal of imperfection,
darkness, and mixture of chaos and confusion, after God first said,
'Let there be light,' before the whole stood in perfect form." Or, less
directly, "The fruits of the earth are first green, before they are ripe,
and come to their perfection gradually."[28] The revivals were but a
stage in the development of God's creation; they should be allowed
to continue to maturity.

In short, then, for James Davenport, Sarah Parsons Moorhead,
and for Jonathan Edwards in his earliest reports on the revivals, the
enthusiasm of the mid-eighteenth-century converts to Calvinism was
not a problem. Indeed, confusion was to be expected when God was
doing something new. At the same time, however, this return of
myth to New England also was increasingly accompanied by overt
criticism of the established clergy. And it was this political dimension to the revivals, and to the opposition, that became increasingly
apparent as the debate over conversion turned more directly to the
problem of free will.

9 "A Strange Revolution"

I

The leading spokesman for the Calvinists opposed to the mid-eighteenth-century revivals was the pastor of First Church in Boston, Charles Chauncy.[1] Chauncy's first *public* antirevivalist production was the 1742 sermon *Enthusiasm Describ'd and Cautioned Against. A Sermon . . . With a Letter to the Rev. Mr. James Davenport.* The sermon had four parts, in which Chauncy defined enthusiasm, established rules for judging when enthusiasm was present, cautioned against becoming involved with enthusiasts, and applied anti-enthusiast doctrine to the present times. The brief letter to Davenport was an appendix to the whole. Throughout, Chauncy linked the revivals both to theological error and to social and political unrest.

Chauncy admitted that the word *enthusiasm* generically meant "inspiration from God," but in modern times, he noted, the term was specifically "used in a bad sense, as intending an imaginary, not a real inspiration." "The enthusiast is one," Chauncy went on, who has a conceit of himself as a person favoured with the extraordinary presence of the Deity. He mistakes the workings of his own passions for the divine communications, and fancies himself immediately inspired by the Spirit of God. . . . The cause of this enthusiasm is a bad temperament of the blood and spirits; 'tis properly a disease, a sort of madness.

Chauncy probably had James Davenport's recent trial behavior in mind.[2] "In nothing does the enthusiasm of these persons discover it self more, than in the disregard they express to the dictates of reason." Enthusiasm, in short, was "a kind of religious phrenzy."[3]

With one swipe Chauncy undercut the rhetoric of fortune. In good Enlightenment fashion, he appealed to a God who was not "the author of confusion, but of peace." Indeed, disorder was the tendency of enthusiasm wherever it appeared:

No greater mischiefs have arisen from any quarter. . . . It has made strong attempts to destroy all property, to make all things common, wives as well as goods.—It has promoted faction and contention; filled the church sometimes with general disorder. . . . It has, in one word, been a pest to the church in all ages.

Or, more succinctly, "there is nothing so wild and frantick, but you may be reconciled to it," once you were caught up in the rhetoric of fortune.[4]

Actually, Chauncy and Edwards agreed on the facts about the revivals; they disagreed over value. The revivals had brought extraordinariness, remarkable conversions, surprising changes, and while for Edwards this was God doing something new, for Chauncy it was simply confusion. Uproar was not the way God worked. "The Spirit of God deals with men as reasonable creatures: And they ought to deal with themselves in like manner."[5] God did not need to balance His orderly rule with occasional dips into chaos: "The veryest fancies, the vainest imaginations, the strongest delusions, they have fathered on [God]," to his eternal "dishonour."[6] For Edwards, God was either the Lord of the extremes or He did not deserve the name God. For Chauncy, there was simply little need to advertise God's wildness, since the average person needed above all to have an example of reason, benevolence, and society-building virtue. Both sides had strong cases, and the issue was anything but decided after this first exchange.

Thus, an anonymous author, probably Chauncy, penned a direct response to Edwards's *Distinguishing Marks*. This work, *The Late Religious Commotions in New England Considered,* defined even more clearly the party line of the antirevivalists. The thesis of the work was simple, but it again undercut the entire revivalist attempt to rebuild a mythic center and all but necessitated the move to ideology: There is, argued the anonymous author, "a natural way, [to] account for the affectings and meltings in the religious assemblies without supposing them the effects of the divine power and presence."[7] Edwards could have his rhetoric of fortune, his surprises, his extraordinary impulses. But they had nothing whatsoever to do with God and everything to do with the powers down below.

In short, power was becoming the issue. Two works published in 1742—Jonathan Edwards's *Some Thoughts Concerning the Present Revival of Religion in New England,* and Chauncy's *Seasonable Thoughts on the State of Religion in New England*—intertwined theology and political ideology in a way not seen in the colonies since the antinomian controversy of 1637. As long as the argument was explicitly about the revivals, nothing was solved. But as Edwards and Chauncy defined what became in effect the party platforms of the aristocracy of grace and the democracy of law, by weaving theological and political themes together, they identified the question of free will as the critical issue over which the colonial struggle for power would be fought.

II

Edwards's *Some Thoughts* directly declared the debate over the revivals a "war." "This is the most important affair that ever New England was called to be concerned in," the Northampton pastor pronounced. "When a people are engaged in war with a powerful and crafty nation, it concerns them to manage an affair of such consequence with the utmost discretion." In a war, in other words, what was needed was a strategy that would win: "We must either conquer or be conquered; and the consequence of the victory, on one side, will be our eternal destruction in both soul and body in hell; and on the other side, our obtaining the kingdom of heaven."[8] Nothing less than salvation was at stake; both of individuals and of the nation.

Much of *Some Thoughts* was completely consistent with Edwards's earlier writings. He reiterated the surprise of the conversions, he repeated the dialectic between chaos and order, and he argued again that in the revivals God had not "taken that course . . . which men in their wisdom would have thought most advisable." The Awakening was "a great and wonderful event, a strange revolution, an unexpected overturning of things, suddenly brought to pass."[9] But Edwards had already displayed the rhetoric of fortune in his earlier writings to little or no effect. Consequently, to really meet the opposers, Edwards had to try a new tack. The "war" imagery was only the beginning.[10]

Edwards readily admitted in *Some Thoughts* that the revivalists had erred. The converted had often been spiritually proud, had relied upon wrong principles, and had been naive to ignore the work of Satan. All three admissions show how Edwards gradually retreated from the rhetoric of fortune and pushed converts away from reliance upon intrinsic grace and toward a reliance upon the extrinsic authority of the community, of Scripture, and of God. If Edwards had advocated an inclusive mythology in his earliest writings on the revivals, in *Some Thoughts* he sought to rebuild the aristocracy of grace around the ideology of predestination.

Spiritual pride, then, was for Edwards the "mainspring, or at least the main support of" the other errors in the revivals. Spiritual pride disposed converts "to speak of other persons' sins," while ignoring their own flaws. A proud convert would affect "singularity in external appearance . . . [and] be singular in voice, or air of countenance of behavior." In short, a proud convert would "assume much to themselves, [and] . . . treat others with neglect." By such abstract accusations, Edwards condemned the extravagant preaching styles of the itinerants and the practice of revived preachers and laity of judging and pronouncing upon the spiritual estate of the unconverted. Such practices overthrew "Christian meekness and gentleness," and thus destroyed community. In short, "the corruption of nature may all be resolved into two things, pride and worldly-mindedness, the Devil and the beast, or self and the world," and the revival had unleashed much that was still worldly, demonic, and natural.[11] Grace had to be extrinsically oriented by the Christian community; not just by the self.

The second cause of error detailed by Edwards followed the same logic. Converts had relied too much upon an erroneous principle, notably the belief that " 'tis God's manner now in these days to guide his saints . . . by inspiration, or immediate revelation . . . by impressions that he by his Spirit makes upon their minds, either with or without texts of Scripture." Edwards himself had earlier countenanced a doctrine of immediacy, and much of his thought still depended upon it, but in this work a retreat was under way.[12]

"Many lay themselves open to delusion," Edwards began, "by expecting direction from heaven in this [immediate] way." Imagine, Edwards went on, some individuals confronted with a difficult choice who are "undetermined what they shall do" and hence wait "for some secret immediate influence on their minds." In such cases, people are often in fact "observing their own minds to see what arises there," and when something decides the case one way or another, "that oftentimes is called an uncommon impression, that is no such thing; and they ascribe that to the agency of some invisible being, that is owing only to themselves."[13]

Like the error of spiritual pride, then, relying upon "immediate revelation" emphasized the intrinsic, rather than extrinsic, sources of grace. Lost in the excitement of the Awakening had been Scripture, "as the words lie in the Bible." And also like spiritual pride, to rely upon self-revelation rather than Scripture "will defend and support all other errors. . . . For what signifies it for poor blind worms of the dust to go to argue with a man . . . that is guided by the immediate counsels and commands of the great Jehovah?"[14]

Finally, then, the third cause of error on the part of converts was "a being ignorant or unobservant of some particular things, by which the Devil has special advantage." In the excitement of the revivals, converts had lost sight of the fact that, not one, but two spiritual powers were operative in the world, and would be until the coming of the kingdom:

It is not to be supposed that Christians ever have any experiences in this world that are wholly pure, entirely spiritual, without any mixture of what is natural and carnal. The beam of light, as it comes from the fountain of light upon our hearts, is pure, but as it is reflected thence, it is mixed: the seed as sent from heaven and planted in the heart, is pure, but as it springs up out of the heart, is impure.[15]

For Jonathan Edwards, following a long line of Christian Platonists, the natural, carnal realm was, predominantly, the realm of the devil. And when the "high affections" of conversion were so mixed with natural imagination and passion, as they always were, "the Devil sets in and works in the corrupt part, and cherishes it to his utmost; till at length the experiences of some persons who began well, come to but little else but violent motions of carnal affections."[16] God may have controlled the world, but the Devil had a hand in it as well and generally managed to control the self.[17] In effect, Edwards was saying, spiritual change needed to conform explicitly to dogma. The rhetoric of fortune had as often as not left people with Lucifer; with an extreme, rather than with the center. Extrinsic authority now needed reinforcements.

Thus, regarding the "extraordinary" effects that Edwards had in 1735 found so delightful, in 1742 he argued that

there ought to be a gentle restraint held upon these things, and there should be prudent care taken of persons in such extraordinary circumstances, and they should be moderately advised at proper seasons, not to make more ado than there is need of, but rather to hold a restraint upon their inclinations; otherwise . . . persons will find themselves under a kind of necessity of making a great ado, with less and less affection of soul, till at length almost any slight emotion will set them going, and they will be more and more violent and boisterous, and will grow louder and louder, till their actions and behavior becomes indeed very absurd.[18]

The revivals needed to be controlled, and the aristocracy of grace that ran the churches, interpreted the Scripture, and defined the proper attributes of God had the means to do so.[19]

Above all, then, Jonathan Edwards's *Some Thoughts Concerning the Present Revival of Religion in New England* sought to revive the public theology of the aristocracy of grace. Edwards advocated this public theology most clearly in two sections of *Some Thoughts*, including one where he suggested that the millennium would probably begin in America.[20] The millennial note was subordinate, however, to the contours of Edwards's public theology, which he developed through a striking metaphor. The revivals, he argued, were like the crowning of a new king. Edwards now linked the revivals, no longer notable primarily for their surprise, to a hierarchical, stratified conception of society, in which each person should pay his or her respects in his or her place. Jonathan Edwards's ideal society—his millennial America—was monarchical, deferential, and aristocratic.[21]

Thus, Edwards first discussed the responsibilities of civil rulers in a time of revival. He simply presupposed a monarchy. And, he pointed out, when a new king is crowned, the king takes particular notice of how his political rivals respond: "God's eye is especially on [civil rulers], to see how they behave." Indeed, "above all others is it expected that the great men" should pay their respects to the king. Indeed, by "neglecting their duty at such a time," rulers "expose themselves to God's great displeasure." And, conversely, "by fully acknowledging God," rulers will "be in the way of receiving peculiar honors and rewards." Indeed, "the days are coming . . . when the saints shall reign on earth."[22] This was both a threat and a promise, but to Edwards civil authorities had the primary duty to honor and to respect the crowning of the new king.

Continuing with the coronation metaphor, Edwards next addressed "ministers of the Gospel." Indeed, as with civil rulers, God's eye was on them, "expecting of them that they should arise and acknowledge and honor him." Ministers were "the officers of Christ's kingdom," the "watchmen over the city," the "keepers of the keys of the gates of Zion," and therefore " 'tis their business to acquaint themselves" with the protocol of entrance into the kingdom. "We that are in this sacred office, had need to take heed what we do, and how we behave ourselves at this time. . . . 'Tis our wisest and best way, fully and without reluctance, to bow to the great God in this work, and to be entirely resigned to him." As the king's procession passed, ministers must "either bow to it or be broken," for the king's "hand will be upon everything that is high, and stiff, and strong in opposition."[23]

Having thus appealed to, and threatened, the civil and religious leadership, Edwards finally extended his political reach to "every living soul," each of whom "is now obliged to arise, and acknowledge

God in this work, and put to his hand to promote it." "All sorts of persons" could contribute, but Edwards mentioned especially the prominent and powerful. "The elder people" of the churches, for instance, were warned to "take heed to themselves, that they partake" in the revivals. Similarly, Edwards singled out for special attention "men that are high in honor and influence," and "rich men," who "have a talent in their hands" by which "they might very much promote such a work as this." Jonathan Edwards was no democrat.[24]

Edwards knew, in fact, that control of social structures was necessary for the aristocracy of grace. Hence, he could encourage coercion. "Great care should be taken that the press should be improved to no purpose contrary to the interest of this work." Colleges should "be so regulated, that they should in fact be nurseries of piety." And even loose speech, notably continual harping upon the "blemishes" of the Awakening, needed to be curbed. "Would it not be very improper, on a king's coronation day, to be much in taking notice of the blemishes of the royal family?"[25]

The point was obvious to anyone who knew anything about the way kings worked:

God doubtless now expects that all sorts of persons in New England, rulers, ministers and people, high and low, rich and poor, old and young, should take notice of his hand in this mighty work of his grace, and . . . everyone doing his utmost *in the place that God has set them in,* to promote it. And God, according to his wonderful patience, seems to be still waiting to give us opportunity, thus to acknowledge and honor him.[26]

Jonathan Edwards sought, through the revivals, to restore the aristocracy of grace—which for him meant a politics of monarchy, hierarchy, deference, and social control.

But why this development now? Why did Edwards at this point retreat from the rhetoric of fortune? The answer to that has to be complex, but the course of Edwards's own career suggests that the preeminent reason was dogmatic. The course of the controversy over the revivals had convinced Edwards that there were aberrancies in the doctrine of some revivalists. Consequently, for all its value, a conversion experience had to be subsumed under, or at least explicitly compatible with, Calvinist dogma.[27] The key to the success of the revivals was to remove the extremes that threatened "to break all in pieces," *and,* at the same time, to avoid both antinomianism and Arminianism.

In short, the members of the aristocracy of grace were not only saints with a peculiar experience, but saints who could articulate that experience in orthodox formulations:

I would now beseech those that have hitherto been something inclining to Arminian principles, seriously to weigh the matter with respect to this work, and . . . to consider whether or no, if it be indeed that this be the work of God, it don't entirely overthrow their scheme of religion; and therefore whether it don't infinitely concern 'em, as they would be partakers of eternal salvation, to relinquish their scheme. Now is a good time for Arminians to change their principles. I would now, as one of the friends of this work, humbly invite 'em to come and join with us, and be on our side.[28]

This appeal by Jonathan Edwards was, of course, more than a call to a political platform. It was a call to "truth" on the question of free will. But insofar as Jonathan Edwards had a public theology, it was consistent with the aristocracy of grace.

III

The degree to which Calvinism had attenuated in the colonies—and therefore mandated Edwards's conservative reaction, becomes apparent when we turn our attention to Charles Chauncy's *Seasonable Thoughts on the State of Religion in New England*. In the main, Chauncy simply rebutted Edwards's argument section by section. At the outset of the 400-page tome, however, Chauncy added a 30-page preface reproducing documents from the 1637 antinomian controversy. In Chauncy's own words, this preface was

a just account of the religious commotion in the country, soon after its first settlement by our fathers. . . . Few, I believe, will venture to disown a likeness between the disturbances then and now: they are indeed surprisingly similar. . . . The boldness and insolency of some of the zealots of this day; their alienations from their old friends; the disturbances, contentions, separations, and schisms . . . are as significantly spoken of, in the words pointing out the sad state of religion in old-time, as any could now adopt language . . . to describe what has happened, of late, in various parts of our land.[29]

"Truth" was historical. In 1742, as in 1637, the center was on trial. The difference was that in 1742, the losers would be neither clear nor, immediately, banished.

Countering Edwards point by point, Chauncy affirmed an Enlightenment alternative to the aristocracy of grace. The "impulses and impressions" of the converts were owing to people mistaking "the motion of their own minds for something divinely extraordinary." The personal visions, "swoonings," "bitter shriekings," "fallings to the ground," and other bodily effects, as well as the more institutional products of the revivals such as itineracy, extempore preaching, and judging of the spiritual state of others, were all simply "disorders" that had nothing to do with a "work of God." When it came to "enthusiasm," " 'tis far more reasonable to look for [its cause] in nature, than in grace."[30]

For Chauncy, humans needed grace, but grace worked by and large through orderly, natural means. The

influence of the Spirit does not consist in sudden impulses and impressions, in visions, revelations, extraordinary missions, and the like; but in working in men the preparations for faith and repentance, by humbling them for sin, and showing them the necessity of a Saviour; then by effecting such a change in them, as shall turn them from the power of sin and Satan, and make them into new Creatures . . . enabling them to grow in grace, and patiently continue doing well, 'till of the mercy of God, through Christ, they are crowned with eternal life: All of which he does in a way agreeable to our make as reasonable creatures.[31]

In short, Edwards was putting the crown on the wrong head.

With grace—a reasonable amount of an extra gift to go along with the innate abilities God gave all humans—any person could be crowned a Christian without frenzy:

When men are effectually wrought upon by divine grace, the roughness of their temper shall be smoothed, their passions restrained and brought into order, so that they shall live together in love and peace, doing to each other all the offices, not only of humanity, but of Christian kindness and charity. . . . There should, in a word, be no more biting, opposing and devouring one another: But this change in men would make them mild and gentle.[32]

Chauncy's gospel focused less on the source of grace and its dogmatic justifications and more on its effects. Grace was available to all, and, if effective, it created a peaceful and inclusive society. Chauncy's own providential ideology of innate liberty criticized Edwards's rhetoric of fortune and the aristocracy of grace for failing to bear real fruit.

Chauncy thus answered Edwards's public theology with one of his own. Chauncy often comes off as an aristocrat; as an ardent proponent of the reasonable and educated against the vulgar.[33] But he also articulated a politics that was considerably more open to individual initiative than Edwardian social control.[34] Like Edwards, Chauncy tried to balance grace and law.[35] But unlike Edwards, Chauncy was reluctant to identify who was among the saved. His basic assumptions were consistent with a democracy of law.

Chauncy could afford to be democratic. As he wrote in 1742, he had behind him the full support of the vested authority of New England. The list of subscribers to *Seasonable Thoughts* ran to eighteen pages and included such figures as William Shirley, governor of Massachusetts, Jonathan Law, governor of Connecticut, and Richard Ward, governor of Rhode Island.

In contrast to Edwards's initial focus on civil rulers, he turned directly to the clergy. This was a religious problem, and it demanded a religious solution. "We are called shepherds," Chauncy began, "and shall we behave as such, if, when the wolf comes to devour the flock, we don't watch in all things?" Ministers had "betrayed a want of courage" in failing to speak out against the extremism of the revivals. Chauncy invoked the example of the founders again, "our fathers in the ministry," who directly "prayed and preached against the errors of the day."[36] Ministers had the preeminent obligation to suppress disorders in religion.

Secondarily, Chauncy addressed "civil rulers." Like Edwards, he occasionally encouraged coercion. Rulers could "do a great deal, not only by their good example, but a wise use of their authority . . . for the suppression of every thing hurtful to society." If necessary, the civil realm could even "restrain some men's tongues with bit and bridle." But this coercion was for the sake, not of religious "truth" alone, but of civil peace. Chauncy nuanced the relationship between religious and political power more subtly than Edwards. The "duty" of civil leaders resided "in keeping peace between those, who unhappily differ in their thoughts about the state of our religious affairs," and not, as Edwards had suggested, by appointing days of thanksgiving and fasting, or controlling presses and colleges.[37]

Chauncy's public theology thus differed from that of Edwards primarily because it assumed enduring differences in the society, including religious differences, and did not seek to impose a principle of uniformity from above, aside from civil peace. Chauncy's appeal was to the responsibility of citizens to contribute to the commonweal notwithstanding their differences. "Private Christians," as Chauncy called them, could continue to pray, parent, serve, or lead in whatever way they saw fit, insofar as they did not disturb the peace. The law, not grace, held together a society in which people would differ over religion.

More significant than what Chauncy made explicit politically, then, was the great deal that he left out. There was no king in Chauncy's political address. The civil rulers were always "they," rather than "he," and there was surely no coronation metaphor uniting the whole. Politics was preeminently the realm of persons in office and of "private Christians." Politics was as much the affair of individuals as of social structures, and of conscience as of Calvinism, although the latter still had its place, too.

And it was for this final reason that Chauncy saved some of his strongest language for those who tried to paint all opposers of the revival as anti-Calvinist Arminians. "It is used to the disadvantage of opposers that they are called men of Arminian and Pelagian principles." But

a more palpable mistake could not have been published to the world. . . . For 'tis notorious to all . . . that the principal opposers are among those of an established reputation for their orthodoxy. Calvinists in principle, now are, and always have been from the beginning, the principle and most inveterate enemies to our growing confusions.[38]

Chauncy admitted that there were, "no doubt," some heretics among the opposers. But "to give it as the character of the principal gentlemen . . . that they are Arminians and Pelagian . . . is very abusive." Indeed, it was no less than a "base slander . . . to publish [Pelagianism] to the world as if any ministers in the country entertained a favourable opinion of it."[39]

In 1742, then, by a seemingly ironic turn of events, Charles Chauncy echoed Cotton Mather's judgment of 1726 about the absence of Arminians in America. They reached the same judgment for radically different reasons, of course, but both had skewed the demographic sample. Neither science nor revivalism had made anti-Calvinists go away, and in fact Chauncy's own arguments had lent the democracy of law increasing credibility. Cotton Mather's attempt to show the compatibility of Newtonian science and the ideology of predestination had been too elitist, and the revivalistic rhetoric of fortune had proven to be too enthusiastic to revive the aristocracy of grace. In the New World, the proper relation between spiritual and political power was proving hard to define.

The real outcome of the Great Awakening, in short, was ideological contention. And the question we are left with, once it is admitted that the controversy over the revivals resolved nothing, is simply, what was the contention really about? And while many answers to this question are possible, the problem of free will was clearly both a catalyst and conclusion to the most intense periods of revivals. Both preceding and following the Great Awakening, the question of free will was debated as never before in the New World. In the workings of this debate, and in the formation of enduring parties on the question, one can see not only contention but a pluralistic consensus emerge. For shortly after the Great Awakening, the leading debaters expressed agreement on one thing: the proper solution to the question of free will avoided the extremes. Reason and the revivals had offered conflicting opposites. Time, and the performances of both Calvinist and Arminian theologians, saw them gradually blended into a harmony in discord.

IV Harmony in Discord, 1735–1760

Nothing that I maintain, supposes that men are at all hindered by any fatal necessity, from doing and even willing and choosing as they please, with full freedom; yea, with the highest degree of liberty that ever was thought of.

JONATHAN EDWARDS

In the 1730s, preceding the Great Awakening, New England Calvinists such as John White, Samuel Moody, Nathaniel Stone, and William Cooper had preached sermons, conducted public heresy trials, and published scholarly tomes designed to warn their audiences about the dangers of Arminian free will. To a degree, they succeeded. Many colonists were mobilized by the perception of an "Arminian threat" and the accompanying strategy of revivalism to support the war of the aristocracy of grace to preserve its power.[1] But if some colonists were converted, and proclaimed the predestinarian ideology, others simply seemed hell-bent for destruction.

Thus, between 1745 and 1750, an American "Arminian controversy" broke out between the leading Anglicans and Calvinists in the colonies that finally resolved the issues revivalism had raised.[2] The names of the debaters are undeservedly obscure. Samuel Johnson, first president of King's College (Columbia), led the Arminians, and Jonathan Dickinson, hired as first president of the College of

New Jersey (Princeton), led the Calvinists. Eventually Jonathan Edwards joined the fray, but by then the question was decided, as his own work all but acknowledged. As Edwards saw it, the "modern prevailing notions" of free will had taken root in America.

10 "Are Not the Saved of the Lord Few?"

When John White, pastor of the First Church, Gloucester, Massachusetts, published his *New England's Lamentations* in 1734, he did so as a "hearty lover of his country." And while White lamented that there had been a deplorable decline in "godliness" in New England, he also offered a more specific social analysis. New England's preachers in training were beginning to "cast a favourable eye upon, embrace, and as far as they dare, argue for, propagate, and preach the Arminian scheme."[1] On the eve of the outbreak of revivals, it was an "Arminian threat" that mobilized Calvinists such as White.[2]

It is now hard to imagine how fear of doctrinal change could be the cause of social unrest, but White had no difficulty describing the unsettling consequences of heterodoxy. When individuals trained in the old Calvinist way abandoned it for Arminianism, they tended to become hypocrites, and hypocrites undeniably went "to hell when

they die, yea to the hottest place in hell." The social consequences
were no more promising than the personal. White pointed to England and Holland, where the "fruits and effects of preaching Arminian doctrines" were rottenly displayed for all to see. In such
places, religion was brought "to a very low ebb." Indeed, there were
"signs of the near approach of [the Apocalypse]," for "soul destructive errors are propagated and spreading."[3] The future of White's
country rested on the revival of true doctrine.

The Gloucester minister detailed thirteen Arminian errors that
were making their insidious way into the hearts and minds of colonists, but these thirteen all reduced to two complex problems. Arminians first erred by emphasizing the intrinsic causes of salvation
too much. Human agency, the "material cause" of salvation, was
exalted by Arminians over God's extrinsic, imputed justice. Arminians maligned grace. They located liberty in the will, and this was
to infringe upon the prerogatives of the omniscient God. Second,
Arminianism eroded the difference between the aristocracy and the
commoner, between the elect and the "natural man," between the
saint and the sinner. The latter development was especially insidious; it was a problem the revivals—with their highly visible conversions, which left no doubt about who was elect and who not—
were designed to address once and for all. The "saved of the Lord"
were few.

White reached that conclusion by a *via negativa,* by defining the
obvious errors of the damned. To begin with, White accused Arminians of being self-centered. They claimed to know that all were offered
salvation and would receive it if they only chose to do so. Consequently, they boasted. "According to Arminian principles we are
justified by our gospel obedience, and inherent righteousness" rather
than by "imputed" grace, White asserted of his opponents. This was
all but to preach works-righteousness, or, at minimum, to say that
"faith is the cause, at least the antecedent, of election." Indeed,
according to White, in the Arminian system, God had to wait on
human choice; Arminians preached "postdestination" rather than
divine "predestination."[4]

And at the root of this error in Arminianism was the doctrine of
the will. "The Arminians," White wrote, "originate the salvation

of such as are saved, in the free motion, option, and determination of their own wills." And this threw salvation up for grabs: "Is it consistent with God's wisdom, to leave it in the power of man, to frustrate all God's gracious intentions, and methods for man's salvation?" Indeed, Arminians "take from free grace, and give to free will," thus setting up a scheme totally "inconsistent" with salvation. "We may as well act rationally, without a rational soul, as exercise grace [and gain salvation] without a supernatural principle of grace."[5] White saw God above all as a savior. Arminians, with their emphasis on human willpower, were challenging God's control.

So White's fundamental aim was to distinguish the supernatural from the natural, those elected to salvation from those not yet elected:

The Arminian scheme makes the way of salvation so plain and easy, that the natural man seeth his way plain before him: 'Tis only assenting to Gospel truths, and setting themselves to obey the precepts, and imitate the examples of the gospel. Yea, the way is so plain, that the heathen by a well improvement of the light of nature, will not fail of heaven. And is this the straight gate and narrow way? . . . And are not the saved of the Lord few, a remnant, and that according to the election of grace?[6]

Indeed, according to White, Arminians believed that "all men are made alive by Christ: and all that they need [for salvation], is the well improvement of free will, and self sufficiency."[7] Not surprisingly, White's work was addressed to the same constituency Edwards later solicited in his revival pieces. He called first upon magistrates, then ministers, then Christians, and finally all parents to guard against the spread of such "soul destructive errors" and to take all means available to inculcate true gospel doctrines. What was needed was reform from the top.

And the attempt to produce that reform came in the form of the revivals. White's work has always been perceived as a catalyst in the outbreak of conversions.[8] How important it was can never be determined. But if, in fact, his alarm was a vital signal for New England's Calvinist theologians to "take up arms," or at least quill pens, then what happened in the Great Awakening was, not just an upsurge of popular piety, but also a strategy to restore some order at

the top by reviving the aristocracy of grace. The Awakening sought
to restore the Saints—that is, good Calvinists—to their proper place
in public life.

I I

And at first the strategy worked—some were both "awakened" and
restored to Calvinism.[9] Samuel Moody, pastor on the frontier in
York, Maine, was among them. In 1737, as if to exemplify the
connection between theology and public life, Moody penned his *A
Faithful Narrative of God's Gracious Dealings, with a Person Lately
Recovered from the Dangerous Errors of Arminius.* The title, of course,
echoed Edwards's *Faithful Narrative* of conversions, which can hardly
be supposed to be coincidental. Moody was so awed by the revivals
that he would not even take the preaching platform with the famous
revivalist George Whitefield when the latter visited his church.[10]

Moody's *Faithful Narrative* recorded his conversion as a matter of
doctrinal orthopedics. "I must acknowledge," the work began, "that
by reading Arminian books, and some of the writings of such as are
called Free-thinkers, I came to be so stumbled at the doctrine of
election, that I could not hear it preached without being very uneasy." Having taken to conversing with "men of wit and learning,"
Moody had become convinced that "our doctrine of election could
not consist with the truth, justice and mercy of God." Indeed,
Moody reported, through such unsavory companionship, "I was led
on in the way of free will, as it stands in opposition to free grace;
quite beside and contrary to the way of salvation."[11] What the effects
of his encounter with "men of wit and learning" implied about the
witlessness and lack of learning of Calvinists did not apparently dawn
upon Moody.

In any event, as he recalled it, the consequences of his apostasy
were immediate and crippling. Moody recalled how his conscience
would "fly in his face" when he recalled his youth and "how sweet
the doctrine of election was then." In time, Moody walked again,
but only after he found his way back to orthodoxy. First he was
"brought to see" Adam's sin, or convinced of the doctrine of innate
depravity. He was "convicted," just as surely as Edwards's revival
converts went through a stage of despair before the joy of conversion.

Then he perceived how "all our hope, now, must be in Christ, and in God's electing love through him."

Moody experienced grace through a moment of doctrinal insight, and what followed was a return to the stability of his youth. "I was brought to bless God for election," he related; in election "I had relief; and on this foundation I desire to build my hope; which hope, cast within the vail, is a sure anchor."[12] Mixed metaphors aside, Calvinism was here a brace that would hold things secure. Moody's work was a personal testimony that outlined the revival strategy at work. The revivals could restore the old order, where God elected a few.

III

Heresy trials were common in New England throughout the 1730s, and many of them centered on Arminianism and the problem of free will.[13] To take just one example, in 1738, Samuel Osborn, pastor of the Second Church in Eastham, Cape Cod, was removed from his pulpit for preaching Arminianism. Nathaniel Stone, pastor at Harwich, was the catalyst in Osborn's prosecution. Free will was a fundamental issue. Osborn was charged with denying unconditional election, and declared in response that people "can do that upon the doing of which they shall certainly be saved." This made salvation dependent upon human agency. As one later commentator puts it: "Osborn was an extreme Arminian, believing in the natural ability of man to meet the legal requirements for salvation."[14]

Stone was appalled. Like Osborn, he was a Harvard graduate at work on Cape Cod.[15] Unlike Osborn, he was growing notorious, or revered, for his orthodoxy.[16] In 1739, just after finally succeeding in his decade-long quest to bring Osborn down, Stone printed his own statement in support of the aristocracy of grace. "If any say, as has been said, that men themselves are the first movers in returning to God . . . this is contrary to evident Scripture." Indeed, "men can't renew their natures, or work grace or holiness in themselves." "Natural men are without strength—dead . . . yea if possible worse than so."[17]

What Stone apparently had in mind by a living state worse than death was the state of bondage to sin, and the pervasiveness of this bondage made it clear that "men do not act freely, but by a fatal necessity when they do either good or evil." And with Osborn in view, Stone's emphasis was on the evil. Granted, humans "know they act freely, without any compunction, when they plant, sow, trade, go on voyages, etc. They will own that they act freely in these things; yet these fall within the compass of the divine predestination as any other that can be mentioned." Nothing escaped the sway of either good or evil, God or Satan.

And yet if humans were obviously free to act, how did one reconcile this freedom with God's predestination? An old scholastic distinction came to Stone's aid:

A necessity of infallibility and of co-action are evidently distinct. The former puts no constraint in any wise on the will, but leaves it to act as freely as if there were not predestination. So God's predestination leaves the will of man still to act freely; tho' men through enmity to God and his truths will needs plead for a compulsion in the case.[18]

Blaming evil on God was the last refuge of the natural human who was unreconciled to the gentle sway of infallible necessity and predestination. In contrast, the chosen few knew their culpability, their responsibility, and their limits.

IV

Nathaniel Stone was undoubtedly ultraorthodox, but when the revivals came, he could not support them. His opposition was not so much doctrinal as procedural. He was concerned about the unsettling consequences of itineracy, or traveling preachers.

A fuller definition of the overall Calvinist strategy came from William Cooper, assistant pastor at the prestigious Brattle Street Church in Boston. If White had stated the doctrinal problem for all of New England, and Moody and Stone gave witness from the frontiers, then Cooper was the chief advocate of the Calvinist strategy in the citadel of Boston. Along with his superior, Benjamin Colman, Cooper was responsible for inviting the revivalist George Whitefield to the colonies. And almost simultaneously, in 1740, Cooper published a four-sermon series in defense of predestination.[19]

The first sermon stated a definition of the doctrine of "predestination to life," making it clear that "all the children of men will not be finally saved. As there are evidently two sorts of persons in the world now, good and bad, so are we sure from the word of God there will be found two ways of dealing with them." The Calvinist preference for the few over the many came through clearly: "Only some of mankind" would be saved—namely, those "personally chosen" by God to live a life of "faith and holiness" through his "certain, infallible, and irrevocable" decision. And this election was "no such conditional uncertain thing"; a definite, albeit secret, number had been "chosen to live forever from before the world was founded."[20] The aristocracy of grace thus found support even on "liberal" Brattle Street.

To be sure, Cooper's defense of predestination, and his support of the overall Calvinist strategy, lacked the intensity some of the frontier zealots preferred. He could just as easily evade an issue as solve it. "To reconcile the divine fore-ordination with human liberty is a thing too hard for us," he claimed, "nor may any one pretend to do it," thereby denying the fact that generations of Calvinists before him had been pretending to do just that. "Yet," Cooper went on, "the matter of fact is certain, that men do act with liberty and freedom in things that are fore-ordained. And tho' we can't reconcile them, there is certainly an agreement between these two." Just as certainly, "though the elect of God are predestinated to faith and holiness, no violence is offered to their wills when they come to believe in Christ, and choose the way of holiness." Belief came "not by a force upon [human] wills, but a change in them."[21] Was there really any question about this? The revivals surely showed not.

The Great Awakening, then, began for some as an ideological strategy, an attempt to restate, reassert, and reestablish the aristocracy of grace. What grated Calvinists about the Arminians was not that they argued for liberty, but that they argued for *too large* a liberty, for too many. "If the salvation of a number is not secured by electing love and grace," Cooper asked, is God not inconsistent, or worse, unjust, in leaving salvation "again to depend upon the will of man, which had ruined him once before?" Indeed, did not this reliance upon such a contingent decree make salvation depend only upon a "common general grace," that "one may improve to equal advantage as another[?]"[22] And was this anything more than throwing pearls before swine, making grace cheap, and suggesting that the saved were as likely to be found in Virginia as in Massachusetts?

To promote common grace, universal salvation, and human free will was, as seen from within the Calvinist fold, to promote anomie, chaos, and uncertainty. The old Puritan bias against contingency was now institutionalized in eighteenth-century America in a revivalist-Calvinist party, the aristocracy of grace, made up of men such as John White, Samuel Moody, and William Cooper. But to the dismay of them all, and especially of the zealots, the Great Awakening went awry and promoted, not only enthusiasm, but ironically Arminianism as well.

V

Samuel Johnson—the same Samuel Johnson who had left the Congregationalist fold as a convert to Anglicanism in 1722 and thereby inspired "Silence Dogood" to speak out in favor of religious change—best identified the irony. As a result of the revivals, Johnson pointed out, "the Church [of England] increased. This growth," the former Yale tutor continued,

> had in great part been occasioned by the obloquy of the dissenters themselves, charging the Church of England with popery, Arminianism, the inventions of men, etc., against which they were obliged in their own defense to procure many books in the Church's vindication, which many of the more candid and inquisitive dissenters read and were surprised to find how many things had been misrepresented. . . . Thus what [the Calvinists] expected would be the ruin of the Church proved the greatest means of its increase and enlargement.[23]

In other words, the revivals inspired at least as many Arminians as Calvinists to make public statements[24]—and, in fact, before long the Arminians themselves learned to use revival techniques. John Wesley, the first prominent champion of Arminian revivalism in America, had been a companion of the Calvinist George Whitefield in England, but broke with his former friend in 1739 over the question of predestination. When Wesley entered into a pamphlet exchange with Whitefield on the topic of grace, the arguments of both sides were published immediately, and often reprinted thereafter, in the colonies.

The critical document was Wesley's sermon *Free Grace*, first preached at Bristol, but reprinted in Philadelphia. Wesley's text was the same one William Cooper chose to defend predestination in Boston, Romans 8. But in Bristol Wesley had focused on verse 32: "God delivered Christ up for us all, how shall he not with him also give us all things." And Wesley turned this into a proof that God offered salvation to all. Indeed, the only "sensible" doctrine was: "I will set before the sons of men, life and death, blessing and curse, and the soul that chooseth life shall live, as the soul that chooseth death shall die." God through Christ "every where speaks, as if he was willing that all men should be saved." Therefore, reasoned Wesley, God must have made the means of salvation—grace—freely available to all. God was no respecter of status.[25]

The movement Wesley began, Methodism, undeniably became a principal agent of democratization in the colonies. Wesley's early sermon, however, was less an argument in support of any democratic "free grace" than it was a diatribe against predestination.[26] It was in many ways a typical anti-Calvinist production. It was atypical, however, in that Wesley was not arguing against Calvinism in order to support "rational" religion, as Franklin and other representatives of the Enlightenment in America had done, but to support the "heart" religion of the revivals. As with the Enlightenment figures, however, Wesley's non-Calvinist "gospel" was based upon virtue—perfectionism was a keynote of his system.[27] In other words, in order to support his gospel of a heartfelt, virtuous life, he presupposed a world where humans had both free choice and ability to effect their choices.

Wesley's basic point in *Free Grace*, echoing Arminius, was that election and predestination were based upon a necessitarian doctrine; that if election was true, some were "infallibly" saved and the rest "infallibly" damned, and that this was a doctrinal system that made God abhorrent to both mind and heart. Absolute predestination made "all preaching vain."[28] If everyone's fate was predetermined one way or the other, there was little purpose in trying to persuade people otherwise. Following the same line, if predestination was true, it tended "to destroy . . . holiness." Predestination "wholly takes away those first motives to follow after" goodness—namely, "the hope of future reward and fear of punishment." Finally, the whole Calvinist system tended "to destroy the comfort of religion, the happiness of Christianity: this is evident as to all those who believe themselves to be reprobated, or who only suspect or fear it."[29] Calvinism left out too many.

Indeed, "how uncomfortable a thought is this, that thousands and millions of men without any preceding offence or fault of theirs, were unchangeably doomed to everlasting burnings?" Wesley was blunt. Predestination was "a doctrine full of blasphemy," for it

represents our blessed Lord, Jesus Christ, . . . as an hypocrite, a deceiver of the people, a man void of common sincerity. For it cannot be denied, that he every where speaks, as if he was willing that all men should be saved. Therefore, to say, *he was not* willing that all men should be saved, is to represent him as a mere hypocrite and dissembler.[30]

Predestination made the promises of God seem vain, and thus made God seem "worse than the devil, as both more false, more cruel, and more unjust. . . . This is the blasphemy clearly contained in the horrible decree of predestination. . . . This is the blasphemy for which . . . I abhor the doctrine of predestination."[31]

It was Wesley's anti-Calvinism that came through most clearly in *Free Grace,* but some colonists also picked up on the constructive implications. For instance, in the wake of Wesley's tract, Philadelphia Anglicans saw fit to republish the best-known American anti-Calvinist publication to date, John Checkley's *Dialogues Between a Minister and an Honest Country-man* (1720).[32] To this, however, was added a new conclusion, probably written by Archibald Cummings, rector of Christ Church, Philadelphia, that attempted to draw out some of the positive implications of the Checkley-Wesley doctrines. Anti-Calvinism was becoming the positive support for innate liberty. "It is Mr. Wesley's opinion," began Cummings,

that mankind are free agents, capable of determining their own actions, and that God freely affords every man . . . a sufficient measure of light and the assistance of his Holy Spirit, to enable him both to see and perform his duty; and that no man shall be punished for not doing what God never afforded him a sufficient power to do.[33]

Humans were self-determining agents within the limits that God had chosen for them. All human beings were enabled by God to perform their duty and had the power to gain their reward. God was still in the picture, but the balance was tilting to the side of the gifts given to all.

And it was in his discussion of causality that Cummings made most clear how he was developing Wesley's ideas. First, people could choose, and thereby actually affect the course of events. "Let us suppose," Cummings began,

> that two valuable objects both equally eligible, were presented before me in order to choose one of them. . . . Now let me choose which I will, it will be that which God foreknew I would choose, yet I am at free liberty to choose either. . . . And as in this so in other cases it is our free choice [that is] sovereign, existing in futurity, that was the cause of God's fore-knowledge of it. Not his fore-knowledge the cause of our choice.[34]

The distinction would become basic. God foreknew all that would happen, but foreknowledge was not causality. Human beings controlled not only action, but motives, and could reflect upon various courses of action in a way that actually altered the courses themselves. Humans were agents in matters left indetermined by God, and this meant matters of the heart as well as matters of action.

Having been given free choice, human beings could in fact contradict what God knew was to come. Foreknowledge was not necessity. Cummings supported a notion of liberty as power to the contrary: "If," the Philadelphia rector wrote, "fore-knowledge does not cause our actions to be unavoidably necessary, then it must be possible for us to act otherwise than God foreknew we would act." Humans not only had free choice, they could actually effect their choices, no matter the foreknowledge of God. "We may do as we will, not withstanding [God's] foreknowledge of what we will do."[35]

Given this assertion, holding together "God's perfection" and God's "moral government of free and accountable agents" was the primary difficulty for Cummings and all the Arminians. If God was not in control, who was? Cummings was hardly ready to leap into absolute chance. Like Benjamin Franklin, he was not about to dispense with some control by the God of the Christian tradition. In fact, he was simply in favor of a mediating doctrine inclined to the side of liberty. He readily admitted that his formulation contained "a paradox," but he also held it was nonetheless "really true." Thus, the argument ran, "if then God is by nature a free agent, man may be also." God was now the moral example of innate human freedom.

Human beings thus possessed liberty as a birthright. If Calvinistical "absolute fatality" made "all religion vain," then it was equally evident that his own "scheme, call it Arminianism, or what you will, has abundantly the advantage over the other." It was "more worthy of God, consistent with our valuable liberty, and inspires the noblest sentiments of virtue."[36] Insofar as Cummings's writing was a typical American interpretation of Wesley, anti-Calvinists were moving toward the democracy of law. God had given all humans freedom in the pursuit of lawful perfection.

In short, almost as the revivals began, they were transformed. By 1745 at the latest, it was clear that Calvinists would have no monopoly on the use of conversion as a political rallying ritual. The issue of fatalism and moral accountability could not be evaded by relocating Calvinist religion in the heart. The aristocracy of grace and the democracy of law were set for their debate. Out of their contention a new culture would be born.

11 "Truths Are Confessed on Both Sides"

Between 1745 and 1754, the leading English writers in the colonies began a debate in which the problem of free will was the central question.[1] The debate had two sides, and as is often the case in such debates, an excluded middle. Both the Calvinist advocates of the aristocracy of grace—most notably Jonathan Dickinson—and the Anglican advocates of the democracy of law—most notably Samuel Johnson—sought to avoid the extremes on the question of free will, and in fact supported a form of free choice. Through their debate, these public theologians exemplified the new ethos that would eventually predominate in American culture.[2]

Although the participants in this Arminian controversy were well known both to one another and to their peers, the course and characters of this controversy are little known today.[3] The debate was started by the Anglicans. In 1745 John Beach, missionary to Newtown and Redding, Connecticut, a position he held continuously until his death in 1782, published *A Sermon, Shewing that Eternal*

Life is God's Free Gift, Bestowed upon Men according to their Moral Behaviour. And that Free Grace and Free Will Concur, in the Affair of Man's Salvation. Beach was a Yale graduate born in 1700 who had converted to the Church of England in 1732.[4] Beach's pamphlet was followed almost immediately by Samuel Johnson's *A Letter from Aristocles to Authades, Concerning the Sovereignty and Promises of God.* At the time, Johnson was the agent of the Society for Propagating the Gospel in Stratford, Connecticut. Johnson had been instrumental in Beach's conversion and served in many ways as the younger man's mentor.[5]

On the Calvinist side, Jonathan Dickinson, the renowned pastor of the Presbyterian Church at Elizabethtown, New Jersey, was the leading spokesman. Dickinson had been a moderate supporter of the revivals and had sought along the lines of Edwards both to restrain the excesses of enthusiasm and to link the revivals to a resurgence of *True-Scripture Doctrine,* as the title of his most famous work had it.[6] Dickinson's initial response to both Beach and Johnson was published in 1745 as *A Vindication of God's Sovereign Free Grace.*[7] These three treatises by Beach, Johnson, and Dickinson set the debate in motion, but when it finally ended years later, Beach, Johnson, and Dickinson had each written at least one more major work, and a dozen other writers across the colonies had contributed to the conversation.[8] By the time Jonathan Edwards published his own thoughts on the problem of free will in 1754, something of a consensus—a harmony in discord—had become clear.

I

This melody was composed in five stanzas, covering the disciplines of rhetoric, theology, ethics, philosophy, and politics. The first was rhetorical. In the midst of this intense debate, both sides found it vital to point up a range of agreement. Much of this was convention, but that was precisely where assumptions came into play. Thus, in the midst of his debate with Johnson over grace, Dickinson acknowledged that there are "truths confessed on both sides of the question . . . Calvinistical [as well as] Arminian."[9] By the time of Dickinson's *Second Vindication,* his patience was wearing thin, and he could only admit that there are "difficulties enough on either side."[10] But the point was the same. Regarding free will, the Calvinists and the Anglicans did not assume absolutely opposite positions.

The Anglicans were, as the minority party, much more eager to make this point, while still pushing their polemic against the powerful Calvinists. "Is it not unmanly and unChristian," asked Beach at one point, "to contend so fiercely, and clamor so loudly for a word [namely, *special grace*] . . . when we are agreed in the sense?"[11] Similarly, Johnson, after criticizing Dickinson for attempting to "cast odium" upon Beach and all Anglicans, charged that Dickinson was "fighting with nothing but a dust of your own raising."[12] Between them, by clearing away the dust, the Calvinists and Anglicans were going to define the "truths confessed on both sides."

II

In addition to being rhetoricians, the participants in this colonial Arminian controversy were, of course, Christian theologians. The old problem of the relationship between grace and works was therefore central to their debate. What roles did grace and virtue play in human salvation and life? Beach's sermon again set the stage for the discussion. "Though eternal life is a gift; yet there are some qualifications requisite" was his most succinct statement of the Anglican thesis.[13] Johnson more explicitly raised the theological aspect of the question. If God was indeed a "moral governor," and not just an arbitrary despot, then the Calvinist doctrine of "absolute determination," or election, "represents Him as laying his creatures under a necessity . . . and so leaves no room for either virtue or vice, praise or blame, reward or punishment."[14] Grace could not be "infallible" without destroying the morality both of God and of human beings. Or, as Beach put it, Christians—not to mention the Christian God—should "excel in all moral . . . virtues," for in such a life was "founded the eternal happiness of a rational creature."[15] Virtue was to take a place of honor alongside grace.

Dickinson had no trouble perceiving the drift of these claims, and in fact a good portion of his *Vindication* was devoted to contrasting passages from Beach's sermon with passages from the Articles of the Church of England. Beach did not fare well in the comparison, and he was in fact called to account for his views by his superiors across the Atlantic shortly after the publication of Dickinson's work. Dickinson's success at depicting Beach as a heretic was not equaled, however, when it came to answering the problem of grace and virtue. In fact, to some, his vindication was too tame. To be sure, Dickinson made it clear that grace was prior to virtue, and that "faith and every other virtue are not the EFFECT of our own choice and pains."[16] But this still implied that grace and virtue were intrinsically related, somehow, to choice.

From the audience, other Calvinists, while respectful of Dickinson's stature, concluded that things were not going well. Jedediah Mills thus penned his own *Vindication of Gospel Truths* in an attempt to state the problem with the Anglicans more sharply. A contradiction was "common to those in the Arminian scheme" such as Beach and Johnson, wrote Mills. The substance of this contradiction was that "they all profess wholly to disclaim the plea of merit" as a cause of salvation, "and yet they assert . . . God's dispensing his efficacious aid or special grace, not as an absolute sovereign benefactor, but as a moral governor and righteous judge of the behaviour and improvements of his creatures." From Mills's vantage, this was to support the efficacy of a "merit of the lower kind," called by the Jesuits "congruent merit," rather than "condign." The simple mention of the Jesuits clinched the case for Mills. "Works and grace can't be blended together," he concluded.[17]

The Arminians were ready for that sort of conclusion. To oppose works and grace as Mills had done was to assert "idle speculations of fate and absolute predestination" and fail ever to touch down with the moral matters that motivated human beings.[18] Beach warned Dickinson in the same way: "Dare you preach that God's grace is such, that he will save men, though they never obey the gospel? What looser doctrine? What broader way to heaven, what ranker Antinomianism was ever preached than this?" Indeed, "if our eternal happiness is not founded or begun in virtue, then a man may have eternal life, and yet be as void of all virtue and goodness as the devil."[19]

Dickinson responded to this charge with care in his *Second Vindication*. He had to avoid both antinomianism and any hint of Arminianism. He did so by trying to define a Calvinist conception of free choice. "Faith and every virtue," he refined his earlier statement on the matter, "are the free gift of God to us in conversion, and are not the effect of our own previous choice and pains, so as to imply or suppose a self-moving principle in the fallen and weak creature."[20] The last clause was the key one. Faith and the virtues were freely given, and in this sense could be connected with free choice, although obviously not with any free choice that meant "self-determination." Calvinists were no more antinomians than the Anglicans. They both valued the virtues, and Beach admitted as much:

Whether it be through weakness or perverseness, or both, I can't determine; but it is notorious, that there is such a distinction kept up, between those who pretend to be preachers of the gospel; as that one sort are styled exalters of free will, and the other are called preachers of free grace: As if grace and free will were directly contrary to each other; as though all who believe man's moral agency, were enemies to the grace of God.[21]

Dickinson would have put the emphasis on the distinction differently. There were some who preached grace and some who preached free will, but it was perverse to depict those who preached grace as if they were enemies to human moral agency.

III

The debate was barely under way. If salvation and the virtues could not be separated, what held them together? What "caused" the two to coincide? To raise this issue pushed the debate more deeply into matters of philosophical theology. Both parties granted that multiple causes were at work, and while they no longer employed Aristotle's distinctions, they nevertheless argued over how God's grace "determined" this or that act, and how the same act might or might not be "contingent." And although there was ample disagreement between the parties, they avoided the extremes of absolute determinism and absolute chance.

Dickinson stated the Calvinist assumption by reducing the idea of a first "free will" in opposition to the will of God to the absurdity of an infinite regress. "Every rational agent must," he began,

be always acted and influenced by the highest motive and inducement before him. But to suppose any higher motive to the eternal God than himself, is to suppose something higher than the highest, which is absurd.

To imagine any cause of God's will or decree out of himself, is to suppose something in God which is an effect, and so to assign a cause of the first cause, which is equally absurd.[22]

An almost identical argument was to be used by Jonathan Edwards just a few years later. Humans were motivated to choose by God, the First Cause, whose motivation had no cause but its own.

Consequently, God's decree was absolute. Election was irrevocable. And yet this was not "determinism," since "although there can be no conditions in God's decrees," Dickinson went on, "yet he has decreed, that the salvation even of the elect themselves shall be conditional." Dickinson explained this paradox by resorting to a distinction between the decree and its enactment. There are, he argued, "conditions of the event, though there be no conditions of the decree."[23] Salvation was caused by God, but its enactment took place in the human being who chose. Dickinson was making room for human liberty.

And his reason for doing so is no longer a surprise. "One of the chief objections against this doctrine [of election] is," Dickinson commented, "that it takes away the liberty of the creature." But this objection was unjust, Dickinson explained. For although "God's decrees are absolute, and without any possible conditions," nevertheless "by experience"—in the actual working out of the decree—we know "that we are at full liberty and freedom, that we act in all our moral behaviour according to our own wills. And don't this consideration make it necessary, that the liberty of the creature is consistent with the decree of God, whether we can see through it or not?"[24] Thus, the human was "compelled and yet willing," attracted by God "so as to necessitate his free compliance with the gospel."[25]

This may have seemed clear to Dickinson, but the Anglicans claimed to find it confused. To Johnson, election and reprobation were simply doctrines of "fatal necessity." To show how this was so, he constructed a hypothetical analogy. Imagine a sovereign ruler, Johnson said, who has before him one hundred criminals. The prince commands one such "unhappy wretch" to lift a ten-thousand-pound weight and throw it one mile. If he can do so, he will go free and gain a huge estate. If he cannot lift the weight, he will hang. "This unhappy wretch," who stands for the reprobate individual, "is under a necessity of disobeying and being hanged," Johnson concluded.

The case with the elect was identical, only the prince now provided to two or three favorites with "engines by which the weight can be easily raised and projected," and the prince "invincibly influences them" to use them. "These persons are under a necessity of doing what they do," namely, gaining their freedom, Johnson concluded. In both cases, the persons were "meerly passive," and their actions were completely necessitated. Election and reprobation were therefore no better than the doctrines of an "infidel" who held that "there is no liberty, and all is fate."[26]

Having thus stated the usual anti-Calvinist critique, Johnson could reconstruct the notion of God's sovereignty in a way that supposedly avoided fatalism. Thus, he contended that a proper notion of God's determination saw in it "one single act, one infinite all-comprehending view," by which God determines all, and sees all, "necessary events as being necessary, and contingent as being such, and the actions of such as he made free agents as being free."[27] By this "one single act," Johnson meant above all creation. Thus, "in the distribution of talents and favors," that is, in creating human beings,

the sovereignty of God as a benefactor does truly take place; but in the future distribution of rewards and punishments, absolute sovereignty is entirely out of the question. As a judge, deciding the eternal condition of men, God never once represents himself as arbitrary, but [as treating people] . . . in exact proportion to their own conduct in the use of the talents committed to their trust.[28]

Here once again was innate liberty. God as Creator and Judge was sovereign. The rest was up to what humans did with their natural gifts and abilities.

But Dickinson refused to allow Johnson to tar Calvinists as extremists: "What does the Dr. mean by *necessity*? If he means, that the sovereignty of God's grace, considered either in his decrees, or in the execution of them, has any necessitating agency upon men, so as to compel or force them to be good, or bad, he knows that this is what the Calvinists have always disclaimed." History may have shown otherwise, but in theory at least orthodox Calvinists regularly denounced coercion. "The sovereign counsels of God's grace do therefore make it evident," argued Dickinson, "that no man can be constrained, either to holiness, or happiness: but both must be his own free choice." Calvinists did not worship a force that compelled human beings. Calvinistic "necessity" was simply "a certainty, that eternal salvation will be the consequence of our participation [in] God's sovereign grace." Thus, "the Dr.'s argument from necessity is really trifling, and has nothing in it."[29]

Having thus preserved Calvinism from the charges of antinomianism and fatalism, Dickinson turned the tables and charged the Arminians with preaching "chance." Johnson and Beach were the true extremists. It was Calvinism that preserved both God's sovereignty and human liberty; Arminians such as Johnson eroded both. Dickinson thus emphasized the contingency in Johnson's system. For instance, "Does [he] indeed think," Dickinson asked of Johnson and his reader, "that there is anything contingent with respect to God? With respect to us indeed, futurities are contingent," but for God no such caprice was conceivable.[30] Did Johnson really believe that God operated by chance?

Johnson answered directly to the point. "By contingent," he wrote to Dickinson, "you will mean uncertain, though I plainly mean events depending on the free actions of the creatures." Human certainty could not be equated with God's. "By contingent events," Johnson explained,

we mean such as depend on our own free wills and self-exertions, as that I am now writing, when I might, if I pleased, visit a neighbor—These things, being fact, are as certain, and as certainly known, as the other; but it by no means follows that they are therefore necessary; nor can they be, because they immediately depend on our free will . . . and not on the will of God, (any otherwise than as our existence depends on his will). . . . [God] knows them as being what they are, i.e. as depending on the free exercises of his creatures, according to that voluntary, self-exerting nature which he hath given them.[31]

In short, God built freedom into human beings, and this did not mean chance as much as it meant responsibility. Every human had a role to play in the cosmic drama.

And in the end, again, the two sides were not in complete disagreement. They both agreed that God's providence did not rule out human free choice. Johnson emphasized the *responsibility* humans had to choose under God in order to defend Anglicanism from the charge of preaching chance. And Dickinson emphasized the *freedom* God's grace gave people to choose in order to defend Calvinism from fatalism and antinomianism:

All are . . . in such a perfect state of freedom, as to be capable of acting their own voluntary inclinations. And though all events will come to pass according to God's eternal counsel and knowledge, this no way infringes the liberty of the creature: nor can any pretences of this kind be justly made, unless it be supposed, that there cannot be an omniscient God, and a creature, notwithstanding, in a state of liberty.

Free choice—"voluntary inclination"—was a Calvinist notion tucked cozily into the traditional category of God's sovereignty, just as free choice was an Anglican ideal tucked safely in the confines of moral responsibility.[32]

I V

So far, then, the colonial Arminian controversy had first established the rhetorical point that the Calvinists and Anglicans agreed on some things. This was followed by the specification of a few of these agreements. Both sides connected grace and the virtuous life. Neither side claimed to support the extremes of antinomianism, fatalism, or chance. Both agreed that the human individual was responsible for his or her choices. The final notes of the debate rang a harmony in dissonance expressing the meaning of free choice in political life. Put succinctly, the Anglicans supported a wide range of liberty for all, captured by such phrases as "self-determination," "power to the contrary," and "free will," while Dickinson defended the traditional Calvinist "liberty of action," or "freedom from coercion," and sought to have the elect few enacting this liberty. The Calvinists had the high range; the Anglicans the low.[33]

The keynote, once again, was "power." Granted that God was First Cause, and that humans chose, how much power did human choice in fact have? The Anglicans were optimistic. Johnson claimed: "We are intuitively certain that we have (and therefore

God has given us) self-exerting, and self-determining powers."[34] Beach was even bolder: "There is in every one a power of self-determining, of choosing, or refusing, by which a man may comply with, or reject . . . the Holy Spirit." This "power," furthermore, was in "the constitution" of the person, so that "when the Spirit of God excites him to consider the things of his eternal peace, he can either apply his heart to them, or turn away his mind to the vanities of this world: and according as we choose the one or the other, so we are like to be eternally happy or miserable." "Every man," just as did Adam, "feels in his breast" a self-determining freedom to become whoever he wanted to be.[35]

Dickinson replied by stressing that humans had first of all a "power to the wicked." Indeed, Article 10 of the Church of England, to which Beach owed loyalty, claimed that

the condition of man after the Fall of Adam is such that he cannot turn and prepare himself, by his own natural strength, and good works, to faith and calling upon God. . . . [Wherefore], we have no power to do good works pleasant and acceptable to God, without the grace of God by Christ preventing [i.e., aiding] us, that we may have a good will; and working with us, when we have that good will.

If this idea of the Fall was taken seriously, then "there is not," Dickinson now contradicted Beach, " 'in every one a power of self-determining, of choosing or refusing, by which a man may comply with, or reject, the suggestions of the Holy Spirit; Man has' not 'this self-moving principle in his constitution,' as Mr. Beach teaches us."[36]

And yet Dickinson still assumed that humans did have power, insofar as they lived a life guided by grace. Humans chose most freely when they chose what had been given them, rather than choosing to strive for what they thought they had to earn. Choice was free and effective to the degree that it was freely given, rather than earned through "self-determining" effort. In light of the obvious tendency of human power to choose evil, human liberty and power had to be derived, hedged, or otherwise treated negatively. Indeed, self-determination was an illusion. "The freedom of a creature does not consist in a power to do everything which he might choose to do . . . but in a power to act of choice in all that he does do." Whatever humans did, and they did plenty, if the act was done by choice, it was done freely. "Freedom therefore is only opposed to coaction or constraint. He that can act according to his own will, and do what he does—of choice, without any constraint, is therein free."[37] Free choice meant the freedom to be who one really was.

V

Who was right? In the context of the colonies, the only answer must be that they both were. Both sides confessed a truth, since both sides had parties lined up behind them. And the disputants were coming to realize at least that much about each other, even while they also felt that their "truth" was the more vital. To Dickinson, it all came down to the question of whether the human could play God. "Where (I beseech you)," he appealed to Beach, "did I ever affirm, that a man has not the power of choosing or refusing?" And yet free choice could not be equivalent to self-determination. "How does it appear," Dickinson asked Beach,

that "a man has not the power to choose or refuse," unless he has a self-determining power, and a self-determining principle . . . ? How does it appear, that a man is no moral agent, but a mere machine, unless he can create himself anew in Christ Jesus unto good works; or unless his renewed nature be his own workmanship, created by his own choice. . . . Can a man have no power to choose or refuse, unless he can choose and exercise the mighty power of God?[38]

Human power had to be derived, but it was no less free thereby.

But who had this freedom, and who deserved it? To the Anglicans, the problem with the Calvinists was that they seemed to claim precisely the power of God for themselves, while leaving the majority of humanity headed nowhere but to hell. Consequently, the Anglicans claimed to want to open up the power of salvation to all. Thus John Beach, who during the revolutionary years was a die-hard Tory, in the 1740s uttered some of the clearest defenses of liberty ever heard in America. Grace was "not confined or restricted to an elect number, but comprehends the whole race of Adam." "There is in *every* one a power of self-determining." "*Every* man, though ever so much inclined, or tempted, to sin, feels in his breast a liberty to forbear, when he commits it." "Men and Angels God governs by laws."[39]

Johnson was no less sure of the matter. Like Beach he had Tory and aristocratic leanings. He admitted that "abilities, capacities, priveledges and advantages" were distributed by God unevenly. But when it came to "rewards and punishments," God was a "universal and irrespective lover of the souls which he hath made, and sincerely and solicitously desirous of their happiness." This universal desire on the part of God to save humans had one primary corollary. When God considered humanity, he considered them "as being what they, and what he himself hath made them, i.e., though frail, yet free, self-exerting and self-determining agents." This power of self-determination, furthermore, was available to all, and of such import that even if some Scriptures contradicted the doctrine, "methinks we should strongly be inclined . . . to get over them."[40]

Dickinson acknowledged that this appeal to the sufficiency of "common grace"—the grace of creation available to all—was "the main plea" of the Anglicans. And he struggled with the implications of the opposite doctrine:

It evidently appears, that although Christ is in some sense the savior of all men, so that all who enjoy the gospel, have the gracious and free offer of salvation, . . . : Yet Christ has wrought out a special and distinguishing Redemption for the elect, whereby they are not only put in a savable state, but shall be actually saved.—He has not only purchased for them a possibility of salvation; but the actual communication of grace here and glory hereafter.—He has not only procured for them, that they may be saved, if they will; but that they shall assuredly have salvation begun in them here, and perfected hereafter, because God will.[41]

The logic here was the logic of the aristocracy of grace. Only a few were given the actual power of salvation. Only for them did God make the possibility inherent in their own choice actual, by conforming that choice to his own.

The problem Calvinists had with the Anglicans was that the latter made too facile a leap from creation to redemption. In between, for Dickinson and every Calvinist, was sin: And "sinners have power to be nothing but wicked creatures . . . [and to] destroy themselves." "It is a visible, undisputed fact, that the greatest part of the world are [sic] left by the Providence of God, in a state of ignorance, impiety, and abominable idolatry." It was a benevolent act of God's

to save any, when he might in fact have damned all. "What im-
peachment then of God's moral government can there be . . . [for]
bestowing that special grace upon some, which none have deserved?"[42]

Indeed, from the American Calvinist point of view, the Anglicans
were the ones impeaching God and trying to set up a different,
human-centered government in God's place. Jedediah Mills put it
succinctly when he said that the Anglicans asserted that humans
have "a right, at least a conditional right, to certain blessings" from
God.[43] Mills was right, but the Anglicans simply countered that
God's sovereignty and human rights were not incompatible. The
Calvinists were confusing God's sovereignty with a set of theologian's symbols.

Consequently, "call no man master" became the rallying cry of
the Anglicans in their defense of the democracy of law. "I am not
insensible," Johnson began *Aristocles to Authades*, "that the odious
name of Arminianism will be the cry against these papers, for those
little minds that are affected with sounds more than sense, and that
are engaged at any rate to support a party. . . . But I do hereby
declare, that I abhor all such party names and distinctions, and
that I will call no man master upon earth."[44] Beach was even more
pointed:

Show yourselves men: See with your own eyes; and judge with your own
reason; which is the candle that God has lighted up, in your own breasts
for your direction. Call no man master or Father upon Earth. Receive
nothing as an article of your faith, because it is the opinion of this, or that
teacher. . . . For a man of common understanding and an honest heart, by
reading the Holy Scriptures, may form a juster notion of the nature of God
and the way to heaven, than . . . some celebrated preachers of grace,
falsely so called.[45]

A Tory in politics, Beach was a democrat when it came to public
theology.[46]

Finally, then, the Great Awakening had ended. It had all come
down to power, where it resided, who had it, and how it was to be
administered. The outcome, to be sure, was not the "revolution"
Jonathan Edwards had anticipated, but it had been a revolution.
Religious groups would contest in America, hotly, but they would

not go to war, at least not with each other. The rhetoric could be extravagant: "I verily believe, this horrible notion . . . propagated by the Calvinistic doctrines, is the principle cause of that malice and ill nature which appears in many New-Light people versus supposed reprobates, called Opposers," Beach declared.[47] And yet the opposers and the Saints had battled this one out with words as their only weapons. They shared enough, the theologians made clear, to make the step beyond verbal violence unnecessary. And what they shared was a harmony in dissonance that sounded like freely given choice. None of the influential elites supported the extremes of fatalism and chance. And, in the end, even Jonathan Edwards added his powerful voice to this rising crescendo.

12 "The Modern Prevailing Notions"

Jonathan Edwards once claimed to abhor the Calvinist doctrine of election. "From my childhood," Edwards recalled, "my mind had been full of objections against the doctrine of God's sovereignty, in choosing whom he would to eternal life, and rejecting whom he pleased; leaving them eternally to perish, and be everlastingly tormented in hell. It used to appear like a horrible doctrine to me."[1] But by the age of 28 and his first published sermon, *God Glorified in the Work of Redemption, By the Greatness of Man's Dependence Upon Him in the Whole of It*, Edwards had apparently overcome his abhorrence. "There is an absolute and universal dependence of the redeemed on God for all their good," Edwards argued before a Boston audience, and "hence those doctrines and schemes of divinity that are in any respect opposite to such an absolute and universal dependence on God, derogate from his glory."[2] And if on that day in 1730 Jonathan Edwards's audience had any doubt which doctrines and systems he felt derogated from God's glory, by the end of his career any ambiguity would seem to have been ended. Edwards was early America's foremost defender of Calvinism.

But his strategies for preserving true doctrine against Arminianism changed over time. In the Great Awakening, his approach was the positive one of encouraging "conversion" through the rhetoric of fortune. But by 1754, when he published A Careful and Strict Enquiry into the Modern Prevailing Notions of that Freedom of Will, Which is Supposed to be Essential to Moral Agency, Vertue and Vice, Reward and Punishment, Praise and Blame, Edwards's retreat from the rhetoric of fortune had advanced. Freedom of the Will was written just two years after Edwards had been forcibly removed from his parish, and while the dispute that had led to his dismissal was about church polity, Edwards, increasingly alert to dogmatic deviance, suspected that it had really been a floodlike tendency of "the younger generation" to reject Calvinism in favor of Arminianism that had swept him out of his church.[3]

So, on one level, Freedom of the Will was Jonathan Edwards's vengeful attack on these Arminians—the younger generation who had deprived him and his substantial family of a living.[4] Somewhat more deeply, the work was Edwards's continued Calvinistic penance for promoting the enthusiastic excesses of the Great Awakening.[5] But beyond both of these relatively superficial explanations, Freedom of the Will is best read as the first systematic treatise in American public theology, and as the most sustained apology ever constructed for the aristocracy of grace.[6]

I

Jonathan Edwards may seem with hindsight to have been predestined to write a defense of the Calvinist solution to the problem of free will, but in fact the work had historical roots. Edwards first perceived the central importance of the problem of free will in the wake of the colonial Arminian controversy between Johnson and Dickinson. When he actually sat down to write Freedom of the Will, Edwards drew primarily on the texts of three British divines, Isaac Watts, Daniel Whitby, and Thomas Chubb. But the American context informed Edwards's thinking throughout. In fact, locating this colonial context of Edwards's work is the key to understanding its significance.[7]

Edwards first claimed to want to write on Arminianism in 1746.[8] At that time, in a letter to his friend Joseph Bellamy, he noted that he was returning to Bellamy "Mr Dickinson's book," and that he wished "further opportunity with Dr. Johnson's." These were none other than the key documents in the colonial Arminian controversy. Edwards was aware of the local debate. Indeed, he concluded his comments to Bellamy on what he himself called "the Arminian controversy" by asking his correspondent to inquire "of Dr Johnson or Mr Beach . . . what is the best Book on the Arminian side, for the defence of their notion of Free will. . . . I don't know but I shall publish something after a while on that Subject."[9] Edwards conceived *Freedom of the Will* in light of the colonial debate.

In fact, Edwards continued to plan his own response throughout the course of the pamphlet exchange between the Calvinists and Anglicans. In the summer of 1747, as the controversy was at its peak, Edwards wrote to Rev. John Erskine, a Scottish minister: "I have thought of writing something particularly and largely on the Arminian controversy."[10] And around the same time, in another letter to Bellamy, Edwards showed a desire to keep up with the colonial contest. "If you have one of Mr. Beach's and Dr. Jonson's last," he requested of Bellamy, "I . . . should be glad if you would lend them to me, after you have used them sufficiently your self, and send them by some safe hand."[11] As far as Edwards was concerned, when he referred to "the Arminian controversy," he meant at least in part the controversy between Beach, Johnson, and Dickinson.

Edwards knew that the Arminian controversy was not just a local event, of course, but he did consider the arguments of Beach and Johnson "notable."[12] "It might be of particular advantage to me here in this remote part of the world," Edwards wrote to his Scottish correspondent, Erskine,

to be better informed what books that are published on the other side of the Atlantic; and especially if there be anything that comes out that is very remarkable. I have seen many notable things that have been written in this country against the truth, but nothing very notable on our side of the controversies of the present day, at least of the Arminian controversy.[13]

Apparently, Edwards thought Johnson and Beach were getting the best of the colonial Calvinists.[14]

Erskine responded by sending Edwards John Taylor's book on original sin. But Edwards's focus was increasingly shaped by what he saw going on around him. "A relish for true religion and piety . . . [are] great strangers [sic] to this part of America," he replied to Erskine. Indeed,

Arminianism . . . , in destruction to the doctrines of free grace, [is] daily propagated in the New England colleges. How horribly and how wickedly, are these poisonous notions rooting out those noble pious principles, on which our excellent ancestors founded those seminaries! And how base a return is it of the present generation, to that God, who is constantly surrounding them with goodness and mercy! and how offensive is it in the eyes of that God, who is jealous of his glory, and will take vengeance on his adversaries, and reserveth wrath for his enemies![15]

Edwards even thought that Arminianism lurked behind the scenes of the debate that led to his removal from Northampton. He described Joseph Hawley, the leader of the party seeking to dismiss him, as "a man of lax principles in religion, falling in, in some essential things, with Arminians, and is very open and bold in it." And Hawley was only one of many. "There seems to be," Edwards claimed one week after his dismissal, "the utmost danger, that the younger generation will be carried away with Arminianism as with a flood. The young gentleman I spoke of [Hawley], is high in their esteem, and is become the leading man in the town . . . ; and we have none able to confront and withstand him in dispute."[16]

And so Edwards himself, pitched into high water, landed at the Stockbridge Indian mission, where he unleashed a torrent of his own. But on the deepest level, *Freedom of the Will* was not a mere vendetta. It was, instead, as he himself entitled it, a "careful and strict inquiry" in direct response to the colonial Arminian controversy.

II

Above all, then, *Freedom of the Will* was an inquiry designed to show the contours and limitations of Arminianism. The center was shifting in America, and Jonathan Edwards was the first to describe in detail the anatomy of this shift. Edwards catalogued and defined the prevailing colonial ideologies, and if on one level he attempted to demolish them, through his presuppositions he in fact contributed to the harmony in discord. The ideology of free choice was left stronger after Edwards supposedly demolished Arminianism. An establishment of mediation—an enduring contest between the anti-extremist parties—was in the making.

Throughout his work, Edwards sought to avoid extreme determinism. This process, as much rhetorical as metaphysical, began as soon as he defined "the will [which] (without any metaphysical refining) is plainly, that by which the mind chooses anything. The faculty of the will is that faculty or power or principle of mind by which it is capable of choosing: an act of the will is the same as an act of choosing or choice."[17] By defining the will in the way that he did, Edwards admitted the central issue at stake. Humans had a "will," they chose, and therefore they had power.

If Edwards in fact supported a form of "free choice," he also, of course, distinguished his sense of free choice from that of the Arminians. The way in which he did so was to show the compatibility of free choice with "necessity." For Edwards, as for every Calvinist before him, a distinction needed to be made between "types" of necessity. For Edwards there were two, natural necessity and moral necessity, and on their difference rested the proper interpretation of Calvinism, indeed, the proper interpretation of the whole question of human power.

Natural necessity was, at base, the compulsion of determinism, and Edwards considered this necessity incompatible with moral responsibility:

By "natural necessity," as applied to men, I mean such necessity as men are under through the force of natural causes. . . . Thus men placed in certain circumstances, are the subjects of particular sensations by necessity: they feel pain when their bodies are wounded; they see the objects presented before them in a clear light, when their eyes are opened . . . so by a natural necessity men's bodies move downwards, when there is nothing to support them.[18]

Put negatively, "natural necessity" was "natural inability" or impossibility. "We are said to be *naturally* unable to do a thing, when we can't do it if we will, because what is most commonly called nature don't allow of it." And Edwards admitted that this sort of necessity was incompatible with praise or blame: "Natural impossibility wholly excuses and excludes all blame." Jonathan Edwards no more sanctioned a violent force on the will than had Jonathan Dickinson, but he did support "moral necessity," defined as "that necessity of connection and consequence, which arises from such *moral causes*, as the strength of inclination, or motives, and the connection which there is in many cases between these, and such certain volitions and actions." Put negatively, moral *inability* therefore was "the want of inclination; or the strength of a contrary inclination; or the want of sufficient motives in view, to induce and excite the act of the will, or the strength of apparent motives to the contrary." In short, "moral inability consists in the opposition or want of inclination."[19] When the will did not will, it was obviously not inclined to will.

Given this distinction between natural and moral necessity, Edwards could argue that all human volitions were both necessary and free. Liberty was ordered, but was still liberty. Freedom was simply the "power, opportunity, or advantage, that anyone has, to do as he pleases. Or in other words, his being free from hindrance or impediment in the way of doing, or conducting in any respect, as he wills."[20] The only thing in the way of liberty was compulsion or restraint—natural necessity. "Let the person come by his volition or choice how he will, yet if he is able, and there is nothing in the way to hinder his pursuing and executing his will, the man is fully and perfectly free."[21]

Edwards was adamant that Calvinism did not make humans "machines."[22] He was opposed to any absolute fatalism:

Man is entirely, perfectly and unspeakably different from a mere machine, in that he has reason and understanding, and has a faculty of will, and so is capable of volition and choice; and in that, his will is guided by the dictates or views of his understanding, and in that his external actions and behavior, and in many respects also his thoughts, and the exercises of his mind, are subject to his will.[23]

The will was "guided" for Edwards, a subject, not an object. To be a human was to have liberty, and to live in accord with human understanding. In his own terms, therefore, Edwards sought to preserve "the highest degree of liberty that ever was thought of, or that ever could possibly enter into the heart of any man to conceive."[24] He was no enemy of human freedom.

But neither was he an advocate of Arminian liberty, and in the most vital part of his work, Edwards set out to define and demolish the Arminian conception of free will. For Edwards, "these several things belong to [the Arminian] notion of liberty":

1. That it consists in a self-determining power in the will, or a certain sovereignty the will has over itself . . . ; 2. Indifference belongs to liberty in their notion of it, or that the mind, previous to the act of volition be, *in equilibrio*. 3. Contingence is another thing that belongs and is essential to it . . . as opposed to all necessity, or any fixed and certain connection with some previous ground or reason of its existence.[25]

Edwards opposed all three conceptions: self-determination, indifference, and contingence.

The case against self-determination came first. Edwards used logical, cosmological, and political arguments. The logical reasoning, in which Edwards reduced the idea of a self-determined will to an infinite regress, is justifiably famous:

If the will determines all its own free acts, then every free act of choice is determined by a preceding act of choice, choosing that act. And if that preceding act of the will or choice be also a free act, then by these principles, in this act too, the will is self-determined; that is . . . it is an act determined still by a preceding act of the will, choosing that. And the like may again be observed of the last mentioned act. Which brings us directly to a contradiction: for it supposes an act of the will preceding the first act in the whole train, directing and determining the rest; or a free act of the will, before the first free act of the will.[26]

The human will could not be sovereign, because no human could will the first free act of will.

Put more concretely, Edwards's point was the obvious one that no human being, the agent of the will, was self-created. Self-determination as a principle could logically go only so far. Just as human individuals had unique parents, unique grandparents, and so on, so every act of the will depended to some extent on a prior act. In other words, Edwards presupposed that "nothing ever comes to pass without a cause. What is self-existent must be from eternity, and must be unchangeable."[27] Self-determination was only sensibly applied to the eternal will. Any particular will was always one will rather than another, and therefore had to have a place in a chain of causes going back to First Cause:

So that it is indeed as repugnant to reason, to suppose that an act of the will should come into existence without a cause, as to suppose the human soul, or an angel, or the globe of the earth, or the whole universe, should come into existence without a cause. . . . 'Tis not the particular kind of effect that makes the absurdity of supposing it has being without a cause, but something which is common to all things that ever begin to be, viz. that they are not self-existent.[28]

So, everything existing—every act of the will, just like every agent—had an appointed "connection."[29] Only the absolute was properly absolute; anything else was partial. And yet the point of human choice was to reflect this absolute as fully as possible. Any other viewpoint led to disaster: "If once this grand principle of common sense be given up . . . all our means of ascending in our arguing from the creature to the Creator, and all our evidence of the being of God, is cut off at one blow." Indeed, if there was not a cause for everything that came to be, then "millions and millions of events are continually coming into existence contingently, without any cause or reason why they do so, all over the world, every day and hour, through the ages."[30] Either the pattern was absolute, and self-determination an illusion, or the cosmos was in fact a chaos.

For Edwards, either all of life was ordered in a causal chain *of some sort*, or all was up for grabs. It all resolved back to either First Cause, the choice of God, or no cause:

Nothing has no choice. And this No-Cause, which causes no existence, can't cause the existence which comes to pass, to be of one particular sort only, distinguished from all others. Thus, that only one sort of matter drops out of the heavens, even water, and that this comes so often, so constantly and plentifully, all over the world, in all ages, shows that there is some cause or reason of the falling of water out of the heavens; and that some-thing besides mere contingence has a hand in the matter.[31]

Edwards's argument against self-determination was, therefore, not simply a logical one. It was also cosmological. Order, harmony, bal-ance, and design were concepts as familiar to the ideology of predes-tination of Jonathan Edwards as they were to the Enlightenment thought of Benjamin Franklin.[32]

But Edwards's critique of self-determination was not only logical and cosmological; it was political. And if in a sense, Edwards was a theocrat who believed that God ruled directly in human affairs, it is more accurate to say that he believed in the political efficacy of the elect. He was, politically, an occasionalist, who believed that God ordered all occasions, while giving humans the freedom to enact them as "second causes."[33] And although Edwards peppered *Freedom of the Will* with appeals to democratic "common sense," which he contrasted with Arminian "pompousness," in fact his political inten-tion was to describe the anarchy of Arminianism and to call America back to the old order of the aristocracy of grace.[34] Only the Saints could enact as second causes the acts of God, the First Cause.

The "conclusion" to Edwards's work made this clear. "As God designedly orders his own conduct, and its connected consequences, it must necessarily be, that he designedly orders all things."[35] But how did God manage this? First, he permitted sin, through moral necessity. Humans were "free" to sin, and naturally did, concluded Edwards.[36] Second, just as inevitably, and yet without contradicting human freedom, God chose "a certain number" to be saved, and "a certain number only." These few, "the saints," would also inevitably and yet by their own acts persevere to earn the reward God had designed for them: "all true saints shall persevere to actual eternal salvation."[37]

Salvation, however, was not just a personal, individualistic matter. It had consequences.

It may also be worthy of consideration, whether the great alteration which has been made in the state of things in our nation, and some other parts of the Protestant world, in this and the past age, by the exploding so generally [of] Calvinistic doctrines, this is so often spoken of as worthy to be greatly rejoiced in by the friends of truth, learning and virtue . . . ; I say, it may be worthy to be considered, whether this be indeed a happy change, owing to any such cause as an increase of true knowledge and understanding in things of religion; or whether there is not reason to fear, that it may be owing to some worse cause.[38]

God had a design for the Saints, for the church, and for America. The Great Awakening had been the occasion; it was now up to the elect to do their part. Leaving the government to the "self-determined" was to leave it to no one, which was simply politically stupid, as well as logically and cosmologically absurd.

The same and more was true of the Arminian claim to ground human liberty in "indifference." According to Edwards, when human chose, the choice involved the entire person, not just a hypostatized faculty of the will: "The very willing is the doing; when once [a person] has willed, the thing is performed."[39] If this seemed counterintuitive, Edwards explained that most people were unaware of the real choices they made. To argue that liberty was grounded in indifference, or in some equilibrium "whereby the will is without all antecedent determination or bias," and is able "either to determine itself or to do anything else, is to assert that the mind chooses without choosing. To say that when it is indifferent, it can do as it pleases, is to say that it can follow its pleasure, when it has no pleasure to follow."[40] The will followed its pleasure, and therefore choice was either passionate, involving the entire person, or it was not choice. A choice, by definition, could not be indifferent.

Arminians supported indifference, Edwards claimed, in order to preserve reward and punishment. A choice had to be one's own, made without prejudice, they argued, in order to earn merit or demerit. "Thus much must at least be intended by Arminians, when they talk of indifference as essential to liberty of will . . . that it is such an indifference as leaves the will not determined already; but free . . . for the will itself to be the determiner of the act that is to be the free act."[41] According to Arminians, one's actions had to be one's own, chosen without prejudice, for them to be worthy of moral praise and blame.

Exactly the opposite was the case, according to Edwards. Any good act deserved praise, regardless of its cause. It was the nature of the act or choice, not its objectivity or sincerity that determined whether it deserved praise or blame.[42] "Some persons are sincerely *bad;* others are sincerely *good.*"[43] If liberty as indifference were necessary to virtue, then habits, inclinations, and "bias" would not be subject to praise or blame. And if this were the case,

> there is no virtue in any such habits or qualities as humility, meekness, patience, mercy, gratitude, generosity, heavenly-mindedness; . . . or in delight in holiness, hungering and thirsting after righteousness, love to enemies, universal benevolence to mankind: and . . . there is nothing at all vicious, or worthy of dispraise, in the most sordid, beastly, malignant, devilish dispositions; in being ungrateful, profane, habitually hating God, and things sacred and holy; or in being most treacherous, envious and cruel towards men. For all these things are dispositions and inclinations of the heart. And in short, there is no such thing as any virtuous or vicious quality of mind; no such thing as inherent virtue and holiness, or vice and sin.[44]

It was a good will, not a free will, that was worthy of praise or blame.

So, just as Edwards sought to demolish self-determined liberty by arguing for a universal, self-existent order in the cosmos prior to individual existence, he likewise sought to demolish "indifference" by arguing for an eternal moral order that established the morality of an act or choice regardless of the cause of that choice. In fact, the closer one reflected that moral order, the closer to goodness, and to freedom. "He that in acting, proceeds with the fullest inclination, does what he does with the greatest freedom. . . . And so far is it from being agreeable to common sense, that such liberty as consists in indifference is requisite to praise or blame."[45] Morality was passionate, or it was not truly moral.

In short, then, Edwards was urging people sincerely to be themselves, and that meant either "sincerely good" or "sincerely bad." And politically, this meant nothing less than that the Saints *would* rule; for "that which is not truly virtuous in God's sight, is looked upon by him as good for nothing."[46] If Edwards had a conception of history as somehow under the sway of God (and all of his apocalyptic writings attest that he did), then he also believed not only that the Saints should, but that they eventually would, rule.[47] For just as "nothing" had no choice, no will, no cause, neither did it have any political effect. "Those things which have no positive virtue, have no positive moral influence."[48] All but the Saints would destroy themselves, and while the Saints might learn something through the negative example of the reprobate, there was surely no sense flattering them.[49] Indifferent liberty was a contradiction in terms. Everyone's acts of choice were biased, but there was only one bias worth having—that of the aristocracy of grace.

In the end, then, Jonathan Edwards was a conservative. The underlying political theme of *Freedom of the Will* was consistency—preservation of the status quo. Edwards's essentially conservative public theology became apparent, especially when he turned to argue against contingence. Arminians, Edwards claimed, argued that contingence was "opposite, not only to constraint, but to all necessity"; an act had to be completely indetermined in order to be free at all. In contrast, Edwards proposed that "the acts of the will are never contingent, or without necessity, in the sense spoken of; inasmuch as those things which have a cause, or reason of their existence, must be connected with their cause."[50]

For Edwards, morality—including politics—was a matter, not of chance, but of design.[51] Goodness was not arrived at casually, any more than the world had been designed carelessly by God. Choice was free, but it was invariably connected with both causes and consequences. First, Edwards argued, contingence was false because acts of free choice had to be connected with the understanding. Humans either chose reasonably, in light of their understanding, or they no more chose than leaves chose to blow in the wind. And the understanding, even Arminians would admit, had to follow some rules. If this were not the case, and if liberty were equal to absolute contingence, then

the freedom of the soul, as a moral agent, must consist in the independence of the understanding on any evidence or appearance of things, or anything whatsoever that stands forth to the view of the mind, prior to the understanding's determination. And what sort of liberty is this! consisting in an ability, freedom and easiness of judging, either according to evidence, or against it; having a sovereign command over itself at all times, to judge, either agreeably or disagreeably to what is plainly exhibited to its own view. Certainly, 'tis no liberty that renders persons the proper subjects of persuasive reasoning, arguments, expostulations, and suchlike moral means and inducements.[52]

The Arminians, of course, claimed that they were the preservers of moral accountability, while Calvinists were antinomians. In fact, suggested the Calvinist Edwards, contingence and moral reasonableness were incompatible.

Contingence was also false because true freedom connected the will to motives, argued Edwards. "There can be no act of will, choice or preference of the mind, without some motive or inducement, something in the mind's view, which it aims at, seeks, inclines to and goes after."[53] What would be the point of a choice with no purpose? Contingence, defined as freedom from all necessity, could not be compatible with human morality. If humans were to be moral agents, they had to admit that their moral choices and acts were connected to their motives.

And where did motives come from? Contingence was false because true freedom connected the human will with the divine. God was omniscient and therefore possessed foreknowledge of all events. Absolute contingence—complete lack of connection between an effect and any cause—obviously ruled out God's omniscient control of events. At the extreme, if events were indeed contingent, then it was conceivable that the world had no purpose; there was no morality, no purpose to creation, no reason for living:

'Tis manifest, the moral world is the end of the natural: the rest of creation is but an house which God hath built, with furniture, for moral agents: and the good or bad state of the moral world depends on the improvement they make of their moral agency, and so depends on their volitions. And therefore, if [volitions] can't be foreseen by God . . . then the affairs of the moral world are liable to go wrong, to any assignable degree; yea liable to be utterly ruined.[54]

A moral world, ruled by a moral God, made for moral humans, was inconsistent with absolute contingence.

Indeed, if liberty consisted in contingence, then liberty was "a full and perfect freedom and liableness to act altogether at random, without the least connection with, or restraint and government by, any dictate of reason, or anything whatsoever apprehended." In contrast,

The notion mankind have conceived of liberty, is some dignity or privilege, something worth claiming. But what dignity or privilege is there, in being given up to such a wild contingence as this, to be perfectly and constantly liable to act unintelligently and unreasonably, and as much without the guidance of understanding, as if we had none, or were as destitute of perception as the smoke that is driven by the wind![55]

The real foes of Jonathan Edwards's *Freedom of the Will* were inconsistency, contradiction, irrationality, and chaos. He did not oppose "free choice," much less freedom in general. And the real subjects of his defense, conversely, were consistency, reason, order, and the status quo. The ironies are ample, for Edwards himself admitted that the status quo was no longer Calvinism. After brilliantly describing the "great alteration" in the American mind, Edwards failed to perceive the consequences of his own argument for consistency. Arminianism was "the modern, prevailing notion of free will."

And, more than he cared to admit, Edwards shared in the Arminians' rationality. Edwards had argued for a universal order to the cosmos in order to criticize the Arminian claim to self-determination. But the Arminians were perfectly comfortable with God as the Creator; and in fact did their best to promote the idea. They simply believed God had created people to be self-determined, not that people created themselves in this way. No Arminian in America advocated the form of self-determination Edwards had effectively ridiculed.

Similarly, Edwards had presupposed the influence of motive, passion, or bias in order to criticize indifference as inconsistent with mortal virtue. But no Arminian was indifferent to moral matters, and indeed, Anglican preachers preached largely the same moral rules as the Calvinists. Even if, as Edwards contended, morality was defined by the nature of the good, rather than its cause, was not preaching the good good enough? No Arminian denied that habits affected the practice of virtue. In fact, Benjamin Franklin's entire life was the attempt to prove the axiom.

And, finally, Edwards advocated a high sense of freedom in order to criticize contingence as opposed to all moral persuasion. But what Arminian actually argued for chance? Samuel Johnson had put it succinctly—contingence was only uncertainty or plurality, not the lack of a cause. Indeed, this uncertainty was in fact the strongest motive to responsibility. Humans had a role to play in the cosmos.

The Arminians were no more indeterminists than Edwards himself was a fatalist.

In a word, then, Jonathan Edwards's *Freedom of the Will* supported the anti-extremist status quo—the establishment of mediation, where human liberty was connected in some way to both the providence of God and moral responsibility. "The doctrine of the Calvinists, concerning the absolute decrees of God, does not at all infer any more fatality in things, than will demonstrably follow from the doctrine of most Arminian divines," he asserted.[56] But by showing the ability of Calvinism to do everything Arminians claimed for their system of doctrine, Edwards only showed the equivalence of the two systems. In so doing, he established that the debate between the aristocracy of grace and the democracy of law over free choice was itself the status quo.

To be sure, Jonathan Edwards's intention was to conserve the aristocracy of grace, not to synthesize a debate in American public theology.[57] But by defining the contours of the problem of free will as clearly as he did, and by arguing so effectively for consistency, cosmic order, and the compatibility of the governance of God with human free choice, Edwards ironically lent legitimacy to the chief reasons the Arminians claimed to be able to define the proper relationship between spiritual and political power. Edwards's *Freedom of the Will*, required reading for fifteen years at Yale, would hardly have kept undergraduates or anyone else who read it from supporting free choice. In fact, by teaching them how to debate about what they loved, it undoubtedly helped them to find their way.

Epilogue

*Let it be tried, then, whether any middle ground
can be taken, which will at once support a due
supremacy of the national authority, and leave in
force the local authorities so far as they can be
subordinately useful.*   JAMES MADISON, 1787

*Almost all extremes are softened or blunted: all that
was most prominent is superseded by some middle
term, at once less lofty and less low, less brilliant
and less obscure, than what before existed in the
world.*   ALEXIS DE TOCQUEVILLE, 1835

I

Studying "the will" today is a bit like studying "the humours." With
a few notable exceptions, the idea of a discrete human will has been
relegated to the intellectual dumpster, along with bloodletting by
leeches, phrenology, the arc reflex, and any number of archaic conceptions of human action and motivation.[1] As an object of antiquarian curiosity, it may be vaguely interesting to ask why the idea
developed, but not too many people consider the problem a matter
of life and death.

In the seventeenth and eighteenth centuries, things were different. Why so? Then, even the most enlightened *philosophes* believed
that first principles—one's theory—had consequences in life—one's
practice. More specifically, in the culture of colonial North America,
the paradoxes of theology mattered, and no issue in theology mattered more than the problem of free will. Obviously, the colonists
would not have bothered to debate so vigorously something they

perceived to be fruitless. Although we might not recognize the utility of leeches, a free will, or the grace of God, they embraced them all.

They were able to do so, in part, because they shared with the other inhabitants of the early modern West a universe that was still largely enchanted.[2] God and the Devil, angels and demons, were as present to most of the colonists of North America as the spouse to whom they made love or the violent deaths they so often observed. And in their effort to understand this universe, which seemed to offer both comfort and terror, they inevitably drew upon myths they had learned that explained the universal patterns. For most of them, the stories they heard told how God gave humans gifts, most notably the gift of His only Son, the Word, so that they could live eternally in a place of delight.

In common with their European ancestors and counterparts, in other words, the colonists of North America believed that "the whole" was worth talking about. They felt that truth was one, thought that ideas mattered, and believed that the effort to express and argue about one's ideas in language was worthwhile. They argued so much about free will, grace, and law, then, because they believed that the beliefs one held about these ultimate questions had consequences. They took their doctrines and myths seriously, not just as a debased or projected materialism, but as in fact the media of reality. Language, mediation, and the Word were as real as matter.

Indeed, the saying of particular words could mean the difference between life and death in early modern Europe or America.[3] Even aside from the incantatory curses with which many colonists believed they could be afflicted, or with which they might try to afflict others, the very political systems of both Europe and the colonies were predicated upon belief in the power of human beings to create networks of sustained relationships through words.[4] For most of the colonists, furthermore, the best source from which to draw the words to build enduring relationships was Holy Scripture.

But the Bible has long been known to promote divergent interpretations, and in early modern Europe, this conflict over the Word had become epidemic. The theologians were not the only ones to quibble over the meaning of grace in Paul's Epistle to the Romans. Protestant soldiers battled Catholic in Central Europe, Jesuits evicted Jansenists from monasteries and convents in France, and

Arminian politicians oppressed Calvinists in England. States were formed, and ended, as one interpretation of the Word prevailed over another. Out of disgust, as much as anything, a few European intellectuals gradually began to suggest that maybe it would be better to separate the power over material life from the control of those who held the power to interpret the words of the spirit.[5] They suggested this, of course, with words.

For most of the colonists of North America, however, separating spiritual power completely from political and material power was really not an option. Many of the settlers brought with them to the New World not only conceptions of an enchanted universe, but particular allegiances that emerged out of the conflicts in the Old. Most of the colonists saw themselves as created in the image of God, and they therefore saw politics as the mirror of salvation. And they thought no issue was more important, both for salvation and for society, than human freedom.

Both the intensity of debate over and the specific answers to the problem of free will that were favored by the colonists can, then, to a degree be traced to the debates going on and the parties that were formed across the Atlantic.[6] But things changed. The range and limits of liberty that prevailed in Europe had to be adapted to new human communities.[7] The very environment of North America, as well as the Indian civilizations the colonists encountered upon landing, first altered the networks they built. The New England Puritans were not the only, or the last, residents of North America to consider the frontier a "howling wilderness," to slaughter the Indians as representatives of demonic chaos, and to equate civilization with political control of both nature and "extremists" like Anne Hutchinson. The "answers" to the problem of free will favored by early Americans—and especially the anti-indeterminism they so often expressed—had roots in the land the settlers encountered, and in their perception of the cultures they met on that land.[8]

But the environmental causes of the debate over free will and its contours in early America inevitably merged with the social causes. Particular socio-religious communities were forming in the colonies—the largest were either Calvinistic or Anglican—and the debate over free will served to legitimate the particular claims and interests of one group over and against the other. Economic interests shaped these claims to power. Churches have always been financial incorporations, and ministers have always needed salaries. And if economic interest does little to explain the recurring intensity of the debate over free will in the colonies (Jonathan Edwards was not a budding religious entrepreneur scheming his way to a best-seller on free will), it may help to explain the ideologies of providence that came to dominate colonial life.

Put succinctly, the anti-extremism of the Calvinist and Anglican establishment of mediation may well have been the first cry of the bourgeois baby in the New World.[9] Max Weber long ago pointed out how "the Puritan ethic" was of a piece with Benjamin Franklin's "Way to Wealth."[10] The anxiety of Protestants about predestination was at the least compatible with their neighbors' economic free action, if not a positive rationalization for their own. Most colonists may have been ready to let God control the extremes of fate and chance, but they also wanted to be sure that they had at least a share of liberty, and most sought Franklin's ideal of "happy mediocrity" with increasing vigor.

Political interests also made the colonial debate over free will distinct from the European one. Almost all of the colonial thinkers, with the possible exception of Benjamin Franklin and some radical sectarians, remained convinced that one religion was preferable for one territory.[11] Calvinists such as Jonathan Edwards clearly hoped Congregationalism would remain the established religion of Massachusetts and Connecticut. Anglicans such as Samuel Johnson and John Beach would have liked nothing better than to see bishops installed throughout the colonies.[12] Jonathan Dickinson was an advocate of the Presbyterian system in New Jersey. The Catholics had strongholds in Maryland and further south and north in Spanish and French America. Even the Quakers had limits to the broad toleration granted in Pennsylvania. Most colonists assumed an inextricable link between the twin powers of religion and politics.[13]

But in the colonies, of course, combining spiritual and political power very quickly became a tricky matter. The combinations simply varied from place to place, and this lent the colonial debate over first principles such as human liberty its peculiar intensity. If the colonial theologians had not found some way to convince themselves that they could live in harmony with people who differed from them on the question of free will, they would have convinced themselves and their politicians that war was the only other option. Being theologically inclined, both Calvinists and Anglicans thought that the claim of their particular group to power was universal, but in practice, and eventually in theory, these claims tended to cancel each other out.[14] What was best for Massachusetts Congregationalists or Virginia Anglicans was best for New Jersey, and Pennsylvania, and New York, since it was best for the cosmos. But let the Anglicans try to gain a foothold in Massachusetts and all hell broke loose. Or at least a debate began.

Finally, then, if one must find some cause beyond the reasons the colonists themselves gave for debating free will, or favoring particular answers to the problem, the best place to look is to the process of culture formation. It was the attempt by the various religio-political parties in early America to *ground* their universal claims to power symbolically that pushed the leaders of the groups into common territory. In order to argue about anything, there had to be some agreement on the fundamental terms of the debate; something like a range of legitimate "solutions" to the problem of free will.[15]

As much as possible, though, it is best to let the voices of the past speak for themselves. And the debaters over free will in seventeenth- and eighteenth-century America offer us the story of a paradox lost. God became a person, they believed, and then they proceeded to build a culture in which they sought to coerce some persons to conform to their own limited formulations of that paradox. They confused the Word with their own words.[16] The individual Christian theologians who wrote about free will in early America knew, of course, that they could not control the Word, but they occasionally pulled together to kill people in its name.[17] In their better moments, these same Christians used words to understand, to appreciate, and to argue with one another. Sometimes words are all human beings have. But sometimes words make history.

II

I have claimed repeatedly that the debate over the question of free will from 1630 to 1760 produced, or exhibited, a new and distinctive culture or ethos for the people who came to live in the American colonies during that time. Another way of saying the same thing is to say free will was the guiding issue in early American thought, and that the prevailing answer, or answers, to the problem of free will produced the "guiding pattern" of this new culture. As such, that problem was part of what Edward Shils has identified as a tradition, the "'tacit component' of rational, moral, and cognitive actions, and of affect" marking a given people in a given time and place. Operating "at the boundaries of deliberate actions, setting the end or the rules and standards," claims Shils, "the traditional stands around the boundaries of the field in which deliberate expediential actions and those which are filled with passion occur."[18] The colonial establishment of mediation—the tendency to avoid extremes on the question of free will in favor of the three ideologies of providence— was this sort of "boundary" of deliberate action for most of the people living in early America (for a succinct summary of the three ideologies of providence, see the table in the introduction to this book). It was an assumption; a cultural presupposition; a "tacit" component in their everyday lives. It was articulated by the elites, and therefore it has been to them that we have largely turned in order to uncover this tradition.[19]

But if, in fact, the "establishment of mediation" was a tradition, how did it work? What was its significance? Again following Shils, we can perceive that the debate over free will produced a "symbolic constellation" that was part and parcel of the tradition of knowledge acquisition in early America. The debates over free will were as "scientific" in the eighteenth-century sense as were Newton's observations on gravity.[20] And just as Newton's work was considered true or orthodox, so too an orthodoxy developed regarding free will. The "establishment of mediation" was this "scientific" orthodoxy, and the extremes of fate and/or chance became "heresy."

Jonathan Edwards clearly labeled his *Careful and Strict Enquiry into . . . Freedom of the Will* a work in "the science of the will," and no one in the eighteenth century even thought to question him on the claim. Edwards observed human agency, and submitted the results of his observation to the community of experts and amateurs who went about working with him in what one historian of science has aptly called the "consensible discipline."[21] And out of Edwards's observations came the orthodoxy of the establishment of mediation—humans could exercise free choice, but were at the same time governed in some way by God. That this conclusion happened to coincide with a watered-down version of theological orthodoxy was so much the better. The verification was mutual, and reciprocal. In the eighteenth-century colonies, the paradoxes of religious myth were considered scientific truth.

The establishment of mediation emerged, then, because it solved any number of problems in early American culture. As Michael Kammen has pointed out, "paradoxes" were peculiar to American culture because of the colonial quest for legitimacy, for a life lived "in accord with law, rule or principle." According to Kammen, this drive for legitimation and the paradoxes it produced separated Americans from their more settled and already "legitimate" European counterparts. In a land where the judicial systems were chaotic, the quest for law was bound to be continuous. In a land where the provisional governments were provisional at best, the quest for rule was inevitably never-ending. And in a land where the churches were all transplanted, all struggling to be established, and all failing to consolidate spiritual and political power, it should hardly be surprising that people debated the questions that they thought would give them stable first principles.[22]

In short, the absence of law, rule, and established orthodoxy in the colonies produced several generations of thinkers (Shils argues that three is the minimum for a tradition) who were forced to face the question of their place in the cosmos, and who answered with the assertion, seemingly undeniable but nevertheless needing to be stated, that they had one. Even more simply, the colonial debate over free will both emerged from and promoted hope and fear. Kammen suggests that there was a "fatalistic optimism, a belief in predestination and God's omnipotence with hope in human striving," at the core of American civilization.[23] This ethos of fatalistic optimism—I believe it was expressed more often by the colonists themselves as "free choice"—held that human liberty was both a gift and a task, free in the sense of a "gift" and a "choice" in the sense of a responsibility. And this paradoxical ethos was embedded in the tradition of knowledge acquisition in the colonies: it was a scientific conclusion and the orthodox result of the best observations of eighteenth-century thinkers.

And if this paradox endured, it also changed. The full paradox was lost. The Calvinists and Anglicans were powerful parties, and through their partisan debate, they defined limits to liberty. They ruled out the extremes and endorsed the establishment of mediation. And if this "agreement" to limit liberty produced a generation of gracious and virtuous citizens who could build a new culture, it also produced anxious and self-righteous moralists who were driven by an overbearing fear of illegitimacy and failure. Ironically, the quest for legitimacy itself became an object of attachment; the answers were in some ways decided before the quest was begun. Americans would be pilgrims, but only certain paths could be followed. And it may have been out of that process of limitation—out of the establishment of mediation, that the American republic was born.[24]

III

Needless to say, republican government in North America did not jump full-fledged out of a debate over free will. In fact, as James T. Kloppenberg has pointed out, three primary sources for the republic have been identified, and argued over, by the scholarly community.[25] First, some have argued that the republic was shaped especially by evangelical Calvinist piety as modified by the Great Awakening.[26] Second, others argue that classical republican political theory, especially as transmitted by radical Whig thinkers from England and Scotland, was the primary source for the shapers of the American political system.[27] Third, yet another group of scholars argue that it was the developing spirit of liberal acquisitiveness, especially as expressed in the philosophy of John Locke, that made the American republic a distinctly "modern" creation.[28]

Of these three sources, the greatest attention of late has been paid to the last two—classical republicanism and liberalism. The debates between advocates of the two arguments have been heated.[29] My work suggests, however, that religious explanations for the origins of the republic have been underestimated. If religion contributed to the ideological origins of the American republic, then more than evangelical Calvinism has to be taken into account.[30]

Nevertheless, the strength of the three-source hypothesis would seem to be that each strand points up a distinctive, potentially definitive, facet of the republic. Calvinism, it is supposed, led some of the founders to argue for commitment to the common good or the whole; these leaders advocated a politics designed to promote a public spirit of benevolence in opposition to self-interest.[31] Classical republicanism, although drawing upon less transcendent sources than the Christians, similarly led the founders to seek restraint upon acquisitive impulses and promoted both the ideal of the virtuous citizen and a secular "science of politics," most notably the writing of the Constitution.[32] And liberalism, notably the belief in "natural rights," promoted the egalitarianism and individualism necessary to support the economic well-being of a diverse new nation.[33] At some point, advocates of all three sources agree, liberalism became the dominant ideology of the republic, and the restraints of both Calvinistic and republican virtue fell by the wayside as America became an empire.

Now, without egregious distortion, this story can be told completely in terms of religious history. Calvinism undoubtedly contributed to the origins of the republic, although the fixation of many scholars on "millennialism" and "evangelicalism" as founts of democracy needs to be curbed. Most converts to evangelicalism in the eighteenth century were Calvinists, and Calvinists thought more about "grace" than they did about the millennium. In short, a conversion to Calvinism may have promoted broader involvement by people in eighteenth-century politics and society, but the usual channel for grace is from the top down; from the few to the many. Calvinists may have supported the "common good," but the aristocracy of grace supported the good first. In early America, the Calvinists were the aristocracy—the elite in the "establishment of mediation." They were, like Edwards, as conservative as they were radical.

The influence of classical republican theory on the founding of the republic cannot be denied. And yet, if the characteristic features of this theory were the "scientific" notion of a balanced government, and the importance of virtue in the citizenry, then here *moderate* Calvinism and Anglicanism both deserve fuller attention as influences inclining the colonists to accept the key tenets of republican theory. It is often forgotten that among the "classical Republicans" identified by Bernard Bailyn were the theologians Benjamin Hoadly, an Anglican, and Philip Doddridge and Isaac Watts, both moderate Calvinists.[34] And, of course, there were numerous Hoadlys and Wattses who supported a distinctive sense of "free choice" among the colonial clergy.[35] Revealed religion could support and promote a science of politics.[36]

And even liberalism may have had religious roots. The idea of "natural rights" did not spring fresh from empiricism any more than did concern for human individuals and their interests. Locke, who wrote as much theology as he did politics, had his religious sources. Moreover, Locke was a source, rather than a blueprint, for the founders of the American republic, just as he was a source, rather than a blueprint, for their thinking about free will. If, in other words, as one strand of the liberal hypothesis has it, Locke was the single most influential source the founders knew, it must be added that when colonial supporters of the democracy of law read Locke's chapter "On Power" and his treatises on politics, they *read into* them an understanding of power adapted to colonial conditions.[37] Locke may have reduced religion to morality in the interest of making it manipulable, but not all of the colonial thinkers were his dupes.[38]

All in all, the hypothesis that there was an interplay between the mentalities of the theologians who debated liberty in religious terms, the people who fought for liberty in the revolution, and the statesmen who ordered liberty into a republic may at the least be worth further study. In fact, such study is already under way. For instance, the Arminian controversy in seventeenth-century England has been traced in part to Protestant anti-Catholicism and fear of a Spanish or French "popish plot."[39] Similarly, it has been suggested that the fear of war with Catholic France may help explain why Protestant theology, and most notably Calvinist "covenant theology," endured in the colonies. At times of crisis—such as the threat of war with "anti-Christ," Catholic France—the notion of a Calvinist "center" could be invoked to rally the forces of Protestantism in defense of truth.[40] In an age of religious wars, an ideological style that described religio-political conspiracies against providential liberty made sense.[41]

Furthermore, if, by the time the American Revolution occurred, it was clear that the threat was no longer just papism but also religious conflict among the colonists themselves, then there must have been a broader logic than fear of foreign conspiracy behind the rebellion. Intracolonial as well as foreign intrigue may have inspired the founding generations with fear of anarchy or tyranny. Indeed, the logic of both the revolution and the founding of the republic may be traceable to the battle against extremes—the enslaving order of tyranny on the one hand and the chaos of licentiousness on the other.[42] And, if so, then this logic was validated by, indeed emerged initially through, the colonial debate over free will.[43]

In short, the history of the competing discourses of religious groups trying to interpret and to apply Christian myth in the colonies provides a contextual template for understanding the broader ideological development of American history. Thus, when the Articles of Confederation failed to achieve the hopes of the people, they, or at least their leaders, came together to form a "more perfect Union." The chief story of that unification may have been, in 1789 as in 1745, the contention between factions—among them the aristocracy of grace and the democracy of law—to settle a way in which liberty could be ordered; in which center and periphery could be balanced; in which freedom could be made to coincide with providence in an American republic of virtue.[44] James Madison's "middle ground" between federal government and state authority may well have been anticipated in the theologians' debates over divine providence and human free will.[45] The origins of the *novus ordo seclorum* may lie, paradoxically, in theology.[46]

IV

But if religion gave us the American republic, it was not only because the "denominations" could not agree with one another, and therefore left the structuring of society to professional politicians. In fact, there have been two great obstacles hitherto preventing historians from identifying the central role of religion in the early American republic. On the one hand, a popular tendency to equate "religion" and "church" spilled over for many years into scholarship, leading to the production of many fine denominational studies of religion in

America, but few syntheses. On the other hand, the "secularization" and the specialization of contemporary life that together breed anti-intellectualism in American culture have worked together to make difficult any attempt to explain the significance of theological first principles for early American thinkers.

Following especially Robert Bellah's essay, "Civil Religion in America," a significant amount of scholarship has been devoted to breaking down the first problem—the equation between denomination and religion in America.[47] The most notable works have explored how America's sense of "destiny" developed out of religious roots. Almost invariably, "millennialism" was the key principle. The colonists, asserted a generation of students of American culture, believed that America was the "new Israel" in God's cosmic historical drama.[48] In other words, so the argument ran, the idea that Israel was God's chosen people was understood self-referentially by Americans; then this understanding of history was communicated to the average colonists by theologians and preachers; and finally this sense of "providential mission" was "secularized" during the revolutionary years into a "civil millennialism." A religious view of history, in short, produced the attempt of Americans to shape political history in their revolution and republic.

Now, while the careful reader will note how much my own work depends upon this interpretation, he or she will also sense by now that I think it needs revision. It should not necessarily be taken as a sign of bad faith that religious historians found a view of religious history to be the fundamental dynamic in their culture's progress, but it does strike even this historian as a particularly self-serving sort of historical explanation. Furthermore, other historians have not failed to point out shortcomings in the millennial hypothesis.[49] Harry S. Stout, for instance, although a historian of religions himself, has claimed that the millennial note "has been abused through overemphasis." According to Stout, it was "*the enduring hold of concepts* like the covenant, Sola Scriptura (Scripture alone), and providential mission" that explains "the ease with which most New Englanders accepted the Revolution and its republican principles."[50]

In contrast to the millennial fixation of many scholars, a detailed and conceptually sophisticated argument for a broad role for religion in the era of the revolution and early republic has come from Catherine Albanese. According to Albanese, there was a full-fledged "civil religion of the American revolution." This religion existed alongside or betweeen the religions of the denominations and promoted a unique view, not only of history, but of space, God, religious leadership, and the ideal social order. This civil religion included, most notably for our purposes, a tendency to think in paradox, or to bring together opposites. Albanese points out, for instance, how liberty (always depicted as a "she") was for the colonists locked in a *hieros gamos,* or "sacred marriage," with providence, understood as the masculine governor of the universe—either Jehovah or the Grand Designer of the Deists.[51] Furthermore, Albanese follows Sidney Mead to show how this civil religion "fostered the idea of individual autonomy," since "all the lines of thinking of the eighteenth century converged on the idea of free, uncoerced, individual consent as the only proper basis for all man's organizations, civil and ecclesiastical."[52]

The virtue of Albanese's contribution, then, is to bring a theoretically sophisticated understanding of religion to bear upon the interrelationship between religion and the American Revolution. She overcomes the denominational anachronism that prevented previous historians from seeing the critical relationships between religious belief and political action in early America.[53] But the second problem impeding an understanding of religion's role in the early republic is just as difficult. Where Albanese (like almost every historian of early America) is weakest is precisely where the colonists themselves, or at least the colonial leaders, were strongest—namely, at understanding the symbols of systematic and philosophical theology.[54] Colonial American intellectuals were literate in the logic of myth, and the modern historian who wants to understand "the civil religion," or as I would prefer to put it, the "public theology" of early America, must therefore undertake to translate their arcane language about God in a way that makes it clear today why that theology was so important.[55]

Theology was a predominant mode of public discourse in the colonies, and theologians were quite arguably the leading group of "public" thinkers in early America.[56] And when these public figures talked, what they talked about was very often the question of free will. Through their debates, the advocates of the aristocracy of grace and the democracy of law taught one another, and themselves, that freedom was both a gift from God and a task demanding a choice. And as the colonies consolidated to battle against the British and to form a republic, far from becoming less important, this theological formula became both rallying cry and paradigm, inspiring both the will to revolt against tyranny and the grace to unite to prevent anarchy.[57] Thus even Thomas Jefferson, perhaps the most radically "secular" and "libertarian" thinker in the colonies, could conclude: "The God who gave us life, gave us liberty at the same time."[58] The tasks to which Jefferson and his peers set themselves in the years after 1760 may have been accomplished, at least in part, because theologians had prepared the people to share in the work that Jefferson's paradoxical proposition set before them.[59]

Notes

Introduction

1. Kees W. Bolle, "Fate," in *The Encyclopedia of Religion*, ed. Mircea Eliade (New York: Macmillan, 1987), 5:290–98. Several general works have been helpful in tracing the history and structure of the problem of free will. Harry J. McSorley, *Luther: Right or Wrong? An Ecumenical-Theological Study of Luther's Major Work*, The Bondage of the Will (New York: Newman Press, 1969), is somewhat tendentious but remains the single best survey of the "Christian" history of the debate. Vernon Joseph Bourke, *Will in Western Thought: An Historico-Critical Survey* (New York: Sheed & Ward, 1964), and Martin Davidson, *The Free Will Controversy* (London: Watts, 1942), are sometimes unreliable. Robert E. Dewey and James A. Gould, *Freedom: Its History, Nature, and Varieties* (London: Macmillan, 1970), is a good collection of readings. Among constructive works addressing the problem, Daniel C. Dennett, *Elbow Room: The Varieties of Free Will Worth Wanting* (Cambridge, Mass.: MIT Press, 1984), is delightful. See also *Free Will*, ed. Sidney Morgenbesser and James Walsh (Englewood Cliffs, N.J.: Prentice-Hall, 1962); *Determinism and Freedom in an Age of Modern Science*, ed. Sidney Hook (New York: New York Univ. Press, 1958); *Free Will*, ed. Gary Watson (New York: Oxford Univ. Press, 1982); and *Free Will and Determinism: Papers from an Interdisciplinary Research Conference*,

1986, ed. Viggo Mortensen and Robert C. Sorensen (Aarhus, Denmark: Aarhus Univ. Press, 1987).

2. A. Leo Oppenheim, *Ancient Mesopotamia: Portrait of a Dead Civilization* (Chicago: Univ. of Chicago Press, 1964), pp. 16, 198–206.

3. "The Code of Hammurabi," trans. T. J. Meeks, in *Ancient Near Eastern Texts Relating to the Old Testament*, ed. J. B. Pritchard (Princeton: Princeton Univ. Press, 1955).

4. See, e.g., the plea of the "friend" in the "Babylonian Theodicy": "Unless you seek the will of God, what luck have you? He that bears his god's yoke never lacks food, though it be sparse," in W. G. Lambert, *Babylonian Wisdom Literature* (Oxford: Clarendon Press, 1960), p. 85.

5. See H. and H. A. Frankfort, *The Intellectual Adventure of Ancient Man: An Essay on Speculative Thought in the Ancient Near East* (Chicago: Univ. of Chicago Press, 1946).

6. This is essentially the response of the "sufferer" in the Babylonian Theodicy: "How have I profited that I have bowed down to my god? I have to bow beneath the base fellow that meets me; The dregs of humanity, like the rich and opulent, treat me with contempt" (Lambert, *Babylonian Wisdom Literature*, p. 87).

7. William Chase Greene, *Moira: Fate, Good, and Evil in Greek Thought* (Cambridge, Mass.: Harvard Univ. Press, 1944).

8. Davidson, *The Free Will Controversy* (London: Watts, 1942).

9. On Aristotle, see W. F. R. Hardie, *Aristotle's Ethical Theory* (Oxford: Clarendon Press, 1968), esp. pp. 152–82. For a broader picture of Greek thought, see Martha C. Nussbaum, *The Fragility of Goodness: Luck and Ethics in Greek Tragedy and Philosophy* (Cambridge: Cambridge Univ. Press, 1986).

10. Epicurus, "Letter to Menoeceus," in *The Philosophy of Epicurus: Letters, Doctrines, and Parallel Passages from Lucretius*, trans. and ed. George K. Strodach (Evanston, Ill.: Northwestern Univ. Press, 1963), p. 185.

11. Walter G. Englert, *Epicurus on the Swerve and Voluntary Action* (Missoula, Mont.: Scholars Press, 1987).

12. A. A. Long, "Freedom and Determinism in the Stoic Theory of Human Action," in *Problems in Stoicism*, ed. A. A. Long (London: Athlone, 1971), pp. 173–99; Josiah B. Gould, "The Stoic Conception of Fate," *Journal of the History of Ideas* 35 (Jan.–Mar. 1974): 17–32.

13. David S. Winston, "Freedom and Determinism in Philo of Alexandria," *Studia Philonica* 3 (1974–75): 47–70; id., "Freedom and Determinism in Greek Philosophy and Jewish Hellenistic Wisdom," *Studia Philonica* 2 (1973): 40–50.

14. Albrecht Dihle, *The Theory of Will in Classical Antiquity* (Berkeley: Univ. of California Press, 1982).

15. Rom. 7:18.

16. Dihle, *Theory of Will*, p. 123.

17. Dom M. John Farelly, *Predestination, Grace, and Free Will* (Westminster, Md.: Newman Press, 1964).

18. See *Saint Augustin's Anti-Pelagian Works*, trans. Peter Holmes and Robert Ernest Wallis, rev. Benjamin B. Warfield (Grand Rapids, Mich.: Eerdmans, 1978 [repr.]); Peter Brown, *Augustine of Hippo* (Berkeley: Univ. of California Press, 1967),

esp. chs. 29–30; John Ferguson, *Pelagius: A Historical and Theological Study* (Cambridge: Cambridge Univ. Press, 1963); Robert F. Evans, *Pelagius: Inquiries and Reappraisals* (New York: Seabury Press, 1968).

19. *Nature and Grace: Selections from the* Summa Theologica *of Thomas Aquinas,* ed. A. M. Fairweather (Philadelphia: Westminster Press, 1977).

20. *Luther and Erasmus: Free Will and Salvation,* trans. and ed. E. Gordon Rupp and Philip S. Watson (Philadelphia: Westminster Press, 1969).

21. For a fascinating study of the rhetorical aspects of this debate, which traces Luther's position in his major work on the topic, *The Bondage of the Will,* to Stoic rhetoric, see Marjorie Boyle O'Rourke, *Rhetoric and Reform: Erasmus' Civil Dispute with Luther* (Cambridge, Mass.: Harvard Univ. Press, 1983).

22. For one brief comment on the import of this development, see Leszek Kolakowski, "The Man Who Made Modernity," review of *Luther: Man between God and the Devil,* by Heiko A. Oberman, *New Republic,* May 6, 1991, pp. 40–41.

23. Richard S. Dunn, *The Age of Religious Wars, 1559–1689* (New York: Norton, 1970).

24. Alexander Sedgwick, *Jansenism in Seventeenth-Century France: Voices from the Wilderness* (Charlottesville: Univ. Press of Virginia, 1977).

25. Douglas Nobbs, *Theocracy and Toleration: A Study of the Disputes in Dutch Calvinism from 1600 to 1650* (Cambridge: Cambridge Univ. Press, 1937).

26. Nicholas Tyacke, "Puritanism, Arminianism and Counter-Revolution," in *The Origins of the English Civil War,* ed. Conrad Russell (London: Macmillan, 1973), pp. 119–43; id., *Anti-Calvinists: The Rise of English Arminianism, c. 1590–1640* (New York: Oxford Univ. Press, 1987).

27. See David D. Hall, *Worlds of Wonder, Days of Judgment: Popular Religious Belief in Early New England* (New York: Knopf, 1989).

28. Mircea Eliade has identified "the mythic pattern" with the paradoxical logic of the "coincidence of the opposites." See Eliade, *The Sacred and the Profane: The Nature of Religion,* trans. Willard R. Trask (New York: Harcourt, Brace & World, 1959), and esp. *Patterns in Comparative Religion,* trans. Rosemary Sheed (New York: Sheed & Ward, 1958), esp. pp. 410–36. Creation stories offer a good example of this logic at work. Many such stories, including Gen. 1:27, depict the Creator as both male and female, "coinciding" the sexual opposites. More profoundly, creation stories, again including accounts in the Hebrew Bible, often depict an encounter or struggle between chaos and order leading to the founding of the cosmos; this struggle is then narrated or ritually reenacted as a way to remind a community of its inclusive ideals and obligations. See here Jon D. Levenson, *Creation and the Persistence of Evil: The Jewish Drama of Divine Omnipotence* (San Francisco: Harper & Row, 1987). The Christian story, although a distinct example of this pattern because of the historicity of its founder, nevertheless represents it in manifold ways. See for instance John Hick, ed., *The Myth of God Incarnate* (Philadelphia: Westminster Press, 1977).

29. For an excellent account of the lasting difficulties Protestants had in applying their theory in practice, see Martin E. Marty, *Protestantism in the United States: Righteous Empire,* 2d ed. (New York: Scribner's, 1986). The inherent instability of mythic paradox is what can lead it to be misused politically, but it also needs to be

added that without such an inclusive pattern, societies may fragment into greater violence. An implicit question behind this study thus is, which better restrains violence, mythic ideals and obligations or rational individualism and interest? On the question of myth and violence, see René Girard, *Violence and the Sacred*, trans. Patrick Gregory (Baltimore: Johns Hopkins Univ. Press, 1972).

30. The work that best describes the struggle between different Christian groups for dominance in the New World is Jon Butler, *Awash in a Sea of Faith: Christianizing the American People* (Cambridge, Mass. Harvard Univ. Press, 1990).

31. By ideology, following Karl Mannheim, I mean the way language becomes distorted, is used, or at the minimum is changed in order to reflect the particular social and political interests of a party or faction in a community. Language is never "just" words; it is about power. For instance, the key terms in the seventeenth- and eighteenth-century debates over free will—*freedom, will, order, choice*, and even, among Puritans, *governance*—were laden with political connotations. It is my contention that the debates over free will both expressed and legitimated particular social structures, group interests, or parties, most notably the parties of Calvinism and Anglicanism in the colonies. See Karl Mannheim, *Ideology and Utopia*, trans. Louis Wirth and Edward Shils (New York: Harcourt, Brace & World, 1936). For a criticism of Mannheim, see Jorge Larrain, *The Concept of Ideology* (Athens, Ga.: Univ. of Georgia Press, 1979). A modified version of Mannheim's notion can be found in Raymond Geuss, *The Idea of a Critical Theory* (Cambridge: Cambridge Univ. Press, 1981).

32. This typology runs the risk of distortion common to all such tools, but it is not without warrant from the period. Note a similar taxonomy used by Benjamin Franklin in 1730, cited in chapter 6.

33. See part 2, chapter 6.

34. See William James, "The Dilemma of Determinism," in *Essays in Pragmatism*, ed. Alburey Castell (New York: Hafner, 1954), pp. 37–64. The relation between theological predestination and philosophical determinism is a central, and complex, question in this work. Suffice it to say that I am persuaded that theological predestination differs fundamentally from philosophical determinism in that theology posits the presence of at least one personal will, namely, God. This mythic element to theology precludes a purely mechanistic view of the cosmos. In fact, a considerable rationale for the colonial favoritism to the "mediating" positions on free will can be found in the increasingly mechanistic assumptions of continental philosophy in the eighteenth century. See for an overview of the issues, on the philosophical side, Richard Taylor, "Determinism," in *The Encyclopedia of Philosophy* (New York: Macmillan, 1967), 2:359–73; for religion, Dewey D. Wallace, Jr., "Free Will and Predestination," in *The Encyclopedia of Religion* (New York: Macmillan, 1987), 5:422–26.

35. *Aristocracy of grace* is a variant on Martin E. Marty's term for the evangelicals on the eve of the American revolution, *aristocracy of the converted*. See *Religion, Awakening, and Revolution* (n.p.: Consortium/McGrath, 1977), p. 99. On "public theology," see esp. John F. Wilson, *Public Religion in American Culture* (Philadelphia: Temple Univ. Press, 1979), and Robert Bellah et al., *Habits of the Heart: Individualism and Commitment in American Public Life* (Berkeley: Univ. of California Press, 1985).

36. A. N. Prior, "Limited Indeterminism," *Review of Metaphysics* 16 (1962): 55–61.

37. Edward Shils, *Tradition* (Chicago: Univ. of Chicago Press, 1981).

38. John Phillip Reid, *The Concept of Liberty in the Age of the American Revolution* (Chicago: Univ. of Chicago Press, 1988).

Part I   The Trial of the Center, 1630–1700

1. Perry Miller first drew attention to the centrality of the covenant in Puritanism. See Miller, "The Marrow of Puritan Divinity," in *Errand into the Wilderness* (New York: Harper & Row, 1956), pp. 48–98; *The New England Mind: The Seventeenth Century* (New York: Macmillan, 1939); and "Preparation for Salvation in Seventeenth-Century New England," in *Nature's Nation* (Cambridge, Mass.: Harvard Univ. Press, 1967), pp. 50–77. For a recent set of evaluations of Miller's legacy, including the focus on the covenant, see James Hoopes et al., "Symposium on Perry Miller's *New England Mind*," *American Quarterly* 34 (Spring 1982): 3–48.

2. My attempt throughout this work is to read covenant theology from the perspective of a historian of religions. From this perspective, the distinctive features that emerge are the mythological shape of the covenant and the use of metaphors of the "center" to describe its function among the Puritans. That is, the purpose of the notion of the covenant was to describe how God drew human beings into the Trinitarian pattern, enabling them to live with both external order and intrinsic spontaneity through the dialectic of a God-man, Christ. The essence of covenant theology was thus a myth bringing together order and spontaneity, Creator and spirit, that sought to establish a "center" or point of mediation in the person of Christ. See the many other variations on Perry Miller's initial insight into covenant theology in New England surveyed in David D. Hall, "Understanding the Puritans," in Herbert J. Bass, ed., *The State of American History* (Chicago: Univ. of Chicago Press, 1970), pp. 330–49; id., "On Common Ground: The Coherence of American Puritan Studies," *William and Mary Quarterly* 44 (Apr. 1987): 193–229. See also William K. B. Stoever, *"A Faire and Easie Way to Heaven": Covenant Theology and Antinomianism in Early Massachusetts* (Middletown, Conn.: Wesleyan Univ. Press, 1978).

3. For one argument identifying the durability of covenant theology, see Harry S. Stout, "The Puritans and Edwards," in *Jonathan Edwards and the American Experience*, ed. Nathan O. Hatch and Harry S. Stout (New York: Oxford Univ. Press, 1988), pp. 142–59.

4. Norman Petit, *The Heart Prepared: Grace and Conversion in Puritan Spiritual Life* (New Haven: Yale Univ. Press, 1966), p. 217.

5. For the notion of the *axis mundi*, see Mircea Eliade, *The Sacred and the Profane: The Nature of Religion*, trans. Willard R. Trask (New York: Harcourt, 1959), pp. 35–37.

6. On this characteristic "abstraction" of Puritanism, see Ann Kibbey, *The Interpretation of Material Shapes in Puritanism* (Cambridge: Cambridge Univ. Press, 1986).

1   "It Overthrows All"

1. John Winthrop, *A Short Story of the Rise, reign, and ruine of the Antinomians, Familists & Libertines* (1644), in David D. Hall, ed., *The Antinomian Controversy, 1636–1638: A Documentary History* (Middletown, Conn.: Wesleyan Univ. Press, 1968), p. 211. The Hall volume is henceforth cited as AC.

2. *The Examination of Mrs. Anne Hutchinson at the Court at Newtown* (1637), in AC, p. 343.

3. Ann Kibbey, *The Interpretation of Material Shapes in Puritanism* (Cambridge: Cambridge Univ. Press, 1986), correctly links the rejection of Hutchinson with the Pequot massacre.

4. See Robert Bellah, *The Broken Covenant: American Civil Religion in a Time of Trial* (New York: Seabury Press, 1975), pp. 13–21; Edmund S. Morgan, *The Puritan Dilemma: The Story of John Winthrop* (Boston: Little, Brown, 1958); Darrett B. Rutman, *Winthrop's Boston: Portrait of a Puritan Town, 1630–1649* (Chapel Hill: Univ. of North Carolina Press, 1965).

5. *Arminianism* was the name given to a variety of movements stemming loosely from the theology of Jacobus Arminius, a liberal Dutch Calvinist. See *The Writings of James Arminius*, trans. James Nichols and W. R. Bagnall (Grand Rapids, Mich.: Baker Book House, 1956), and Carl Bangs, *Arminius: A Study in the Dutch Reformation*, 2d ed. (Grand Rapids, Mich.: Francis Asbury, 1985).

6. William Twisse, *A Treatise of Mr. Cottons, Clearing certaine Doubts Concerning Predestination, Together with an Examination Thereof* (London: J. D. Crook, 1646), p. 63.

7. Twisse was, along with John Owen, probably the leading exponent of High Calvinism in seventeenth-century Britain. See Dewey D. Wallace, Jr., *Puritans and Predestination: Grace in English Protestant Theology, 1525–1695* (Chapel Hill: Univ. of North Carolina Press, 1982), and esp. Peter Toon, *God's Statesman: The Life and Work of John Owen, Pastor, Educator, Theologian* (Exeter: Paternoster, 1971).

8. John Cotton, *A Treatise I. of Faith. II. Twelve Fundamental Articles of Christian Religion. III. A Doctrinal Conclusion. IV. Questions and Answers Upon Church Government* ([Boston: B. Green?], 1713), p. 18. The last section of this work bears the date "25.11, 1634," and both Larzer Ziff and Everett Emerson date its composition from around this time, that is, shortly after Cotton arrived in New England. See Larzer Ziff, *The Career of John Cotton: Puritanism and the American Experience* (Princeton: Princeton Univ. Press, 1962); and Everett Emerson, *John Cotton* (New York: Twayne, 1965).

9. Ziff, *Career of John Cotton*, p. 55.

10. Calling Cotton "deterministic" is both inaccurate and anachronistic, but he was clearly more deterministic in New England than he had been in Old. See Frank H. Foster, *A Genetic History of New England Theology* (Chicago: Univ. of Chicago Press, 1907), pp. 25–27; Pettit, *Heart Prepared*, pp. 133–41; Miller, "Preparation for Salvation," pp. 61–63; and Emerson, *John Cotton*, pp. 85–90.

11. This phrase is from a "doctrinal conclusion" appended to Cotton's *A Treatise*, p. 10, and may therefore date from later than the treatise itself.

12. See Marilyn Westerkamp, "Anne Hutchinson, Sectarian Mysticism, and the Puritan Order," *Church History* 59 (Dec. 1990): 482–96.

13. The incomprehensibility of Aristotle's notion of cause to most moderns is a major impediment to understanding any discussion of free will prior to 1800. No simple synopsis of the four causes is likely to gain wide assent, but David D. Hall presents the following very helpful working definitions: efficient—"that by which a change is wrought"; material—"that in which a change is wrought"; formal— "that into which something is changed"; final—"the end or purpose for which a change is made"; in AC, p. 35.

14. Peter Bulkeley and John Cotton, "On Union with Christ" (1636), in AC, p. 38.

15. Ibid., p. 39.

16. Ibid.

17. The phrase is Larzer Ziff's but the perception was widespread, because Cotton had held a prestigious appointment prior to emigrating. See Ziff, Career of John Cotton, p. 115.

18. Sixteene Questions of Serious and Necessary Consequence, Propounded unto Mr. John Cotton . . . , Together with His Answers to each Question (London, 1644), in AC, p. 53.

19. Max Weber, The Protestant Ethic and the Spirit of Capitalism, trans. Talcott Parsons (New York: Scribner's, 1958), p. 232.

20. "The Elders Reply," in AC, p. 65.

21. "Mr. Cotton's Rejoynder" (1636–37), in AC, p. 78.

22. Ibid., p. 127.

23. Ibid., p. 133.

24. Ibid., p. 129.

25. Bulkeley and Cotton, "On Union with Christ," in AC, p. 40.

26. Ibid.

27. One of the strengths of Westerkamp's "Anne Hutchinson, Sectarian Mysticism, and the Puritan Order" is that she correctly identifies this "mystical" strand in Hutchinson's thought. Unfortunately, Westerkamp does not devote the same attention to Cotton.

28. Bulkeley and Cotton, "On Union with Christ," in AC, pp. 40–41.

29. "Mr. Cotton's Rejoynder," in AC, p. 98.

30. Ibid., p. 102.

31. Ibid. Nicolas Grevinchovius was one of the signers of the "Remonstrance" that was the original document of Dutch Arminianism. See Carl Bangs, Arminius: A Study in the Dutch Reformation, (1971), 2d ed. (Grand Rapids, Mich.: Zondervan, 1985).

32. "Mr. Cotton's Rejoynder," in AC, p. 103.

33. Ibid., pp. 144–45.

34. Yet another line of interpretation, supportive of the two traced here, would follow the debates over "absolute" and "conditional" promises. See Stoever, "A Faire and Easie Way to Heaven," pp. 46–52.

35. Cotton had a reputation in some circles for doctrinal shifts. The enthusiast Samuel Gorton, who at least was consistent in his enthusiasm, and with whom Cotton had had a run-in shortly after arriving in New England, was probably less than completely objective when he charged that "Mr. Cotton . . . ordinarily

preacheth that publickly one year, that the next year he publickly repents of." But
the perception of inconsistency was so widespread that it called forth *A Defence of
Mr. John Cotton From the imputation of Selfe Contradiction* a year before his death in
1652. See Samuel Gorton, *Simplicities Defence Against Seven-Headed Policy* (London,
1646), cited by Ziff, *Career of John Cotton,* p. 207. On the interesting career of
Gorton, see Philip F. Gura, "The Radical Ideology of Samuel Gorton: New Light
on the Relation of English to American Puritanism," *William and Mary Quarterly,*
3d ser., 36 (Jan. 1979): 78–100.

36. Two contending images reign among scholarly interpretations of Anne
Hutchinson. On the one side there are those who see Hutchinson as the advocate
of a "radical spiritual message of equality" that would have "changed profoundly
the thrust of the Massachusetts experiment" had she not been ruthlessly "defeated."
See, e.g., Mary Maples Dunn, "Saints and Sisters: Congregational and Quaker
Women in the Early Colonial Period," in *Women in American Religion,* ed. Janet
Wilson James (Philadelphia: Univ. of Pennsylvania Press, 1980), p. 30, and Lyle
Koehler, "The Case of the American Jezebels: Anne Hutchinson and Female Agita-
tion during the Years of Antinomian Turmoil, 1636–1640," *William and Mary Quar-
terly* 31 (Jan. 1974): 55–78.

On the other side are those who take the perspective of the elders and see in
Hutchinson a justifiably condemned "anarchistic subjectivism." The best advocate
of this view remains Emery Battis, *Saints and Sectaries: Anne Hutchinson and the
Antinomian Controversy in the Massachusetts Bay Colony* (Chapel Hill: Univ. of
North Carolina Press, 1962), p. 286.

These may not be completely exclusive perspectives. There is little question
that Hutchinsonianism would have changed the character of the Massachusetts
"experiment," and that her condemnation was motivated as much by matters distinct from doctrine, such as her sex, as by what she actually said. At the same
time, records of her position do suggest that she not only had a positive program
for increased "equality" but was also inclined to subvert the current order. The
existing texts suggest a predominance of the latter motive. But those very texts
were recorded and passed down by the authorities. Hence, they inevitably portray
Hutchinson through the eyes of the bias established after the controversy. The
historian's work must begin from this point. That is, *given* the bias evident in the
record, what does the record tell us about the impact of her views on New England
culture? And aside from all of that, what would a plausible reconstruction of her
views be?

37. Winthrop had to depict Hutchinson as dangerous and seditious in order to
find her guilty. Throughout her trial, though, Hutchinson denied charging the
ministers with preaching works-righteousness, although she did admit to drawing a
relative distinction between Cotton as a preacher of grace and the other ministers.
See *The Examination of Mrs. Hutchinson,* in AC, p. 324.

38. Winthrop claimed to be troubled by Hutchinson's "haughty carriage" from
the moment he met her. See Amy Schrager Lang, *Prophetic Woman: Anne Hutchinson and the Problem of Dissent in the Literature of New England* (Berkeley: Univ. of
California Press, 1987), p. 17. See also Schrager-Lang's provocative "Antinomian-

ism and the 'Americanization' of Doctrine," *New England Quarterly* 54 (Sept. 1981): 225–42.

39. Westerkamp, "Anne Hutchinson, Sectarian Mysticism, and the Puritan Order," accurately develops Stoever's insight into the way Hutchinson's views were continuous with doctrines popular as early as the 1620s in England. See Stoever, *"A Faire and Easie Way to Heaven,"* pp. 138–60, where Hutchinsonianism is connected with the doctrines of John Eaton, John Traske, and Tobias Crisp. See also notes 46–50 below.

40. *Examination of Mrs. Hutchinson,* in AC, pp. 336–37.

41 Ibid.

42. Stoever's chapter on the impulse behind the English antinomians is instructive here. He points out that the tenets of Crisp, Eaton, Traske, and, perhaps, Hutchinson, "tended to make a person's own estate in grace the proper object of his faith" (*"A Faire and Easie Way to Heaven,"* p. 157). Just how far Cotton was from such a conception is plain when he stresses, as he does continually in his controversial writings, the unmediated *objectivity* of Christ to believers. See "Mr. Cotton's Rejoynder," in AC, p. 96; and cf. pp. 99–100, 121–22.

43. *Examination of Mrs. Hutchinson,* in AC, pp. 336–38, emphasis added.

44. Ibid., p. 332.

45. Ann Fairfax Withington and Jack Schwartz, "The Political Trial of Anne Hutchinson," *New England Quarterly* 51 (June 1978): 226–40.

46. The modern historian must be careful not to impose post-Kantian conceptions of autonomy on seventeenth-century individuals. For instance, Ann Fairfax Withington and Jack Schwartz, in an otherwise excellent review of the trial ritual, pull up short of showing how binding the religious roles were for both Cotton and Hutchinson in the trial. Marilyn J. Westerkamp does better by pointing out that Hutchinson's doctrine of immediacy was part of a tradition of Puritan mysticism that appealed especially to women, but she goes on to say that the violence against Hutchinson was "understandable" because of her gender and because of the threat her ideology posed to Winthrop. All of this is true, but making violence "understandable" still fails to highlight how the religious roles of Hutchinson and Cotton were shaped by a unique process of social construction in 1637 Boston. Traditions were being transformed in New England, and this is especially clear in the antinomian controversy: High Calvinism and mysticism were ritually represented in the trial by Cotton and Hutchinson in a way that allowed Winthrop and the rest of the culture to produce a new ideology and constellation of power. Neither gender nor religious roles such as "mysticism" just endure or are consciously assumed by individuals; more often they are created by social relations and they change. See on the "social construction" of gender (and implicitly, all other roles in society), Linda K. Kerber et al., "Beyond Roles, Beyond Spheres: Thinking about Gender in the Early Republic," *William and Mary Quarterly,* 3d. ser., 46 (July 1989): 565–85.

47. Significantly, the increasing awareness of the transcontinental character of Puritan and antinomian controversies has led several historians to see their paradigmatic and invented aspects. See Stephen Foster, "New England and the Challenge of Heresy, 1630–1660: The Puritan Crisis in Transatlantic Perspective," *Wil-*

liam and Mary Quarterly, 3d ser., 38 (Oct. 1981): 624–60, and Dewey D. Wallace, *Puritans and Predestination. Grace in English Protestant Theology*, 1525–1695 (Chapel Hill: Univ. of North Carolina Press, 1982). Wallace writes, speaking of English Puritans, that "like Voltaire's God, had there been no Antinomianism, it would have been necessary to invent it" (p. 114). The suggestion here is that it was necessary to "invent" both High Calvinism and its opposite in New England, and that Cotton and Hutchinson did so, hoping that their new society could embrace them both.

48. René Girard, *Violence and the Sacred*, trans. Patrick Gregory (Baltimore: Johns Hopkins Univ. Press, 1972) gives the clearest description of how myth becomes violence, although Girard neglects to show how myth can also preserve and enhance the concrete by differentiating people from one another under a transcendent ideal and persuading them toward it.

49. See *Examination of Mrs. Hutchinson*, in AC, pp. 340–43.

50. Ibid., p. 343.

51. René Girard, *The Scapegoat*, trans. Yvonne Freccero (Baltimore: Johns Hopkins Univ. Press, 1986). On the connection between gender and the scapegoating of witches, see Carol F. Karlsen, *The Devil in the Shape of a Woman: Witchcraft in Colonial New England* (New York: Norton, 1987). For a disturbing account of domestic violence against a woman in colonial New England, see *Religion and Domestic Violence in Early New England: The Memoirs of Abigail Abbot Bailey*, ed. Ann Taves (Bloomington: Indiana Univ. Press, 1989).

52. Winthrop, *A Short Story*, in AC, p. 274.

53. Ann Kibbey puts it well: "The crises of the late 1630's were less a breakdown of social order than a struggle to institute a particular kind of social order by defining acceptable forms of prejudicial violence and beliefs" (*Interpretation of Material Shapes in Puritanism*, p. 120).

54. *A Report of the Trial of Mrs. Anne Hutchinson*, in AC, pp. 354, 357. On the soul's dying, see J. F. Maclear, "Anne Hutchinson and the Mortalist Heresy," *New England Quarterly* 54 (Mar. 1981): 74–103.

55. Urian Oakes, *The Soveraign Efficacy of Divine Providence; Overruling and Omnipotently Disposing and Ordering all Humane Counsels and Affairs* (Boston: Sewall, 1682), pp. 2–3.

56. *Trial of Mrs. Anne Hutchinson*, in AC, p. 373.

57. Fortunately, scholars have been undoing the limitations the Puritans established by showing the resiliency of radical movements such as Hutchinson's throughout the history of the colonies. See, most notably, Stephen A. Marini, *Radical Sects of Revolutionary New England* (Cambridge, Mass.: Harvard Univ. Press, 1982).

2   "There Is Chance, There Is Not"

1. For the most balanced treatment of Puritan-Indian relations, see esp. James Axtell, *The Invasion Within: The Contest of Cultures in Colonial North America* (New York: Oxford Univ. Press, 1986).

2. On the Pequot massacre, see Francis Jennings, *The Invasion of America: Indi-*

ans, *Colonialism, and the Cant of Conquest* (Chapel Hill: Univ. of North Carolina, 1975).

3. *God's Plot: The Paradoxes of Puritan Piety. Being the Autobiography & Journal of Thomas Shepard*, ed. Michael McGiffert (Amherst: Univ. of Massachusetts Press, 1972), pp. 66–68, cited in part by Ann Kibbey, *The Interpretation of Material Shapes in Puritanism* (Cambridge: Cambridge Univ. Press, 1986), p. 99.

4. William Greenhill and Samuel Mather, "To the Christian Reader," in *Subjection to Christ, In All His Appointments, The Best Means To Preserve Our Liberty*, vol. 3 of *The Works of Thomas Shepard* (Boston: Doctrinal Tract and Book Society, 1853; repr., New York: A.M.S., 1967), p. 283.

5. Ibid., p. 279.

6. By the time Shepard wrote, the extremes were not so much juxtaposed or in equipoise as they were "dimmed." Extraordinary religion had become ordinary, and hence the antinomian controversy was remembered by later generations and Shepard's sermons were all but forgotten. On the "extraordinary" and "ordinary" distinction, see Catherine Albanese, *America: Religions and Religion* (Belmont, Calif.: Wadsworth, 1981).

7. See, on this point, Mary Cappello, "The Authority of Self-Definition in Thomas Shepard's *Autobiography* and *Journal*," *Early American Literature* 24 (Jan. 1989): 35–51.

8. At one point in the controversy, Cotton, quoting Calvin, admitted that "to will is of nature; to will aright is of grace," and if he had consistently argued for such a position, he and Shepard would have had little reason for dispute. The quotation is, however, isolated, and not representative of the main thrust of Cotton's writings on the will and related questions. Cf. "Mr. Cotton's Rejoynder," in AC, pp. 145–46.

9. Shepard, *Subjection to Christ*, in *Works*, 3:294.

10. Ibid., p. 354.

11. Ibid., p. 298.

12. Again, this is true for the most part only of Cotton's writings during the antinomian controversy, and would need to be qualified if we were speaking of Cotton's position as a whole.

13. See, in this connection, Jesper Rosenmeier, "New England's Perfection: The Image of Adam and the Image of Christ in the Antinomian Controversy," *William and Mary Quarterly* 27 (July 1970): 435–59, who traces the dispute between Cotton and Shepard on this point.

14. Thomas Shepard, *Certain Select Cases Resolved; Specially Tending to the Right Ordering of the Heart*, in *Works*, 1:311.

15. Greenhill and Mather, "To the Christian Reader," p. 277.

16. *God's Plot*, ed. McGiffert, pp. 42–43.

17. Cappello, "Authority of Self-Definition," puts it nicely: There was "a troubling indeterminacy between Shepard's relation to the world and his relation to the self" (p. 44).

18. Shepard, *Certain Select Cases*, p. 321.

19. Ibid., p. 323.

20. Greenhill and Mather, "To the Christian Reader," p. 279.

21. Christopher Hill's apt phrase for the various sectaries to emerge during the Glorious Revolution of 1688, "masterless men," captures exactly the philosophical tenor of those opposed by thinkers such as Shepard. Whether, as Hill urges, this opposition also followed class lines is, especially in the case of New England, a far more problematic question. See Hill, *The World Turned Upside Down: Radical Ideas during the English Revolution* (New York: Viking, 1972).

22. Shepard, *Subjection to Christ*, in *Works*, 3:287, 286–87, 312.

23. Ibid., p. 334.

24. Shepard, *Certain Select Cases*, p. 330; *The First Principles of the Oracles of God*, in *Works*, 1:339; *Theses Sabbaticae*, in *Works*, 3:96–97 as cited in part by William K. B. Stoever, *"A Faire and Easie Way to Heaven": Covenant Theology and Antinomianism in Early Massachusetts* (Middletown, Conn.: Wesleyan Univ. Press, 1978), p. 103.

25. Robert F. Berkhofer, Jr., *The White Man's Indian: Images of the American Indian from Columbus to the Present* (New York: Knopf, 1978), p. 72, has a succinct discussion of this "primitivist" strain among the colonizers. Theodore Dwight Bozeman has argued that this "primitivist" strand was predominant among the first Puritans. As Bozeman depicts it, though, the Puritans took themselves as the types of Adam and Eve; not the natives. More study of why this occurred would be valuable. See *To Live Ancient Lives: The Primitivist Dimension in Puritanism* (Chapel Hill: Univ. of North Carolina Press, 1988).

26. See James Axtell, *The Invasion Within: The Contest of Cultures in Colonial North America* (New York: Oxford Univ. Press, 1985).

27. Francis Jennings, *The Invasion of America: Indians, Colonialism, and the Cant of Conquest* (Chapel Hill: Univ. of North Carolina Press, 1975), p. 213.

28. *So Dreadfull A Judgment: Puritan Responses to King Phillip's War, 1676–1677*, ed. Richard Slotkin and James K. Folsom (Middletown, Conn.: Wesleyan Univ. Press, 1978), pp. 3–4.

29. *The Puritans*, ed. Perry Miller and Thomas H. Johnson (New York: American Book Company, 1938), p. 350.

30. *So Dreadfull A Judgment*, ed. Slotkin and Folsom, p. 4.

31. Richard R. Johnson, "The Search for a Usable Indian: An Aspect of the Defense of Colonial New England," *Journal of American History* 64 (Dec. 1977): 623–51.

32. Perry Miller, *The New England Mind: The Seventeenth Century* (New York: Macmillan, 1939), p. 235, calls Oakes's sermon "perhaps the most eloquent discussion" of free will in colonial America.

33. Urian Oakes, *The Soveraign Efficacy of Divine Providence; Overruling and Omnipotently Disposing and Ordering all Humane Counsels and Affairs* (Boston: Sewall, 1682), p. 27.

34. Ibid., p. 3.

35. Ibid., p. 5.

36. Ibid., pp. 20, 5, 5, 15; emphasis mine.

37. Ibid., p. 6.

38. Ibid., p. 8.

39. In this connection, see Sacvan Bercovitch, *The American Jeremiad* (Madison: Univ. of Wisconsin Press, 1978), p. 12, who was the first to point out the "both/and" character of jeremiads. Oakes's application of Eccles. 9:11 supports Bercovitch's reading.

40. See also, in this connection, many of the captivity narratives, which suggest the same motive. The most famous is, of course, Mary Rowlandson's, and the title alone, *The Soveraignty and Goodness of God,* is illustrative of the point at hand. See *Puritans among the Indians: Accounts of Captivity and Redemption, 1676–1724,* ed. Alden T. Vaughan and Edward W. Clark (Cambridge, Mass.: Harvard Univ. Press, 1981), pp. 29–75.

41. Oakes, *Soveraign Efficacy,* p. 21.

42. From an accounting of the Puritan inability to recognize Native American religion as anything but heathenism or atheism, see Frank Shuffleton, "Indian Devils and Pilgrim Fathers: Squanto, Hobomok, and the English Conception of Indian Religion," *New England Quarterly* 49 (Mar. 1976): 108–16.

43. Oakes, *Soveraign Efficacy,* p. 34. Oakes seems to make a great deal of "second causes" in this work, and for this reason Perry Miller reads him as part of a gradual decline in Puritan piety away from the doctrine of the sovereignty of God and toward human autonomy. This reading of the sermon seems to be mistaken. Some of Oakes's statements about second causes do ring stronger than Shepard's, but the distinction is fine, and it is clear in any event that what Oakes wanted to preserve was nothing more than a liberty of action, on which point Shepard and the tradition would have been largely in agreement. Oakes did not, to my knowledge, publish anything in New England discussing causality in Aristotelian terms, and hence the grounds for a broader comparison are lacking. Texts examined were *The Unconquerable, All-Conquering and More-Than Conquering Soldier* (Cambridge: Samuel Green, 1674), which was an earlier, highly militaristic artillery address, quite possibly the reason he was asked back in 1677; *New England Pleaded With, and Pressed to Consider the Things Which Concern Her Peace* (Cambridge: Samuel Green, 1673), which was an election sermon; and *A Seasonable Discourse Wherein Sincerity and Delight in the Service of God is Earnestly Pressed Upon Professors of Religion* (Cambridge: Samuel Green, 1682).

44. Benjamin Tompson, "The Town Called Providence Its Fate," in *So Dreadfull a Judgment,* ed. Slotkin and Folsom, p. 228.

45. See Peter N. Carroll, *Puritanism and the Wilderness: The Intellectual Significance of the New England Frontier, 1629–1700* (New York: Columbia Univ. Press, 1969).

3   "The True Middle"

1. The standard biography, in need of updating, is Ethyn Williams Kirby, *George Keith (1638–1716)* (New York: D. Appleton-Century, 1942). See also Jon Butler, " 'Gospel Order Improved': The Keithian Schism and the Exercise of Quaker Ministerial Authority in Pennsylvania," *William and Mary Quarterly,* 3d ser., 31 (July 1974): 431–52.

2. On the latter's role in eroding Calvinism throughout the English-speaking

world, see Rosalie L. Colie, *Light and Enlightenment: A Study of the Cambridge Platonists and the Dutch Arminians* (Cambridge: Cambridge Univ. Press, 1957).

3. For the origins of the Society of Friends, see Hugh Barbour, *The Quakers in Puritan England* (New Haven: Yale Univ. Press, 1964). On the Friends in the colonies, see Rufus Jones, *The Quakers in the American Colonies* (New York: Norton, 1966).

4. Kirby, *George Keith*, p. 50.

5. On Puritan-Quaker relations, see Kai T. Erikson, *Wayward Puritans: A Study in the Sociology of Deviance* (New York: Wiley, 1966), esp. pp. 107–36; David S. Lovejoy, *Religious Enthusiasm in the New World: Heresy to Revolution* (Cambridge, Mass.: Harvard Univ. Press, 1985); and esp. Carla Gardina Pestana, "The City upon a Hill under Siege: The Puritan Perception of the Quaker Threat to Massachusetts Bay, 1656–1661," *New England Quarterly* 56 (Sept. 1983): 323–53.

6. See Jonathan M. Chu, *Neighbors, Friends, or Madmen: The Puritan Adjustment to Quakerism in Seventeenth-Century Massachusetts* (Westport, Conn.: Greenwood Press, 1985).

7. George Keith, *The Presbyterian and Independent Visible Churches Brought to the Test* (Philadelphia: Bradford, 1689), p. 58.

8. Ibid., p. 70. The quotation is verbatim from the Westminster Confession, ch. 3, sec. 1. See *Creeds of the Churches*, ed. John H. Leith, 3d ed. (Atlanta: John Knox, 1982), p. 198.

9. Keith, *Presbyterian Churches Brought to the Test*, p. 70.

10. Ibid., pp. 75–74 (page numbers inverted in MSS).

11. Ibid., p. 76.

12. Ibid., pp. iii–iv, 62.

13. James Allen, Joshua Moody, Cotton Mather, and Samuel Willard, *The Principles of the Protestant Religion Maintained* (Boston: Richard Pierce, 1690), p. A.2.

14. Ibid., p. A.

15. Ibid., p. 70, 71.

16. Ibid., p. 159.

17. See Kirby, *George Keith*, pp. 95–116.

18. George Keith, *A Refutation of a Dangerous and Hurtful Opinion Maintained by Mr. Samuel Willard* (New York: n.p., 1703), p. 2.

19. This background to the controversy is traced nicely by Seymour Van Dyken, *Samuel Willard, 1640–1707: Preacher of Orthodoxy in an Era of Change* (Grand Rapids, Mich.: Eerdmans, 1972), p. 119–21.

20. Perry Miller, *The New England Mind: The Seventeenth Century* (New York: Macmillan, 1939), p. 233.

21. Keith, *Refutation of a Dangerous and Hurtful Opinion*, p. 3.

22. Ibid., pp. 3–4.

23. Samuel Willard, *A Brief Reply to Mr. George Keith* (Boston: Samuel Green, 1703), p. 8.

24. Ibid., pp. 20–21, 38, 23. See here also Norman Fiering, *Moral Philosophy at Seventeenth-Century Harvard: A Discipline in Transition* (Chapel Hill: Univ. of North Carolina Press, 1981). Fiering's work traces the depreciation of classical, Aristotelian, and Stoic ethics at Harvard between 1675 and 1725, which he attributes

partly to "the failure of those systems to find a positive role for the affections" in ethics (p. 5). This close study might bear affinities to the more general claim here concerning the Puritan reaction to indeterminism. For Fiering, however, the "famous" question of "free will versus determinism" was "a relatively dormant issue in New England" (p. 105). This may have been true at Harvard, as evidenced by theses and in the development of a more or less "secular" discipline of moral philosophy, but in the wider culture there were at least implicitly active rumblings concerning the "famous" question of free will throughout the seventeenth century.

25. Willard, *Brief Reply*, pp. 28, 14, 15, 46.

26. According to Willard's modern biographer, he was a "preacher of orthodoxy in an era of change" (Van Dyken, *Samuel Willard, 1640–1707*). See for ample confirmation of this fact the 900-plus pages of Willard's posthumously published lectures on the Westminster Catechism, *A Compleat Body of Divinity* (Boston: B. Green & S. Kneeland, 1726; repr., New York: Johnson Reprint Company, 1969).

27. See here the argument of Richard R. Johnson, *Adjustment to Empire: The New England Colonies, 1675–1715* (New Brunswick, N.J.: Rutgers Univ. Press, 1981), which traces the effects of increasing English control over New England, and especially Massachusetts.

28. Willard, *Brief Reply*, pp. 4–5.

29. Keith, *Refutation of a Dangerous and Hurtful Opinion*, p. 7.

30. Willard, *Brief Reply*, p. 52.

31. Ibid., p. 57; emphasis his.

32. Ibid., pp. 55–56.

Part II   Anti-Calvinism in America, 1700–1735

1. The term *anti-Calvinist* is Nicholas Tyacke's; see *Anti-Calvinists: The Rise of English Arminianism, c. 1590–1640* (New York: Oxford Univ. Press, 1987). Anti-Calvinism was an enduring rhetoric of dissent in America, as Nathan O. Hatch shows in *The Democratization of American Christianity* (New Haven: Yale Univ. Press, 1989).

2. A fourth potential source of anti-Puritanism was within Calvinism itself, in what James W. Jones has identified as "Puritan Liberalism" (see Jones, *The Shattered Synthesis: New England Puritanism before the Great Awakening* [New Haven: Yale Univ. Press, 1973]).

4   "Little Love and Charity to God or Man"

1. Stanley Elkins, *Slavery: A Problem in American Institutional and Intellectual Life* (1959) 2d ed. (Chicago: Univ. of Chicago Press, 1968), p. 38.

2. Edmund S. Morgan asserts that "the central paradox of American history" is "how a people could have developed the dedication to human liberty and dignity exhibited by the leaders of the American Revolution and at the same time have developed and maintained a system of labor that denied human liberty and dignity every hour of the day" (*American Slavery, American Freedom: The Ordeal of Colonial Virginia* [New York: Norton, 1975], pp. 4–5). My contention would be a little

different—that the "paradox" of slavery represented a replacement of inclusive myth with an ideology centered upon paternalistic control.

3. Samuel Willard, *A Complete Body of Divinity, Sermon CLXXIX* (Aug. 24, 1703) (New York: Johnson Reprints, 1969), p. 614. For Winthrop's charge, see *A Short Story of the Rise, Reign, and Ruine of the Antinomians, Familists and Libertines,* in *The Antinomian Controversy, 1636–1638: A Documentary History,* ed. David D. Hall (Middletown, Conn.: Wesleyan Univ. Press, 1968), p. 266.

4. Ibid., p. 616.

5. Cotton Mather, "An Essay to Excite and Assist that Good Work, the Instruction of Negro-Servants in Christianity" (1706), in *Racial Thought in Early America: From the Puritans to Abraham Lincoln,* ed. Louis Ruchames (Amherst: Univ. of Massachusetts Press, 1969), p. 60.

6. Eugene D. Genovese, *Roll, Jordan, Roll: The World the Slaves Made* (New York: Random House, Vintage Books, 1972).

7. See Winthrop D. Jordan, *White over Black: American Attitudes toward the Negro, 1550–1812* (Baltimore: Penguin Books, 1969); James Oakes, *The Ruling Race: A History of American Slaveholders* (New York: Random House, 1983); and Joseph R. Washington, Jr., *Anti-Blackness in English Religion, 1500–1800* (New York: E. Mellen Press, 1984).

8. On Sewall, see David D. Hall, *Worlds of Wonder, Days of Judgment: Popular Religious Belief in Early New England* (New York: Knopf, 1989), pp. 213–38, and the standard biography by T. B. Strandness, *Samuel Sewall: A Puritan Portrait* (n.p.: Michigan State Univ. Press, 1967).

9. Samuel Sewall, "The Selling of Joseph: A Memorial" (1700), in *Racial Thought in America,* p. 47.

10. Ibid., pp. 48–49.

11. John Saffin, "A Brief and Candid Answer to a Late Printed Sheet Entituled, 'The Selling of Joseph' " (1701), in *Racial Thought in America,* ed. Ruchames, p. 54.

12. Economic and other social factors may have been primary in "justifying" the practice of slavery, but the ideological or symbolic elements also deserve attention. Jordan, *White over Black,* argues that "negro slavery never really flourished in New England," and that the establishment of the practice was generally an "unthinking decision" (pp. 66–71). He also refuses to draw any link between ideas of providence and the practice of slavery, but he does note a certain affinity between Puritan "tribalism" and the justification of the practice (pp. 198–212). I would draw the connection even more strongly. From contemporary history, the connection between Calvinism in the Dutch Reformed Church and the practice of apartheid in South Africa would provide one obvious analogy to the relationship between providential ideologies and race relations in the American colonies. For one exploration of the origins of slaveholders' paternalism in Calvinist theology, see Alan Gallay, "The Origins of Slaveholders' Paternalism: George Whitefield, the Bryan Family, and the Great Awakening in the South," *Journal of Southern History* 53 (Aug. 1987): 369–94.

13. "Germantown Friends Protest against Slavery" (1688), in *Racial Thought in America,* ed. Ruchames, p. 38.

14. George Keith, "An Exhortation and Caution to Friends Concerning Buying or Keeping of Negroes" (1693), in *Racial Thought in America,* ed. Ruchames, pp. 44, 41–42.

15. Ibid., p. 42. Keith's doctrines of free will and a universal offer of salvation even led him to argue that escaped slaves should never be returned to their masters, and that blacks "should have liberty to dwell amongst us, where it liketh [them] best." Nothing like this appeared, to my knowledge, in Puritan writings. Sewall expressed the prevailing opinion when he wrote that "there is such a disparity in their [the blacks'] conditions, color and hair, that they can never embody with us, and grow into orderly families." See "Selling of Joseph," p. 48.

16. See Jean R. Soderlund, *Quakers and Slavery: A Divided Spirit* (Princeton: Princeton Univ. Press, 1985); Thomas E. Drake, *Quakers and Slavery in America* (New Haven: Yale Univ. Press, 1950); and Lester B. Scherer, *Slavery and the Churches in Early America, 1619–1819* (Grand Rapids, Mich.: Eerdmans, 1975).

17. John Hepburn, *The American Defence of the Christian Golden Rule, or An Essay to Prove the Unlawfulness of Making Slaves of Men* ([New York: William Bradford], 1715), p. 51.

18. For what can be reconstructed of Hepburn's life, see Henry J. Cadbury, "John Hepburn and His Book against Slavery," *Proceedings of the American Antiquarian Society* 59 (Apr.–Oct. 1949): 89–112.

19. Hepburn, *American Defence,* p. 1.

20. Ibid., p. 3.

21. There is some question whether the Lowry pieces (the work includes one other in addition to the antipredestinarian tract) were part of the original manuscript. Hepburn's preface does not mention them, and they are lacking in the Boston Public Library copy. The only full copy is in the British Museum. It may be that the Lowry pieces were simply added by the publisher as an afterthought, after having been sent by Hepburn or Lowry as a separate book. Whatever the text-critical problems here, both external evidence (the family relationship between Hepburn and Lowry) and the internal evidence (of continuity of thought and language), suggest that the antislavery and antipredestination pieces share a common worldview and logic. See Cadbury, "John Hepburn and His Book against Slavery," pp. 102–3, for the manuscript difficulties. The text used for this work was that of Charles Evans's *American Imprints,* a microcard reproduction of the British Museum document.

22. Ibid., p. 54.

23. Thomas Lowry, "A Short Answer to that Part of Predestination, which Asserts that Christ Died for None but the Elect," in Hepburn, *American Defence,* p. 56.

24. Ibid., p. 55.

25. And by the 1750s Quakers led the antislavery movement, notably Benjamin Lay (1677–1759), Ralph Sandiford (1693–1733), and above all John Woolman (1720–1772).

26. See table, p. 12.

5   "The Armies of the Philistines"

1. John F. Woolverton, *Colonial Anglicanism in North America* (Detroit: Wayne State Univ. Press, 1984), p. 21.

2. Ibid., p. 25. Jon Butler's work suggests the need to integrate the study of Anglicanism in early American culture more fully. See most notably his *Awash in a Sea of Faith: Christianizing the American People* (Cambridge, Mass.: Harvard Univ. Press, 1990).

3. *Dictionary of American Biography*, ed. Allen Johnson and Dumas Malone (New York: Scribner's, 1930), 4:46.

4. John Checkley, *Choice Dialogues Between a Godly Minister, and an Honest Country-Man, Concerning Election & Predestination* ([Boston: T. Fleet], 1720; repr. in *John Checkley; or the Evolution of Religious Tolerance in Massachusetts Bay*, Publications of the Prince Society, vol. 22 (Boston: John Wilson & Son, 1897), pp. 143–49.

5. See chapter 10.

6. Checkley, *Choice Dialogues*, pp. 151–52.

7. Ibid., pp. 152, 145.

8. Ibid., pp. 153–54.

9. For some confirmation of Checkley's observations about the Puritan conscience, see David D. Hall, *Worlds of Wonder, Days of Judgment: Popular Religious Belief in Early New England* (New York: Knopf, 1989).

10. Checkley, *Choice Dialogues*, p. 161.

11. Ibid., pp. 161–62.

12. Ibid., p. 174.

13. Ibid., pp. 145, 164.

14. Admittedly, there were precedents. Checkley was apparently responding to the writings of a certain Dissenter turned Arian named James Peirce, who had exhibited the typically Calvinist iconoclasm in a diatribe against the practice of bowing. But in this case the precedent is less important than the principle; namely, Checkley's commitment to the High Church liturgy in the attempt to restore mediation to the Puritan system by reviving its explicitly symbolic elements, over and against a system of strict causality that suppressed them.

15. Ibid., p. 174.

16. For Walter's brief career, see Frederick Lewis Weis, *The Colonial Clergy and the Colonial Churches of New England* (Lancaster, Mass.: Society of Descendants of the Colonial Clergy, 1936), p. 145, and Perry Miller, *The New England Mind: From Colony to Province*, pp. 334–35, 469–70.

17. Miller, *New England Mind: From Colony to Province*, p. 470.

18. [Thomas Walter], *A Choice Dialogue Between John Faustus A Conjurer, and Jack Tory His Friend. Occasioned by some* Choice Dialogues *Lately Published, Concerning Predestination and Election* (Boston: B. Gray & J. Edwards, 1720), p. ii.

19. Ibid., p. 8.

20. Ibid., p. 20.

21. See again, Tyacke, *Anti-Calvinists*, and Dewey D. Wallace, *Puritans and Pre-*

destination: Grace in English Protestant Theology, 1525–1695 (Chapel Hill: Univ. of North Carolina Press, 1982).

22. [Walter], *Choice Dialogue,* p. 16.

6 "The Doctrine of Devils"

1. Franklin's most recent biographer, Esmond Wright, focuses primarily on Franklin's later career, and thus takes Franklin's oft-stated disdain for "metaphysics" and organized religion too literally. Wright thus follows an approach to Franklin more or less established by Carl van Doren. See Wright's *Franklin of Philadelphia* (Cambridge, Mass.: Harvard Univ. Press, 1986), p. 44, and van Doren's classic, *Benjamin Franklin* (New York: Viking, 1938), pp. 51–52. Franklin needs a biographer sensitive to his religious life.

2. Benjamin Franklin, *The Autobiography of Benjamin Franklin,* ed. Leonard W. Labaree et al. (New Haven: Yale Univ. Press, 1964), p. 145. Henceforth cited as Franklin, *Autobiography.*

3. See chapter 7.

4. Franklin, *Autobiography,* p. 58.

5. Franklin to Samuel Mather, May 12, 1784, in *The Writings of Benjamin Franklin,* ed. Albert Henry Smyth (New York: Macmillan, 1905–7), 9:210.

6. Monographs exploring the relationship between Franklin and the Puritans are not lacking. See most notably Phyllis Franklin, *Show Thyself A Man: A Comparison of Benjamin Franklin and Cotton Mather* (Paris and the Hague: Mouton, 1969), who argues that "Mather was less and Franklin more the Puritan than has been generally supposed" (p. i); Mitchell Robert Breitwieser, *Cotton Mather and Benjamin Franklin: The Price of Representative Personality* (Cambridge: Cambridge Univ. Press, 1984), who makes a more specifically literary, less theological, and more polemical comparison; and William Pencak, "Benjamin Franklin's *Autobiography,* Cotton Mather, and a Puritan God," *Pennsylvania History* 53 (Jan. 1986): 1–25.

7. The pseudonym Silence Dogood is widely taken to be a blast at Mather's *Essays* by the young Franklin, before the latter became convinced of their utility. See *The Political Thought of Benjamin Franklin,* ed. Ralph Ketcham (Indianapolis: Bobbs-Merrill, 1965), p. 1.

8. "Silence Dogood, No. 14" (1722), in *The Papers of Benjamin Franklin,* ed. Leonard W. Labaree and William B. Willcox et al. (New Haven: Yale Univ. Press, 1959–), 1:43. Henceforth cited as Franklin, *Papers.*

9. Ibid.

10. The circle of what Franklin called his brother's "writing friends" would surely have given "young Benjamin a partiality toward the Episcopal church," as John F. Woolverton argues in *Colonial Anglicanism in North America* (Detroit: Wayne State Univ. Press, 1984), p. 122.

11. Much has been made of Franklin's youthful conversion to "Deism," which he reports in his *Autobiography,* pp. 114–15. And while it is unquestionable that Franklin abandoned Puritanism when still a youth, there is reason to doubt whether the conversion to Deism was as "thorough" as Franklin reports. The *Autobiography*

was, of course, written primarily during the years of conflict with Great Britain, when the Church of England was, to say the least, in disfavor in America. There are ample hints from Franklin's writings and later course of life, however, to suggest that his "conversion" may have been as much to liberal Anglicanism as to "thorough" Deism.

12. "Silence Dogood, No. 14," in Franklin, *Papers*, 1:43. Admittedly, much of this letter was addressed to the Anglican converts, who had disavowed the validity of Presbyterian ordination generally out of zeal for their own recent conversion. One theme of the work, therefore, not touched upon here but surely characteristic of the later Franklin as well, is a general repudiation of zealotry. Still, insofar as "Silence Dogood" takes sides, she does consider the Church of England "the Established Religion of our Nation," and she concludes with two lengthy quotations from Anglican theologians. Franklin may have been expressing a new loyalty here.

13. As quoted in the editor's introduction to *A Dissertation on Liberty and Necessity*, in Franklin, *Papers*, 1:57.

14. Van Doren, *Benjamin Franklin*, p. 52; Franklin, *Autobiography*, p. 115.

15. *Dissertation on Liberty and Necessity*, in Franklin, *Papers*, 1:59.

16. Ibid., p. 60.

17. Ibid., pp. 61–62, 63.

18. Ibid., p. 71.

19. For an interesting comparison of Franklin with another creative thinker, Voltaire, see Thomas J. Schlereth, *The Cosmopolitan Ideal in Enlightenment Thought* (Notre Dame, Ind.: Univ. of Notre Dame Press, 1977).

20. Alfred Owen Aldridge, "Benjamin Franklin and Philosophical Necessity," *Modern Language Quarterly* 12 (June 1951): 292–309.

21. Free thought was, of course, known about in the colonies, but especially prior to 1760, it was characteristically expressed in moderate forms. See Herbert F. Morais, *Deism in Eighteenth-Century America* (New York: Russell & Russell, 1960); and esp. Henry F. May, *The Enlightenment in America* (New York: Oxford Univ. Press, 1976).

22. Franklin to Benjamin Vaughan, Nov. 9, 1779, in *Writings of Benjamin Franklin*, ed. Smyth, 9:412–13. See also *Autobiography*, p. 106, for Franklin's comments on this period of his life.

23. Franklin, "Plan of Conduct," in *Papers*, 1:99–100.

24. Labaree, in Franklin, *Papers*, dates the treatise to 1732 because of its position in Franklin's notebook. Aldridge has argued persuasively for 1730 in his review of vol. 1, *American Literature* 32 (Mar. 1960): 208–10.

25. A. O. Aldridge, *Benjamin Franklin and Nature's God* (Durham, N.C.: Duke Univ. Press, 1967), p. 34, correctly perceives the shift in basic ideology, but goes on to argue that "the pendulum of [Franklin's] thought had moved to the opposite extreme from his necessitarian pamphlet," and that "On Providence" was "designed to prove the freedom of the will." Despite inaccurately describing Franklin's new position as an "extreme," Aldridge's work remains the best single guide to Franklin's religious life.

26. "On the Providence of God in the Government of the World," in Franklin, *Papers*, 1:266.

27. Ibid., p. 267.

28. Ibid.

29. Franklin to Benjamin Vaughan, Nov. 9, 1779, in *Writings of Benjamin Franklin*, ed. Smyth, 9:412, cited by Aldridge, *Benjamin Franklin and Nature's God*, p. 40.

30. "On Providence," in Franklin, *Papers*, 1:268.

31. Ibid., p. 266. Emphasis mine.

32. This position is akin to what William James would much later call "soft determinism." See James, "The Dilemma of Determinism," in *The Will to Believe* (New York: Dover, 1956), p. 149.

33. "On Providence," in Franklin, *Papers*, 1:269.

34. Franklin, *Autobiography*, pp. 147–48, 167.

35. In the midst of the trial, and in an apparent attempt to influence it, Franklin published a "Dialogue between Two Presbyterians," one of them (clearly the protagonist) a supporter of Hemphill, the other one of Hemphill's orthodox detractors. It is impossible to say how much of Franklin's indignation was because of the treatment of Hemphill, and how much owing to the fact that his own opinions were ignored. See Franklin, *Papers*, 2:27–33.

36. On Franklin's activity in relation to the trial, and for a more general survey of Franklin's relations with Calvinists, see Melvin H. Buxbaum, *Benjamin Franklin and the Zealous Presbyterians* (University Park: Pennsylvania State Univ. Press, 1975).

37. *Observations on the Proceedings against Mr. Hemphill*, in Franklin, *Papers*, 2:50–51. This emphasis on the purpose of virtue has often anachronistically been called utilitarian. A better word is the classical *hedonistic*. The most famous expression of this ethical approach of Franklin's is from the *Autobiography*: "Vicious actions are not hurtful because they are forbidden, but forbidden because they are hurtful," and "certain actions might not be bad because they were forbidden by [Revelation], or good because it commanded them; yet probably those Actions might be forbidden because they were bad for us, or commanded because they were beneficial to us" (pp. 158, 114–15).

38. *Observations*, in Franklin, *Papers*, 2:56.

39. Ibid.

40. Ibid., p. 57, 64.

41. "A Letter to a Friend," in Franklin, *Papers*, 2:66–67.

42. *A Defence of the Rev. Mr. Hemphill's Observations: or, an Answer to the Vindication of the Reverend Commission*, in Franklin, *Papers*, 2:92, 98, 103.

43. Ibid., p. 107, 109.

44. Ibid., p. 114, 117.

45. For perhaps the most succinct statement of these assumptions, see one of the few positive passages in the *Defence*: "The main design and ultimate end of the christian revelation, or of Christ's coming into the world, was to promote the practice of piety, goodness, virtue, and universal righteousness among mankind, or the practice of the moral duties both with respect to God and man, and by these means to make us happy here and hereafter" (p. 105).

46. See Norman S. Fiering, "Benjamin Franklin and the Way to Virtue," *American Quarterly* 30 (Summer 1978): 199–223. And see also David M. Larson, "Frank-

lin on the Nature of Man and the Possibility of Virtue," *Early American Literature* 10 (Fall 1975): 111–20, arguing persuasively that Franklin's view of human nature was a "middle way" between pessimism and optimism.

47. Franklin, *Proposals Relating to the Education of Youth in Pennsylvania*, excerpted in *The Political Thought of Benjamin Franklin*, ed. Ralph L. Ketcham (Indianapolis: Bobbs-Merrill, 1965), pp. 55–56.

48. *Albany Plan of Union*, in ibid., pp. 83–88; *Articles of Confederation*, in ibid., p. 294.

49. Franklin to Peter Collinson, Apr. 30, 1764, in *Writings of Benjamin Franklin*, ed. Smyth, 4:243, cited by Ketcham, *Political Writings of Benjamin Franklin*, p. 167.

Part III   The Prelude to Debate, 1721–1743

1. For further examples of anti-Calvinist tracts, see [Anon.], *Some Short Observations Made on the Presbyterian Doctrine of Election and Reprobation. By some of the Believers of the Good Tidings and Joyful Doctrine of Christ's Dying for All Men* (Philadelphia: Andrew Bradford, 1721), and Benjamin Eastburn, *The Doctrine of Absolute Reprobation, According to the Westminster Confession of Faith, Refuted: and the Universality of the Saving Grace of God Asserted* (Philadelphia: Samuel Keimer, 1723). And for an eloquent credit to Calvinist irenicism, see the reply to the anonymous tract above by Connecticut's Joseph Morgan, *Letter to the Authors of a Discourse, entitled Some Short Observations Made on the Presbyterian Doctrines of Election and Reprobation* (New London: T. Green, 1724).

2. The most provocative study of Mather remains Sacvan Bercovitch, *The Puritan Origins of the American Self* (New Haven: Yale Univ. Press, 1975). The most complete is Kenneth Silverman, *The Life and Times of Cotton Mather* (New York: Harper & Row, 1984).

3. The following are instructive in tracing the effect of scientific thought on the question of free will: Edwin Arthur Burtt, *The Metaphysical Foundations of Modern Physical Science*, rev. ed. (Garden City, N.Y.: Doubleday, 1954); I. Bernard Cohen, *Revolution in Science* (Cambridge, Mass.: Harvard Univ. Press, 1985); id., "Isaac Newton's *Principia*, the Scriptures, and the Divine Providence," in *Philosophy, Science, and Method: Essays in Honor of Ernest Nagel*, ed. Sidney Morgenbesser, Patrick Suppes, and Morton White (New York: St. Martin's Press, 1969), pp. 523–48; Elizabeth Flower and Murray G. Murphey, *A History of Philosophy in America*, vol. 1 (New York: Putnam's, 1977), esp. ch. 2, "The Impact of Science"; Henry Guerlac, "Theological Voluntarism and Biological Analogies in Newton's Physical Thought," *Journal of the History of Ideas* 44 (June 1983): 219–29; and P. M. Heimann, "Voluntarism and Immanence: Conceptions of Nature in Eighteenth-Century Thought," *Journal of the History of Ideas* 39 (Apr.–June 1978): 271–83.

4. Marilyn J. Westerkamp, *Triumph of the Laity: Scots-Irish Piety and the Great Awakening, 1625–1760* (New York: Oxford Univ. Press, 1988), has argued that the Great Awakening was not the eruption of a novel piety in America but rather the continuation and expansion of Scots-Irish lay piety in the New World.

5. The phrase is a variant on *aristocracy of the converted* in Martin E. Marty, *Religion, Awakening and Revolution* (n.p.: Consortium/McGrath, 1977), p. 99.

6. On "public theology," see John F. Wilson, *Public Religion in American Culture.* (Philadelphia: Temple Univ. Press, 1979), for the most general statement of the concept.

7 "Holy Epicurism"

1. Cotton Mather, *Ratio Disciplinae Fratrum Nov Anglorum: A Faithful Account of the Discipline Professed and Practised in the Churches of New-England* (Boston: S. Gerrish, 1726; repr., New York: Arno Press, 1972), p. 5. The utility of the term *Arminian* for historians is limited, since it was an ill-defined, catchall term of abuse. As used here, the term does not necessarily signify a lineage with the Dutch theologian Jacobus Arminius, but only a species of the genus anti-Calvinist. For the original "Arminianism," see *The Writings of James Arminius,* trans. James Nichols and W. R. Bagnall (Grand Rapids, Mich.: Baker Book House, 1956).

2. Cotton Mather, *Free Grace Maintained and Improved. Or, the General Offer of the Gospel . . . and the Illustrious Doctrines of Divine Predestination and Humane Impotency, Rescued from the Abuses, which they too Frequently Meet Withal . . .* (Boston: B. Green, 1706), pp. 2–4, 32.

3. John F. Woolverton, *Colonial Anglicanism in North America* (Detroit: Wayne State Univ. Press, 1984).

4. Mather, *Free Grace,* p. 2.

5. Ibid., pp. 23–24.

6. Richard Lovelace nicely understates the case when he calls *Free Grace* "an apologia for the retention of the received tradition"; see *The American Pietism of Cotton Mather: Origins of American Evangelicalism* (Grand Rapids, Mich.: Christian Univ. Press, 1979), p. 87.

7. Mather, *Free Grace,* pp. 24, 25.

8. Sacvan Bercovitch, *The American Jeremiad* (Madison: Univ. of Wisconsin Press, 1978).

9. The descriptions of the workings of foreknowledge and the covenant take up more than sixteen pages in the text, whereas reprobation receives a much shorter treatment. Mather, *Free Grace,* pp. 5–21, 39–41.

10. Ibid., p. 28.

11. Ibid., pp. 2, 23.

12. Ibid., pp. 22–23.

13. Other Mather works in the same vein are *The Good Old Way* (Boston: B. Green, 1706), and *The Old Paths Restored. In a Brief Demonstration that the Doctrines of Grace Hitherto Preserved in the Churches of the Non-Conformists, are . . . in the Sacred Scriptures, [and] . . . the Articles and Homilies of the Church of England* (Boston: T. Green, 1711).

14. See *Grace Defended. A Censure of the Ungodliness, by which the Glorious Grace of God is too Commonly Abused* (Boston: B. Green, 1712); *The Man of God Furnished. The Way of Truth, Laid Out; with a Threefold Catechism* (Boston: B. Green, 1708); and *Icono-clastes. An Essay upon the Idolatry, too often Committed under the Profession of the most Reformed Christianity* (Boston: John Allen, 1717), and others.

15. See here Robert Middlekauff, *The Mathers: Three Generations of Puritan In-*

tellectuals, 1596–1728 (New York: Oxford Univ. Press, 1971), pp. 191–208, who takes the image of "Virtuous Epicure" as an apt introduction to Mather's entire career.

16. For a succinct sketch of the European scene, see Franklin L. Baumer, *Modern European Thought: Continuity and Change in Ideas, 1600–1950* (New York: Macmillan, 1977).

17. Cotton Mather, *The Christian Philosopher: A Collection of the Best Discoveries in Nature, With Religious Improvements* (1721; Gainesville, Fla.: Scholars' Facsimiles and Reprints, 1968). Winton U. Solberg's "Science and Religion in Early America: Cotton Mather's *Christian Philosopher*," *Church History* 56 (Mar. 1987): 73–92, was indispensable in pointing out explicitly the design elements in Mather's book; more indirectly, Solberg highlights the critique of Epicureanism.

18. The malleability of Newtonianism for social purposes is nicely underscored by Margaret C. Jacob, *The Newtonians and the English Revolution, 1689–1720* (Ithaca, N.Y.: Cornell Univ. Press, 1976).

19. Mather, *Christian Philosopher*, p. 8. In fact, Mather's conclusion was consonant with Newton's own "System of the World" and "General Scholium" to the *Principia*, although Mather was perhaps a bit quicker to explain matter by God than Newton himself would have warranted.

20. Mather, *Christian Philosopher*, p. 36, cited by Solberg, "Science and Religion," p. 82.

21. I. Bernard Cohen, *The Newtonian Revolution* (Cambridge: Cambridge Univ. Press, 1980), pp. 115–19. For the degree to which Newton himself was an antimechanist, see Middlekauff, *The Mathers*, pp. 286–89.

22. Mather, *Christian Philosopher*, pp. 81–82, 85. There is more than a little irony in the fact that Mather was here quoting Samuel Clarke, who was by the time Mather's book was published well known as an Arminian who had defended free will, along with theism, against Anthony Collins's materialistic determinism. See Clarke's *Remarks upon a Book entituled, "A Philosophical Enquiry concerning Human Liberty"* (London: 1717), as cited by James O'Higgins, S.J., *Anthony Collins: The Man and His Works.* (The Hague: Martinus Nijhoff, 1970).

23. In European thought, and most notably in France, harmonizing science and faith was a more difficult matter. See, for the contrast, Aram Vartanian, "Necessity or Freedom? The Politics of an Eighteenth-Century Metaphysical Debate," in *Studies in Eighteenth-Century Culture*, ed. Roseann Runte (Madison: Univ. of Wisconsin Press, 1978), 7:153–74. In England, John Toland had applied scientific paradigms to Christianity in *Christianity Not Mysterious* (1696), and even earlier, in 1656, Hobbes had been convicted by the Anglicans of fatalism in his famous debate with Bishop Bramhall; see *The Questions Concerning Liberty, Necessity, and Chance*, in *The English Works of Thomas Hobbes*, ed. Sire William Molesworth (London: John Bohrn, 1841), 7:2–175. The freethinker Anthony Collins would be another candidate for Mather's hit list. See once again the works of O'Higgins on Collins and the determinist tradition in Europe, notably Anthony Collins's *A Philosophical Inquiry Concerning Human Liberty* (The Hague: Martinus Nijhoff, 1976), where O'Higgins provides in his introduction a fine sketch of the lineage of seventeenth- and early eighteenth-century determinist philosophy.

24. Mather, *Christian Philosopher*, p. 222.

25. This is one of the mistakes of Jeffrey Jeske, "Cotton Mather: Physico-Theologian," *Journal of the History of Ideas* 47 (Oct.–Dec. 1986): 583–94.

26. Mather, *Christian Philosopher*, p. 225.

27. Ibid., pp. 278–79.

28. Mather's God was never an absentee First Cause only. See *Christian Philosopher*, p. 85, and elsewhere for assertions of direct and continuous involvement of God with matter.

29. Ibid., p. 295.

30. Robert E. Schofield has nicely described the type of thinking Mather represents as "theological Newtonianism"; see "An Evolutionary Taxonomy of Eighteenth-Century Newtonianisms," in *Studies in Eighteenth-Century Culture*, ed. Runte, 7:175–92.

8   "God Gone Out of His Ordinary Way"

1. This is not to say that Mather's legacy was unremarkable; he clearly contributed. Scholars rightly see links between Mather and Franklin, and by extension between Mather and the entire Enlightenment strand of do-good piety joined to an Epicurean life-style. But the links between Mather and "pietism," or evangelicalism, are if anything even clearer. See Richard F. Lovelace, *The American Pietism of Cotton Mather: Origins of American Evangelicalism* (Grand Rapids, Mich.: Christian College Consortium, 1979).

2. The phrase *rhetoric of fortune* might well remind scholars of Perry Miller's description of Edwards's "rhetoric of sensation," but the connection is accidental. If anything, the two rhetorics are diametrical opposites; the "rhetoric of sensation" grounded Edwards's idealism, whereas the "rhetoric of fortune" balanced his "determinism." See Perry Miller, "The Rhetoric of Sensation," in *Errand into the Wilderness* (New York: Harper Torchbooks, 1956), pp. 167–83. It ought to be pointed out that the term *rhetoric* is used here to refer to linguistic strategy generally, rather than in the "oral" sense of rhetoric proper. The topic could be called second-order rhetoric, insofar as it primarily concerns polemical descriptions of events, rather than the addresses that constituted the events, such as sermons. For a study of sermonic rhetoric, see Harry S. Stout, *The New England Soul: Preaching and Religious Culture in Colonial New England* (New York: Oxford Univ. Press, 1986), and Teresa Toulouse, *The Art of Prophesying: New England Sermons and the Shaping of Belief* (Athens, Ga.: Univ. of Georgia Press, 1987).

3. Jonathan Edwards, *A Faithful Narrative of the Surprising Work of God in the Conversion of Many Hundred Souls in Northampton, and the Neighbouring Towns . . .* , 3d ed. (Boston: S. Kneeland & T. Green, 1738), in Jonathan Edwards, *The Great Awakening*, vol. 4 of *The Works of Jonathan Edwards*, ed. C. C. Goen (New Haven: Yale Univ. Press, 1972), p. 149.

4. Ibid., pp. 149–50. Much emphasis has been made on Edwards's morphology of conversion, or delineation of the usual stages in the process of the new birth, but at least as prominent are the images of variety he uses to describe what took place. See esp. pp. 168–85.

5. Ibid., pp. 149–50, 157. Perhaps the most telling passage in *A Faithful Narrative* is where Edwards reports that "there has been much talk in many parts of the country, as though the people have symbolized [sic] with the Quakers, and the Quakers themselves have been moved with such reports; and came here, once and again, hoping to find good waters to fish in" (p. 189). The link between the Calvinists and the Quakers was inevitable, given Edwards's rhetoric of fortune. The significance of this perception has not, to my mind, been adequately appreciated as yet by scholars.

6. The logic also worked in reverse; fortune had to be balanced with order for it to be from God, rather than from a delusion. Hence Edwards quickly sought to reduce the great variety of conversions to a set form. See the lengthy section on "the morphology of conversion" in ibid., pp. 159–91.

7. Ibid., p. 191.

8. Ibid., pp. 193–94. Emphasis added.

9. It is no coincidence that Edwards's great collection of sermons on justification by faith dates from these years. See *Discourses on Various Important Subjects, Nearly concerning the great Affair of the Soul's Eternal Salvation . . .* (Boston, 1743).

10. This apparent denial of the value of material life accords with the "indeterminism" expressed by Anne Hutchinson nearly 100 years earlier. For an interpretation of "material shapes" in earlier Puritanism, see Ann Kibbey, *The Interpretation of Material Shapes in Puritanism: A Study of Rhetoric, Prejudice, and Violence* (Cambridge: Cambridge Univ. Press, 1986). Kibbey suggests that the iconoclasm of Puritanism was an enduring one, manifest especially against women, and evident in both fear of chaos and the assertion of "hierarchic" order. I am inclined to agree, although I give more credence to the claims of theology than Kibbey and therefore disagree with Kibbey that this "rhetoric" necessarily promoted violence. It was the distortion of this theology into an ideology that promoted the violence; not the theology itself.

11. Jon Butler cautions against "homogenizing" the different revivalists, and attempts especially to distinguish Tennent from Whitefield. Suffice it to say that I think this is among the weaker arguments in an otherwise superb book, *Awash in a Sea of Faith: Christianizing the American People* (Cambridge, Mass.: Harvard Univ. Press, 1990), p. 178. For all of their ethnic and regional diversity, the early "Grand Itinerants" were all seeking to add some "enthusiasm" to Calvinism. The term *Grand Itinerants* is Edwin Scott Gaustad's, whose *The Great Awakening in New England* (New York: Harper, 1957) remains the best synthesis of the pivotal New England occurrences. This should be compared with the even older, but still useful, works by Charles Hartshorn Maxson, *The Great Awakening in the Middle Colonies* (Chicago: Univ. of Chicago Press, 1920), and Wesley M. Gewehr, *The Great Awakening in Virginia, 1740–1790* (Durham, N.C.: Duke Univ. Press, 1930). Three collections of primary sources make countless documents from the Awakening period readily available: *The Great Awakening: Documents on the Revival of Religion, 1740–1745*, ed. Richard L. Bushman (New York: Atheneum, 1970); David S. Lovejoy, *Religious Enthusiasm and the Great Awakening* (Englewood Cliffs, N.J.: Prentice-Hall, 1969); and esp. *The Great Awakening: Documents Illustrating the Crisis and Its Consequences*, ed. Alan Heimert and Perry Miller (Indianapolis: Bobbs-Merrill, 1967).

12. In an influential article, "Enthusiasm Described and Decried: The Great Awakening as Interpretive Fiction," *Journal of American History* 69 (Sept. 1982): 305–25, Butler argues cogently that the Great Awakening was "a short-lived Calvinist revival in New England during the early 1740s." Furthermore, Butler argues, seeing the development of a spirit of democracy in these years is simply fictitious: "Tumult should not be confused with democracy" (pp. 309, 317). Basically, I agree with the first of Butler's assertions, while questioning the second. The helpful corrective of Butler's article is to highlight the eclecticism of the times and to prevent facile generalization. But Butler is somewhat deaf to theological tunes, and he thereby misses the intellectual significance of the attempt at a Calvinist revival. For a Calvinist, tumult was always significant.

13. *Great Awakening*, ed. Heimert and Miller, p. 201. On Davenport's escapades, see Harry S. Stout and Peter Onuf, "James Davenport and the Great Awakening in New London," *Journal of American History* 70 (Dec. 1983–84): 556–78.

14. Gaustad, *Great Awakening in New England*, p. 38. Again, with minor differences, this pattern was the same in all of the itinerants. See the classic sermon by Gilbert Tennent, *The Danger of an Unconverted Ministry, Considered in a Sermon on Mark VI. 34* (1741), reprinted in its entirety in *Great Awakening*, ed. Heimert and Miller, pp. 71–99.

15. James Davenport, *A Song of Praise for Joy in the Holy Ghost* (Boston, 1741), in *Great Awakening*, ed. Heimert and Miller, p. 201.

16. Editor's introduction to *Great Awakening*, ed. Goen, p. 60; *Boston Weekly News-Letter*, July 1, 1742, in *Great Awakening*, ed. Bushman, p. 46.

17. *The Christian History, containing Accounts of the Revival and Propagation of Religion in Great Britain & America*, ed. Thomas Prince, vol. 1 (Boston, 1744), pp. 412–16; vol. 2 (Boston, 1745), pp. 80–91, cited by Gaustad, *Great Awakening in New England*, p. 39.

18. *The Declaration of A Number of the associated Pastors of Boston and Charles-Town relating to the Rev. Mr. James Davenport, and his Conduct* (Boston: S. Kneeland & T. Green, 1742), pp. 4–5.

19. On Moorhead, see Pattie Cowell, "Sarah Parsons Moorhead," in *American Writers before 1800: A Biographical and Critical Dictionary*, ed. James A. Leverneir and Douglas R. Wilmes (Westport, Conn.: Greenwood Press, 1982), 2:1026–27. Moorhead also wrote a letter criticizing the excesses of Gilbert Tennent, *New England Weekly Journal*, Mar. 17, 1741, p. 1.

20. Sarah Parsons Moorhead, *To the Rev. Mr. James Davenport, on his Departure from Boston, by Way of a Dream. With a Line to the Scoffers at Religion* (Boston: [Charles Harrison], 1742), pp. A–2.

21. Ibid., pp. 3–4.

22. James Davenport, *The Reverend Mr. James Davenport's Confession and Retractions* (Boston, 1744), in *Great Awakening*, ed. Heimert and Miller, pp. 257–61.

23. Moorhead, *To the Rev. Mr. James Davenport*, pp. 4–5.

24. Jonathan Edwards, *The Distinguishing Marks of a Work of a Spirit of God* (Boston: S. Kneeland & T. Green, 1741), in *Great Awakening*, ed. Goen, p. 260.

25. Ibid., pp. 228, 234, 235, 241. Emphasis added.

26. Ibid., p. 242.

27. Ibid., pp. 266–67.

28. Ibid., pp. 268, 269.

9   "A Strange Revolution"

1. The treatment of Chauncy to follow inevitably focuses only upon an isolated aspect of a long and fruitful career. The debates with Edwards inevitably made Chauncy appear less Calvinistic than he was at this stage of his career, and more "Anglican" and liberal. For the full story of this fascinating figure, see Edward M. Griffin, *Old Brick: Charles Chauncy of Boston, 1705–1787* (Minneapolis: Univ. of Minnesota Press, 1980), and Charles H. Lippy, *Seasonable Revolutionary: The Mind of Charles Chauncy* (Chicago: Nelson-Hall, 1981).

2. On Davenport, see chapter 8 above.

3. Charles Chauncy, *Enthusiasm Described and Caution'd Against*, in *The Great Awakening: Documents Illustrating the Crisis and Its Consequences*, ed. Alan Heimert and Perry Miller (Indianapolis: Bobbs-Merrill, 1967), pp. 231–34.

4. Charles Chauncy, *Enthusiasm Describ'd and Cautioned Against* (Boston: J. Draper, 1742), pp. 14–15.

5. Ibid., pp. 19–20.

6. Ibid., p. 15.

7. [Charles Chauncy], *The Late Religious Commotions in New England Considered. An Answer to the Rev. Mr. Jonathan Edwards's Sermon, entitled, The Distinguishing Marks* (Boston: C. Russel, 1743), p. 7.

8. Jonathan Edwards, *Some Thoughts Concerning the Present Revival of Religion in New England*, in *The Great Awakening*, vol. 4 of *The Works of Jonathan Edwards*, ed. C. C. Goen (New Haven: Yale Univ. Press, 1972), p. 384.

9. Ibid., pp. 294, 344.

10. Perry Miller also noted a progressive rigidity in Edwards's writings on the Awakening. See Miller, *Jonathan Edwards* (New York: Sloan, 1949), p. 178.

11. Edwards, *Some Thoughts*, in *Great Awakening*, ed. Goen, pp. 414–16, 418, 421, 419, 415.

12. Ibid., p. 432. For the continuity of "immediacy" as an idea in Edwards's thought, see Douglas J. Elwood, *The Philosophical Theology of Jonathan Edwards* (New York: Columbia Univ. Press, 1960).

13. Edwards, *Some Thoughts*, in *Great Awakening*, ed. Goen, pp. 438–39.

14. Ibid., pp. 432–33.

15. Ibid., pp. 458, 459.

16. Ibid., p. 467.

17. Christopher R. Peaske has argued that while Edwards was interested in the Devil throughout his career, his interest peaked during the revivals. See Peaske, "The Devil and Jonathan Edwards," *Journal of the History of Ideas* 33 (Jan. 1972): 123–38.

18. Edwards, *Some Thoughts*, in *Great Awakening*, ed. Goen, p. 473.

19. In this reading, Edwards's *A Treatise Concerning Religious Affections*, vol. 2 of *The Works of Jonathan Edwards*, ed. John E. Smith (New Haven: Yale Univ. Press, 1959), while undoubtedly the more substantive work intellectually, is less

historically significant than Edwards's earlier works on the Great Awakening for revealing the course of the development of Edwards's thought. *Religious Affections* can be read in continuity with the development sketched here. The entire purpose of the book—to distinguish true from false affections in religion—can be read as yet another step back from the wholesale acceptance of passion, and so on, implied by Edwards's rhetoric of fortune. This development is most clear in the following sections of *Religious Affections:* the preface, where Edwards distinguishes "common" and "gracious" works of the spirit, in contrast to the position in *Distinguishing Marks;* p. 98, where he distinguishes affections and passions; pp. 138–42, and 197–239, where he expressly traces grace to "the powerful and efficacious operation of an extrinsic agent, or divine efficient out of ourselves"; pp. 151–62 where he makes some extraordinary statements concerning "God's ordinary manner of dealing with" humans through a regular order, thus "taming" the indeterminist impulse he had endorsed during the revivals; and, finally, in the emphasis on "symmetry" and "proportion" that runs like a thread throughout the entire work (but see esp. pp. 365–76).

20. This theme of millennialism has been mined thoroughly by scholars, if not exhausted. See, among many, Alan Heimert, *Religion and the American Mind: From the Great Awakening to the Revolution* (Cambridge, Mass.: Harvard Univ. Press, 1966); Nathan O. Hatch, *The Sacred Cause of Liberty: Republican Thought and the Millennium in Revolutionary New England* (New Haven: Yale Univ. Press, 1977); and Patricia U. Bonomi, *Under the Cope of Heaven: Religion, Society and Politics in Colonial America* (New York: Oxford Univ. Press, 1986). Whatever novelty my approach to Edwards and early American theological debate offers lies in the fact that it takes as central Edwards's work on freedom. Freedom (space), not millennialism (time), was the central category of theology in early America. See, along these lines, Sidney E. Mead, *The Lively Experiment: The Shaping of Christianity in America* (New York: Harper & Row, 1963).

21. For a helpful warning about the concept of "deference" in prerevolutionary American politics, see Joy B. and Robert R. Gilsdorf, "Elites and Electorates: Some Plain Truths for Historians of Colonial America," in *Saints and Revolutionaries: Essays on Early American History,* ed. David Hall, John Murrin, and Thad W. Tate (New York: Norton, 1984), pp. 207–44.

22. Edwards, *Some Thoughts,* in *Great Awakening,* ed. Goen, pp. 370–73.

23. Ibid., pp. 374–79.

24. Ibid., pp. 506, 513. In light of this fact, and in light of the ensuing discussion, I believe David L. Weddle's "The Democracy of Grace: Political Reflections on the Evangelical Theology of Jonathon [sic] Edwards," *Dialog* 15 (Autumn 1976), is off the mark. Roland A. Delattre's attempt to describe Edwards's politics as a "pluralism" is better, but still too optimistic. See "Beauty and Politics: A Problematic Legacy of Jonathan Edwards," in *American Philosophy from Edwards to Quine,* ed. Robert W. Shahan and Kenneth R. Merrill (Norman: Univ. of Oklahoma Press, 1977), pp. 20–48. More accurate in my estimation are Gerhard T. Alexis, "Jonathan Edwards and the Theocratic Ideal," *Church History* 35 (Sept. 1966): 328–43; and esp. Jerald C. Brauer, "The Rule of the Saints in American Politics," *Church History* 27 (Sept. 1958): 240–55, who clearly labels Puritan politics "aristrocratic."

25. Edwards, *Some Thoughts*, in *Great Awakening*, ed. Goen, pp. 380, 511, 383. The suggestion regarding press restrictions was later restated positively by Edwards (p. 529) as a call for the publication of a journal devoted to revival accounts. This was probably the only one of his political proposals that gained acceptance when *The Christian History*, a journal detailing revivals, was published in 1744 and 1745.

26. Edwards, *Some Thoughts*, in *Great Awakening*, ed. Goen, p. 380. Emphasis added.

27. See Patricia J. Tracy, *Jonathan Edwards, Pastor: Religion and Society in Eighteenth-Century Northampton* (New York: Hill & Wang, 1979), who traces Edwards's increasing emphasis on extrinsic control and orthodox formulation in his parish, and the tragic consequences this emphasis held for him and his family.

28. Edwards, *Some Thoughts*, in *Great Awakening*, ed. Goen, p. 503.

29. Charles Chauncy, *Seasonable Thoughts on the State of Religion in New England* (Boston: S. Eliot, 1743), pp. A2, xxvi.

30. Ibid., pp. 178, 278, 107. The emphasis on "disorder" is the main theme of *Seasonable Thoughts*.

31. Ibid., p. 218.

32. Ibid., pp. 16–17.

33. For instance: "Good order is the strength and charity of the world.—The prosperity of both church and state depends very much upon it. And can there be order where men transgress the limits of their station?" (ibid., p. 366).

34. The case for Chauncy's "democratic" side does not need to rest simply upon *Seasonable Thoughts*, of course. For an early suggestive work, see *The Only Compulsion* (Boston: J. Draper, 1739), and for later works, Chauncy's ardent prerevolutionary sermons are well known. See esp. *A Discourse On The Good News From a Far Country* (Boston: Kneeland & Adams, 1766), Chauncy's sermon on the Stamp Act.

35. For a crisp presentation of the mediating character of Chauncy's politics, as well as his religion, see John Corrigan, *The Hidden Balance: Religion and the Social Theories of Charles Chauncy and Jonathan Mayhew* (Cambridge: Cambridge Univ. Press, 1987).

36. Chauncy, *Seasonable Thoughts*, pp. 337, 358, 341.

37. Ibid., pp. 367–68.

38. Ibid.

39. Ibid., pp. 398; 388–89; 399.

Part IV   Harmony in Discord, 1735–1760

1. This role of the elites in creating the symbolic structure of revivalism is stressed throughout chapter 10. In other words, revivalism was at least as conservative as it was progressive. See, for a similar interpretation, Jon Butler, *Awash in a Sea of Faith: Christianizing the American People* (Cambridge, Mass.: Harvard Univ. Press, 1990), who argues persuasively that the revivals were in part a Dissenting strategy to stave off Anglican state church control: "For better or worse, the state church tradition, rather than Dissenting evangelicalism or voluntaryism, gave Christianity its primary shape in eighteenth-century colonial American society, at least through

1740" (p. 165). My reading of the Great Awakening in this chapter in many ways confirms some of Butler's suspicions about the revivals, although in the end I am more interested in the intellectual and symbolic origins and significance of the Great Awakening than in its social roots.

2. Here, Butler and I diverge in our interpretations. Studying the debates surrounding the revivals has led me to conclude that the way that debate was *resolved* illumines as much about the emerging limits of the culture as the differing opinions of the revivalists and their opponents illumine plurality. To borrow language from the anthropologist Victor Turner, Butler's interpretation (in continuity with an earlier school) still emphasizes the antistructural character of the revivals, whereas mine emphasizes the resolution of the revival process in new structure. See Victor Turner, *The Ritual Process: Structure and Anti-Structure* (Ithaca, N.Y.: Cornell Univ. Press, 1969), and Victor and Edith Turner, *Image and Pilgrimage in Christian Culture: Anthropological Perspectives* (New York: Columbia Univ. Press, 1978).

10   "Are Not the Saved of the Lord Few?"

1. John White, *New England's Lamentations under these three heads. The Decay of the Power of Godliness; the Danger of Arminian Principles; the Declining State of our Church-Order, Government, and Discipline* (Boston: T. Fleet, 1734), p. 17.

2. See editor's introduction to Jonathan Edwards, *The Great Awakening*, ed. C. C. Goen (New Haven: Yale Univ. Press, 1972), pp. 4–18, which sketches in detail the range of complaints about Arminianism on the eve of the Awakening.

3. White, *Lamentations*, pp. 2, 29, 13.

4. Ibid., pp. 23, 18–19.

5. Ibid., pp. 20, 21, 23.

6. Ibid., p. 24.

7. Ibid., p. 23.

8. See editor's introduction to Edwards, *Great Awakening*, ed. Goen, p. 8.

9. The anti-Calvinists and revival opposers constantly complained about this coalition. See, e.g., John Bass, *A True Narrative of an Unhappy Contention in The Church of Ashford . . .* (Boston: 1751), in *The Great Awakening: Documents Illustrating the Crisis and Its Consequences,* ed. Alan Heimert and Perry Miller (Indianapolis: Bobbs-Merrill, 1967), pp. 465–579.

10. Clifford K. Shipton, "Samuel Moody," in *Sibley's Harvard Graduates*, vol. 4, *1690–1700: Biographical Sketches of Those Who Attended Harvard College.* (Cambridge, Mass.: Harvard Univ. Press, 1933), pp. 356–65.

11. Samuel Moody, *A Faithful Narrative of God's Gracious Dealings, with A Person Lately Recovered from the Dangerous Errors of Arminius* (Boston, 1737), pp. 1–2.

12. Ibid., pp. 3–4.

13. See Joseph J. Ellis, *The New England Mind in Transition: Samuel Johnson of Connecticut, 1696–1772* (New Haven: Yale Univ. Press, 1973), pp. 124–25; Robert J. Wilson III, *The Benevolent Deity: Ebenezer Gay and the Rise of Rational Religion in New England, 1696–1787* (Philadelphia: Univ. of Pennsylvania, 1984); and Conrad Wright, *The Beginnings of Unitarianism in America* (Boston: Starr King/Beacon Press, 1955).

14. Wilson, *Benevolent Deity*, pp. 74–75. And see Samuel Osborn, *The Case and Complaint of Mr. Samuel Osborn, Late of Eastham* (Boston, 1743).

15. J. M. Bumsted, "A Caution to Erring Christians: Ecclesiastical Disorder on Cape Cod, 1717 to 1738," *William and Mary Quarterly*, 3d ser., 28 (July 1971): 413–38.

16. See Stone's defense of original sin, *A Very Brief Account of the Wretched State of Man by the Fall. Added, A Discourse of the Absolute Freedom of Grace* (Boston: B. Green, 1731), written more than twenty years before Jonathan Edwards's.

17. Nathaniel Stone, *On Account of Pleas of Late Made, that tend to subvert the New Covenant Constitution . . . [A Plea for Truth, in Opposition to Arminian Principles]* (Boston: S. Kneeland, 1739), pp. 14, 5, 9.

18. Ibid., p. 12.

19. On the intellectual significance of Brattle Street Church, see Norman Fiering, "The First American Enlightenment: Tillotson, Leverett, and Philosophical Anglicanism," *New England Quarterly* 54 (Sept. 1981): 307–44.

20. William Cooper, *The Doctrine of Predestination unto Life, Explained and Vindicated* (Boston: J. Draper, 1740), pp. 13–15.

21. Ibid., pp. 92–93.

22. Ibid., pp. 113, 116.

23. Samuel Johnson, *Autobiography*, in *Samuel Johnson, President of King's College, His Career and Writings*, ed. Herbert and Carol Schneider (New York: Columbia Univ. Press, 1929), 1:27–28.

24. For the range of opposition, see again *Great Awakening*, ed. Heimert and Miller.

25. John Wesley, *Free Grace. A Sermon Preach'd at Bristol* (Philadelphia: Reprinted by Edward Pleadwell, 1740–41), pp. 28, 21–22.

26. See Nathan O. Hatch, *The Democratization of American Christianity* (New Haven: Yale Univ. Press, 1989). On Methodism in America, see Frederick A. Norwood, *The Story of American Methodism: A History of the United Methodists and Their Relations* (Nashville, Tenn.: Abingdon Press, 1974), and the still helpful works of William Warren Sweet, *Methodism in American History* (Nashville, Tenn.: Abingdon Press, 1953).

27. Leo George Cox, *John Wesley's Concept of Perfection* (Kansas City, Mo.: Beacon Hill, 1964).

28. Wesley, *Free Grace*, pp. 9–10.

29. Ibid., pp. 10–12.

30. Ibid., pp. 15, 21–22. Emphasis in original.

31. Ibid., pp. 24–25.

32. See part 2 for a detailed discussion of this work.

33. An Enquirer after Truth [Archibald Cummings], *Dialogues Between a Minister and an honest Country-man, concerning Election and Predestination, Very Suitable to the Present Times. To which is annexed, Divine Prescience Consistent with Human Liberty: Or Mr. Wesley's Opinion of election and Reprobation, Prov'd to be not so absured as represented in a late letter. . . . But to be clear of those destructive consequences that will forever attend the Calvinistical doctrine of absolute fatality* (Philadelphia: Andrew Bradford, 1741), p. 29.

34. Ibid., p. 35.
35. Ibid., p. 34.
36. Ibid., p. 38.

11   "Truths Are Confessed on Both Sides"

1. In fact, the topic of free will had been contested throughout the 1740s. The works of Beach, Dickinson, and Johnson were simply the most significant of many. See Samuel Blair, *The Doctrines of Predestination Truly and Fairly Stated . . . and Defended Against All the Material Arguments and Objections Advanced Against It* (Philadelphia: Benjamin Franklin, for the author, 1742); Isaac Chanler, *The Doctrines of Glorious Grace Unfolded, Defended, and Practically Improved* (Boston: S. Kneeland & T. Green, 1744); Samuel Cooke, *Divine Sovereignty in the Salvation of Sinners, Consider'd and Improved* (Boston: G. Rogers, 1741); Experience Mayhew, *Grace Defended, in a Modest Plea for an Important Truth* (Boston: B. Green, 1744); and Edward Wigglesworth, *The Sovereignty of God in the Exercises of His Mercy; and How He is Said to Harden the Hearts of Men* (Boston: Rogers & Fowle, 1741).

2. My point is not only the idealistic one that there is usually an "excluded middle" to all two-sided debates; rather, it is the historical point that in America after 1745 the most obvious feature in the debate over free will was a tacit, but clear, agreement on a "mediating" solution to the problem. As Dorothy L. Sayers pointed out: "The first task, when undertaking the study of any phenomenon, is to observe its most obvious feature; and it is here that most students fail" (*Unpopular Opinions* [London, 1946], cited by Nathan O. Hatch, *The Sacred Cause of Liberty: Republican Thought and the Millennium in Revolutionary New England* [New Haven: Yale Univ. Press, 1977], p. 6).

3. The disputants were familiar with one another through an earlier pamphlet debate on the nature and benefits of episcopal church government. The best scholarly discussion of the debate over free will to date is in Claude M. Newlin, *Philosophy and Religion in Colonial America* (New York: Philosophical Library, 1962), pp. 106–10, 135–39.

4. On Beach, see Franklin Bowditch Dexter, *Biographical Sketches of the Graduates of Yale College*, vol. 1, *1701–1745* (New York: Holt, 1885), pp. 239–43.

5. Joseph J. Ellis, *The New England Mind in Transition: Samuel Johnson of Connecticut, 1696–1772* (New Haven: Yale Univ. Press, 1973), is a reliable recent biography. More venturesome is Peter N. Carroll, *The Other Samuel Johnson: A Psychohistory of Early New England* (Rutherford, N.J.: Fairleigh Dickinson Univ. Press, 1978). See also the helpful synthesis of Norman Fiering, "President Samuel Johnson and the Circle of Knowledge," *William and Mary Quarterly*, 3d ser., 28 (Apr. 1971): 199–236. Primary works are collected in *Samuel Johnson, President of King's College, His Career and Writings*, ed. Herbert and Carol Schneider (New York: Columbia Univ. Press, 1929).

6. Jonathan Dickinson, *The True-Scripture Doctrine Concerning some Important Points of Christian Faith, Particularly Eternal Election, Original Sin, Grace in Conversion . . . Justification by Faith, and the Saints Perseverance* (Boston: G. Rogers, 1741), p. 8.

7. Dickinson is sadly not the subject of a modern biography. See, however, Keith J. Hardiman, "Jonathan Dickinson and the Cause of American Presbyterianism, 1717–1740" (Ph.D. diss., Univ. of Pennsylvania, 1974). Dickinson's role in the Great Awakening has been highlighted in two recent articles: David C. Harlan, "The Travail of Religious Moderation: Jonathan Dickinson and the Great Awakening," *Journal of Presbyterian History* 61 (Winter 1983): 411–26; and Leigh Eric Schmidt, "Jonathan Dickinson and the Making of the Moderate Awakening," *American Presbyterians* 63 (Winter 1985): 341–53.

8. From among the other works published in the colonies on the topic between 1745 and 1754, see esp. *A Letter Concerning the Two Different Schemes of Divinity, viz. Calvinism and Arminianism, Preached at this Day by Different Ministers* (Boston: Rogers & Fowle, 1746); Andrew Croswell, *Heaven Shut Against Arminians and Antinomians* (Boston: Rogers & Fowle, 1747); Experience Mayhew, *A Letter to a Gentleman on that Question Whether Saving Grace be Different in Species from Common Grace, or in Degree Only?* (Boston: S. Kneeland & T. Green, 1747); *The Doctrine of Universal Free Grace Proved from the Scriptures* (New York: DeForest, 1748); Robert Seagrave, *The True Protestant: A Dissertation, Shewing the Necessity of Asserting the Principles of Liberty in their Full Extent* (Philadelphia: William Bradford, 1748); Lemuel Briant, *The Absurdity and Blasphemy of Depretiating Moral Virtue* (Boston, 1749); John Porter, *The Absurdity and Blasphemy of Substituting the Personal Righteousness of Men in the Room of the Surety-Righteousness of Christ* (Boston, 1750); Lemuel Briant, *Some Friendly Remarks on a Sermon Lately Preach'd at Braintree . . . by the Rev'd Mr. Porter of Bridgwater* (Boston: J. Green, 1750); Moses Dickinson, *An Inquiry into the Consequences both of Calvinistical and Arminian Principles* (Boston: Daniel Fowle, 1750); John Porter, *A Vindication of a Sermon Preached at Braintree Third Parish* (Boston: S. Kneeland, 1751); Briant, *Some More Friendly Remarks on Mr. Porter & Company* (Boston: J. Green, 1751); and Samuel Niles, *A Vindication of Divers Important Gospel-Doctrines . . . Against the Injurious Reflections and Misrepresentations . . . of the Rev. Lemuel Briant* (Boston: S. Kneeland, 1752). On the Briant-Porter debate, see Conrad Wright, *The Beginninings of Unitarianism in America* (Boston: Starr King, 1955), pp. 67–71.

9. Jonathan Dickinson, *A Vindication of God's Sovereign Free Grace* (Boston: Rogers & Fowle, 1746), p. 69.

10. Jonathan Dickinson, *A Second Vindication of God's Sovereign Free Grace* (Boston: Rogers & Fowle, 1748), p. 68.

11. John Beach, *Remarks Upon Mr. Mills's Letter* (Boston: Rogers & Fowle, 1748), p. 22.

12. Samuel Johnson, *A Letter to Mr. Dickinson* (Boston: G. Rogers, 1747), p. 7.

13. John Beach, *A Sermon, Shewing, that Eternal Life is God's Free Gift, Bestowed Upon Men According to their Moral Behaviour. And that Free Grace and Free Will Concur, in the Affair of Man's Salvation* (Newport, R.I.: Widow Franklin, 1745), p. 29.

14. Samuel Johnson, *A Letter from Aristocles to Authades, Concerning the Sovereignty and Promises of God* (Boston: T. Fleet, 1745), in *Samuel Johnson, President of King's College: His Career and Writings*, ed. Herbert and Carol Schneider (New York: Columbia Univ. Press, 1929), 3:163.

15. Beach, *Sermon*, pp. 37–38.

16. Dickinson, *Vindication*, p. 18.

17. Jedediah Mills, *A Vindication of Gospel Truth . . . Containing a reply to what the author of a late letter from Aristocles to Authades, has offer'd* (Boston: Rogers & Fowle, 1747), p. 57.

18. John Beach, *Remarks Upon Mr. Mills's Letter* (Boston: Rogers & Fowle, 1748), p. 20.

19. Beach, *God's Sovereignty and His Universal Love to the Souls of Men Reconciled. In a reply to Mr. Jonathan Dickinson's Remarks Upon a Sermon, Intitled, Eternal Life is God's Free Gift* (Boston: Rogers & Fowle, 1747), pp. 56, 60.

20. Dickinson, *Second Vindication*, p. 21.

21. Beach, *Sermon*, p. 3.

22. Dickinson, *True-Scripture Doctrine*, p. 8.

23. Ibid., p. 17.

24. Ibid., pp. 31–32.

25. Dickinson, *Vindication*, p. 43.

26. Samuel Johnson, *A Letter to the Rev. Jonathan Dickinson in Defence of Aristocles and Authades, Concerning the Sovereignty and Promises of God* (Boston: Rogers & Fowle, 1747), pp. 15–16, 13.

27. Ibid., p. 170.

28. Ibid., p. 176.

29. Dickinson, *Vindication*, pp. 67–68. Emphasis in original.

30. Ibid., p. 77.

31. Johnson, *Letter to the Rev. Jonathan Dickinson*, pp. 10–11.

32. Dickinson, *Vindication*, p. 68. That this was a subtle change in Calvinism, or at least appeared to be, did not escape the notice of the more hard-line Calvinists, notably Andrew Croswell, who openly charged Dickinson with preaching "Arminianism." See both *Mr. Croswell's Reply to a Book lately Publish'd, Entitled, A Display of God's Special Grace* (Boston: Rogers & Fowle, 1742) and *Heaven Shut Vs. all Arminians and Antinomians* (Boston: Rogers & Fowle, 1747).

33. See, for some social confirmation of this intellectual hypothesis, Bruce E. Steiner, "New England Anglicanism: A Genteel Faith?" *William and Mary Quarterly*, 3d ser., 27 (Jan. 1970): 122–35.

34. Johnson, *Aristocles to Authades*, p. 170.

35. Beach, *Sermon*, pp. 21–22.

36. Dickinson, *Vindication*, p. 9.

37. Dickinson, *True-Scripture Doctrine*, pp. 34–36.

38. Dickinson, *Second Vindication*, pp. 14–15.

39. Beach, *Sermon*, pp. 6, 21–22. Emphasis added.

40. Johnson, *Aristocles to Authades*, in *Samuel Johnson*, ed. Schneider, pp. 166, 164.

41. Dickinson, *Vindication*, pp. 26–27.

42. Ibid., pp. 38, 66–67.

43. Mills, *Vindication of Gospel Truth*, p. 20.

44. Johnson, *Aristocles to Authades*, p. 161.

45. Beach, *God's Sovereignty*, p. 67.

46. That historically the Anglicans became loyalists and the Calvinists revolutionaries makes no difference to my thesis about the "establishment of mediation"; in fact, it strengthens my argument that there was an agreement between the parties on the matter of free choice. By the 1760s enough "cross-fertilization" had occurred for the two camps to switch ideological sides, and much of the "revolutionariness" of the revolution resided precisely in this switch.

47. Beach, God's Sovereignty, p. 66.

12   "The Modern Prevailing Notions"

1. Jonathan Edwards, "Personal Narrative," in Jonathan Edwards: Representative Selections, ed. Clarence H. Faust and Thomas H. Johnson (New York: Hill & Wang, 1962), p. 58.

2. Jonathan Edwards, God Glorified in the Work of Redemption, By the Greatness of Man's Dependence Upon Him in the Whole of It (Boston, 1731), in vol. 2 of The Works of Jonathan Edwards, ed. Sereno E. Dwight and Edward Hickman (Carlisle, Pa.: Banner of Truth, 1979), pp. 3, 6. Henceforth cited as Edwards, Works [BT].

3. See Jonathan Edwards, Freedom of the Will, vol. 1 of The Works of Jonathan Edwards, ed. Paul Ramsey (New Haven: Yale Univ. Press, 1957). Henceforth cited as FW.

4. On this theme of vengeance, see David Levin's claim that scholars have been blinded to the "human" Edwards by the power of his intellect ("Edwards, Franklin, and Cotton Mather: A Meditation on Character and Reputation," in Jonathan Edwards and the American Experience, ed. Nathan O. Hatch and Harry S. Stout [New York: Oxford Univ. Press, 1988], pp. 34–49).

5. My reading of Edwards diverges here from the line of thought, launched by Perry Miller, that reads Edwards's career and thought as a seamless "system," gathered essentially around a hybrid of the philosophy of John Locke and Neoplatonism. "It is no exaggeration to say that the whole of Edwards's system is contained in miniature within some ten or twelve of the pages in [A Divine and Supernatural Light, Immediately imparted to the Soul by the Spirit of God, Shown to be both a Scriptural, and Rational Doctrine]," Miller claims in Jonathan Edwards (New York: William Sloane, 1949), p. 44. Even though Miller's motives for stressing this tract on the immediacy of the divine light deserve to be treated with suspicion (he discovered it), most scholars have agreed with his reading of Edwards's career as a continuity. The result has been a series of works seeking to distill the essence of Edwards. See, e.g., Douglas J. Elwood, The Philosophical Theology of Jonathan Edwards (New York: Columbia Univ. Press, 1960), who takes "immediacy" as the key to Edwards's thought; and, with a somewhat revisionist intention, Roland Delattre, who focuses on Beauty and Sensibility in the Thought of Jonathan Edwards (New Haven: Yale Univ. Press, 1968). Most recently, see too Sang Hyun Lee, The Philosophical Theology of Jonathan Edwards (Princeton: Princeton Univ. Press, 1988), who traces the importance of the idea of "habit" in Edwards. To my mind, there are ample signs of shifting emphases in Edwards's thought, which are at least as interesting as the "unity" of his system. Of the unitary views, Lee's strikes me as most persuasive.

6. Here I follow those interpreters of Edwards who highlight his continuity with the "federal theology" of New England. See esp. Harry S. Stout, "The Puritans and Edwards," in *Jonathan Edwards and the American Experience*, ed. Hatch and Stout, pp. 142–59.

7. I disagree here again with one predominant trend of Edwards scholarship, which has sought to locate the broader significance of Edwards's work in the philosophical-literary world, and especially in British thought. See, above all, Norman Fiering, *Jonathan Edwards's Moral Thought and Its British Context* (Chapel Hill: Univ. of North Carolina Press, 1982), who makes what to me is a somewhat tenuous claim to find a connection between Edwards and the French philosopher Nicolas de Malebranche. Paul Ramsey may have initiated this approach to Edwards scholarship with his introduction to *The Freedom of the Will* (New Haven: Yale Univ. Press, 1958), in which he identifies the British textual sources most explicitly used by Edwards, while for the most part ignoring the colonial situation.

8. Of course, Edwards pondered the problem of the will throughout his life, and most notably in the *Scientific and Philosophical Writings*, vol. 6 of *The Works of Jonathan Edwards*, ed. Wallace E. Anderson (New Haven: Yale Univ. Press, 1980). See esp. pp. 129–36 of Anderson's introduction. Following Miller, scholars have tended to read *The Freedom of the Will* in light of these earlier writings. See esp. Alan Guelzo, *Edwards on the Will: A Century of American Theological Debate* (Middletown, Conn.: Wesleyan Univ. Press, 1989). I believe these early writings are like the sketches for an oil painting. For all of their interest, the miscellaneous writings on "the will" do not highlight the significance of Edwards on free will as fully as does awareness of the colonial debate leading up to Edwards's work, or as fully as a close reading of the text itself does. Edwards was not just arguing with himself in *Freedom of the Will*. He was not developing his "system" as much as he was attempting to develop a solution to what he perceived to be, in his own words, a distinctly "modern" or contemporary problem.

9. Edwards to Joseph Bellamy, Jan. 15, 1746/47, in "Six Letters of Jonathan Edwards to Joseph Bellamy," *New England Quarterly* 1 (Apr. 1928): 230–31. One of the reasons the significance of this date, and the relation of Edwards's work to the colonial debate, has not so far been appreciated is the fact that one of the leading introductions to Edwards on Arminianism misdates the letter to 1741. See *Jonathan Edwards: Representative Selections*, rev. ed., ed. Clarence H. Faust and Thomas H. Johnson (New York: Hill & Wang, 1962), p. xlii.

10. The original letter from Edwards to Erskine is lost; we depend here upon a recollection of the contents of the letter conveyed by Sereno Dwight, *Memoirs of Jonathan Edwards*, in Edwards, *Works* [BT], 1:xcv.

11. Edwards to Joseph Bellamy, June 11, 1747, in "Six Letters of Jonathan Edwards to Joseph Bellamy," p. 234.

12. Another classical article on Edwards may have dissuaded scholars from tracking down the colonial significance of *Freedom of the Will*. See Thomas H. Johnson, "Jonathan Edwards' Background of Reading," *Publications of the Colonial Society of Massachusetts* 28 (Dec. 1931): 193–222, and esp. pp. 200–201, where Johnson cavalierly dismisses the value of Edwards's correspondence for understanding his thought.

13. Edwards to John Erskine, Aug. 31, 1748, in Edwards, *Works* [BT], 1:xcv.

14. Still, when Jonathan Dickinson died in the midst of writing his *Second Vindication*, Edwards could describe his passing as "a great loss" (Edwards to John Erskine, May 20, 1749, in Edwards, *Works* [BT], 1:civ.

15. Edwards to John Erskine, May 31, 1748, in ibid., p. cii.

16. Edwards to John Erskine, July 5, 1750, in ibid., p. cxx.

17. *FW*, p. 137. Edwards's definition was essentially that of John Locke, and while the entire relation between Locke's *Essay concerning Human Understanding* and Edwards's work is a fascinating problem, here it is simply worth pointing out that Locke, on the basis of his definition, eventually developed in a more "Arminian" direction in subsequent editions of his *Essay*. This may give more credence to the idea that this definition was inherently "mediating." For the heated scholarly discussion on this topic, see Miller, *Jonathan Edwards*; Ramsey, *FW*, pp. 47–65; and, most recently, Norman Fiering, "The Rationalist Foundations of Jonathan Edwards's Metaphysics," in *Jonathan Edwards and the American Experience*, ed. Hatch and Stout, pp. 73–101.

18. *FW*, p. 157. At one point Edwards refers to this as "compulsion or extrinsical necessity" (p. 280). See Ramsey's lucid description of natural necessity as compulsion (p. 37).

19. Ibid., pp. 159, 297, 156, 159. Emphasis added.

20. *FW*, p. 163. Nothing in the *Scientific and Philosophical Writings* anticipated this definition of liberty. Edwards did indicate in his earlier writings an intention to consider the question of "liberty, wherein it does consist" as part of a larger treatise on the mind. And he frequently took up the problem of the will in philosophy (see esp. pp. 348, 352, 375, 385). But none of these writings work out the rigorous definitions found in *FW*. The implications of this are plentiful, but foremost among them is the suggestion that he drew his sense of liberty from nothing stranger than Calvinism.

21. *FW*, p. 164.

22. This definition of liberty has caused some commentators to describe antimaterialism, and particularly fear of being lumped together with the freethinker Thomas Hobbes, as the mainspring of Edwards's attempt to restate the Calvinist doctrine on the will. See Guelzo, *Edwards on the Will*, who claims that Arminians were turning Arminian in order "to avoid being tarred with the brush of Hobbesian determinism," and who claims that Edwards's work was a "defense against atheistic materialism" (pp. 40, 72). In fact, wrote Edwards, "it happens I never read Mr. Hobbes" (*FW*, p. 374). The problem Edwards addressed was not atheism, but a partial, distorted sense of liberty. The debate was between theological parties, not between atheists and theists.

23. *FW*, p. 370.

24. *Remarks on the* Essays on the Principles of Morality and Natural Religion, *in a Letter to a Minister of the Church of Scotland*, in *FW*, p. 457.

25. *FW*, pp. 164–65.

26. *FW*, p. 172. See also Dickinson's use of the same logic, cited in chapter 11 above, and Jonathan Dickinson, *The True-Scripture Doctrine Concerning some Important Points of Christian Faith, Particularly Eternal Election, Original Sin, Grace in Con-*

version . . . Justification by Faith, and the Saints Perseverance (Boston: G. Rogers, 1741), p. 8.

27. *FW,* p. 182.

28. *FW,* p. 185.

29. Again, this was not determinism, because Edwards carefully built an ambiguity into his use of the term *cause.* At times, Edwards spoke of causality as sufficient; at others, showing a kinship with Hume, simply as "connection." The latter notion, which is not incompatible with human liberty, is more distinctive in Edwards, and is therefore the central notion of causality in his work. On this tricky question, see Ramsey, introduction, *FW,* and esp. Clyde A. Holbrook, "Edwards Re-Examined," *Review of Metaphysics* 13 (June 1960): 623–41. See also David Hume, *An Enquiry concerning Human Understanding* (1748; Indianapolis: Hackett, 1977).

30. *FW,* pp. 183–84.

31. *FW,* p. 184.

32. Highlighting this emphasis on "harmony" and "balance" in Edwards, albeit from a theological rather than a cosmological focus, is one of the virtues of Robert W. Jenson, *America's Theologian: A Recommendation of Jonathan Edwards* (New York: Oxford Univ. Press, 1988).

33. Edwards's "occasionalism" is nicely highlighted by Fiering, "Rationalist Foundations of Jonathan Edwards's Metaphysics," in *Jonathan Edwards and the American Experience,* ed. Hatch and Stout, pp. 73–101.

34. The literature on Edwards as a politician is surprisingly scant. On Edwards as a "democrat," see esp. Alan Heimert, *Religion and the American Mind: From the Great Awakening to the Revolution* (Cambridge, Mass.: Harvard Univ. Press); and Roland A. Delattre, "Beauty and Politics: A Problematic Legacy of Jonathan Edwards," in *American Philosophy from Edwards to Quine,* ed. Robert W. Shahan and Kenneth R. Merrill (New York: Oxford Univ. Press, 1975). And for the most egregious example, see David L. Weddle, "The Democracy of Grace: Political Reflections on the Evangelical Theology of Jonathon [sic] Edwards," *Dialog* 15 (Autumn 1976): 248–52. I believe this reading of a "democratic" Edwards results from a confusion of Edwards's intention (reconstructed of course) with the lasting significance of his writing on freedom. For the best reconstruction of the whole of Edwards's social thought, see Gerald R. McDermott, "One Holy and Happy Society: The Public Theology of Jonathan Edwards" (Ph.D. diss., Univ. of Iowa, 1989). On the problem of intention and significance in intellectual history and the history of religions, see Robert A. Segal, "How Historical Is the History of Religions?" *Method and Theory in the Study of Religion* 1 (Spring 1989): 2–19.

35. *FW,* p. 432.

36. In this light, Edwards's *Original Sin,* vol. 3 of *The Works of Jonathan Edwards,* ed. Clyde A. Holbrook (New Haven: Yale Univ. Press, 1970), becomes the logical sequel to *FW,* as it was. If, in fact, Edwards's case against Arminianism depended upon this distinction between the election of a few and the damnation of most, then it was incumbent upon Edwards to show that the conditions for damnation of all were actual, in order to prepare the way for God's grace. *Original Sin* was an indictment of all forms of "innate liberty," and thus was a specification of the critique Edwards began in *FW.*

37. *FW*, p. 436.

38. *FW*, p. 438.

39. *FW*, p. 162. The use of "faculty" language by Edwards is another tricky subject. Perry Miller initiated the tendency to see Edwards's conception of the human as "unified," and while I to some extent agree, at times the emperor seems to be wearing no clothes. Edwards used faculty language freely, and this linguistic fact can only be evaded to a point. A substantial effort is required to read *Freedom of the Will* as "the assertion of the unitary and functional nature of the organism," as Miller claims in *Jonathan Edwards* (p. 254).

40. *FW*, pp. 203, 198.

41. *FW*, p. 204.

42. Edwards developed this facet of his argument in *FW* more fully in *The Nature of True Virtue*, in *Ethical Writings*, vol. 8 of *The Works of Jonathan Edwards*, ed. Paul Ramsey (New Haven: Yale Univ. Press, 1989).

43. *FW*, p. 315. This emphasis on the inherent good may have had roots in the British "moral sense" philosophers. See Mark Valeri, "The New Divinity and the American Revolution," *William and Mary Quarterly*, 3d ser., 46 (Oct. 1989): 741–69.

44. *FW*, p. 325.

45. *FW*, p. 359.

46. *FW*, p. 315.

47. See Jonathan Edwards, *Apocalyptic Writings*, vol. 5 of *The Works of Jonathan Edwards*, ed. Stephen J. Stein (New Haven: Yale Univ. Press, 1977).

48. *FW*, p. 315.

49. See on this theme, among others, the sermon "Wicked Men Useful in their Destruction Only," in Edwards, *Works* [BT], pp. 125–29.

50. *FW*, p. 213.

51. For a contemporary account arguing for the compatibility of morality and contingency, see Martha Nussbaum, *The Fragility of Goodness: Luck and Ethics in Greek Tragedy and Philosophy* (Cambridge: Cambridge Univ. Press, 1986).

52. *FW*, pp. 223–24.

53. *FW*, p. 238.

54. *FW*, p. 255.

55. *FW*, pp. 272–73.

56. *FW*, p. 269.

57. Alongside his appeal to the Saints, an appeal to the Fathers was the fundamental appeal of Edwards's conclusion, thus suggesting again the basic conservatism of his work. See esp. *FW*, pp. 436–37.

Epilogue

1. A notable exception to this trend is the work of the philosophers of action. See esp. Brian O'Shaughnessy, *The Will: A Dual Aspect Theory* (Cambridge: Cambridge Univ. Press, 1980); Robert Dunn, *The Possibility of Weakness of Will* (Indianapolis: Hackett, 1987); and William Charlton, *Weakness of Will* (Oxford: Basil Blackwell, 1988). If the faculty psychology that for so long supported the idea of a

discrete "will" has for the most part been abandoned, the problem of how necessity, chance, and human action relate is as lively as ever in the arts and sciences. See, e.g., Jacques Monod, *Chance and Necessity: An Essay on the Natural Philosophy of Modern Biology*, trans. Austryn Wainhouse (New York: Random House, Vintage Books, 1971); Karl Popper, *The Open Universe: An Argument for Indeterminism* (Totowa, N.J.: Rowman & Littlefield, 1982); *Free Will and Determinism: Papers from an Interdisciplinary Research Conference*, 1986, ed. Viggo Mortensen and Robert C. Sorensen (Aarhus, Denmark: Aarhus Univ. Press, 1987); Martha C. Nussbaum, *The Fragility of Goodness: Luck and Ethics in Greek Tragedy and Philosophy* (Cambridge: Cambridge Univ. Press, 1986).

2. See, for one work that stimulated increased interest in this topic, Keith Thomas, *Religion and the Decline of Magic in Early Modern Europe* (New York: Scribner's, 1971). For the colonies, see David D. Hall, *Worlds of Wonder, Days of Judgment: Popular Religious Belief in Early New England* (New York: Knopf, 1989), and Jon Butler, *Awash in a Sea of Faith: Christianizing the American People* (Cambridge, Mass.: Harvard Univ. Press, 1990).

3. See Hall, *Worlds of Wonder, Days of Judgment*, ch. 2, pp. 71–116.

4. This insight into the power of language has been one of the chief discoveries of the past decade or so of intellectual history. See, among many, Dominick LaCapra, *Rethinking Intellectual History: Texts, Contexts, Language* (Ithaca, N.Y.: Cornell Univ. Press, 1983); Quentin Skinner, *The Foundations of Modern Political Thought* (Cambridge: Cambridge Univ. Press, 1978); J. G. A. Pocock, *Virtue, Commerce, and History: Essays on Political Thought and History, Chiefly in the Eighteenth Century* (Cambridge: Cambridge Univ. Press, 1985); and *The Languages of Political Theory in Early-Modern Europe*, ed. Anthony Pagden (Cambridge: Cambridge Univ. Press, 1987).

5. For the most provocative account of this split between civic and Christian values, see J. G. A. Pocock, *The Machiavellian Moment: Florentine Political Thought and the Atlantic Republican Tradition* (Princeton: Princeton Univ. Press, 1975).

6. For the best survey of the English theological debates, see Dewey D. Wallace, Jr., *Puritans and Predestination: Grace in English Protestant Theology, 1525–1695* (Chapel Hill: Univ. of North Carolina Press, 1982). For a broader picture, see the helpful synthesis by Franklin Baumer, *Modern European Thought: Continuity and Change in Ideas, 1600–1950* (New York: Macmillan, 1977).

7. On this issue of "boundary maintenance," and the creation of new paradigms synthesizing spiritual and political power, see David Chidester, *Patterns of Power: Religion and Politics in American Culture* (Englewood Cliffs, N.J.: Prentice-Hall, 1988), esp. pp. 35–48.

8. Given what we now know about the "peopled" character of the frontier, Turner's frontier thesis is in need of radical revision. Put succinctly, Turner's hypothesis may need to be completely reversed; the frontier, with its conflicts and "chaos," may in its own way have promoted an emphasis on aristocracy, hierarchy, and order; the civilized cities produced the conditions in which responsible political liberty could flourish. Along these lines, see Oscar and Lillian Handlin, *Liberty and Power, 1600–1760*, vol. 1, *Liberty in America, 1600 to the Present* (New York: Harper & Row, 1986), who present the Turner thesis in its original form: the wilderness

promoted liberty. See esp. pp. 23–52. For the original, see Frederick Jackson Turner, *The Frontier in American History* (New York: Holt, 1920).

9. For a highly critical reading of Weber's impact on the historiography of early America, see Thomas L. Pangle, *The Spirit of Modern Republicanism: The Moral Vision of the American Founders and the Philosophy of Locke* (Chicago: Univ. of Chicago Press, 1988), pp. 17–19.

10. Max Weber, *The Protestant Ethic and the Spirit of Capitalism*, trans. Talcott Parsons (New York: Scribner's, 1958).

11. On the separatists, see C. C. Goen, *Revivalism and Separatism in New England, 1740–1800: Strict Congregationalists and Separate Baptists in the Great Awakening* (New Haven: Yale Univ. Press, 1962).

12. Carl Bridenbaugh, *Mitre and Sceptre: Transatlantic Faiths, Ideas, and Politics, 1689–1775* (New York: Oxford Univ. Press, 1962).

13. For a contemporary polemic lamenting the loss of this connection, see Thomas Molnar, *Twin Powers: Politics and the Sacred* (Grand Rapids, Mich.: Eerdmans, 1988).

14. See Sidney E. Mead, *The Lively Experiment: The Shaping of Christianity in America* (New York: Harper & Row, 1963), esp. ch. 2, "From Coercion to Persuasion: Another Look at the Rise of Religious Liberty and the Emergence of Denominationalism" (pp. 16–37).

15. This is essentially the argument of William Lee Miller, *The First Liberty: Religion and the American Republic* (New York: Knopf, 1986). As Miller concludes, "The American democratic society does have metaphysical [I would add, theological] presuppositions. It is not a wholly empty 'process' " (p. 352).

16. Pointing out this confusion has been a central task of my work, which thus lands it, I suppose, in the field of ideology critique. On this topic, see Raymond Guess, *The Idea of A Critical Theory: Habermas and the Frankfurt School* (Cambridge: Cambridge Univ. Press, 1981).

17. Reinhold Niebuhr, *Moral Man and Immoral Society: A Study in Ethics and Politics* (New York: Scribner's, 1932).

18. Edward Shils, *Tradition* (Chicago: Univ. of Chicago Press, 1981), p. 33.

19. Shils has, to my mind, refined this concept in a highly illuminating way. For an earlier attempt to define a "tradition" in American religious history, see Winthrop Hudson, *The Great Tradition of the American Churches* (New York: Harper Torchbooks, 1963).

20. On this notion, see Theodore Dwight Bozeman, *Protestants in an Age of Science: The Baconian Ideal and Antebellum American Religious Thought* (Chapel Hill: Univ. of North Carolina Press, 1977), a work covering an even later period and detailing the compatibility of religion and science in America.

21. See John Ziman, *Public Knowledge: An Essay concerning the Social Dimension of Science* (Cambridge: Cambridge Univ. Press, 1968), pp. 82–83, cited by Shils, *Tradition*, p. 114.

22. Michael Kammen, *People of Paradox: An Inquiry concerning the Origins of American Civilization* (New York: Knopf, 1973), pp. 32–47.

23. Ibid., p. 177.

24. This follows Shils's description of how "the past holds the present in its grip" closely. See Shils, *Tradition*, pp. 195–209.

25. James T. Kloppenberg, "The Virtues of Liberalism: Christianity, Republicanism, and Ethics in Early American Political Discourse," *Journal of American History* 74 (June 1987): 9–33.

26. The most notable recent cases for the impact of Calvinism on the early republic are John P. Diggins, *The Lost Soul of American Politics: Virtue, Self-Interest and the Foundation of Liberalism* (New York: Basic Books, 1984), and Patricia U. Bonomi, *Under the Cope of Heaven: Religion, Society, and Politics in Colonial America* (New York: Oxford Univ. Press, 1986). See also, however, the original manifesto of the "religious" interpretation of the origins of the republic, Alan Heimert's *Religion and the American Mind: From the Great Awakening to the Revolution* (Cambridge, Mass.: Harvard Univ. Press, 1966).

27. The most notable are Bernard Bailyn, *The Ideological Origins of the American Revolution* (Cambridge, Mass.: Harvard Univ. Press, 1967), and Gordon S. Wood, *The Creation of the American Republic, 1776–1787* (Chapel Hill: Univ. of North Carolina Press, 1969).

28. On liberalism, see the dated but still indispensable work of Louis Hartz, *The Liberal Tradition in America: An Interpretation of American Political Thought since the Revolution* (New York: Harcourt, Brace, 1955), and for a more nuanced assessment of the liberal tradition, Joyce Appleby, *Capitalism and a New Social Order: The Republican Vision of the 1790s* (New York: State Univ. of New York Press, 1984). Pangle's *Spirit of Modern Republicanism* offers another variant of the liberal hypothesis.

29. See again Kloppenberg, "Virtues of Liberalism," who details the various disputes, along with Colin Gordon, "Crafting a Usable Past: Consensus, Ideology, and Historians of the American Revolution," *William and Mary Quarterly*, 3d ser., 46 (Oct. 1989): 671–95, who invokes a plague on all three houses for their failure to consider the primacy of economic and class interests in the early republic. Gordon thus draws on the line of interpretation first advocated by Charles A. Beard, *An Economic Interpretation of the Constitution* (New York: Macmillan, 1913).

30. Bonomi, *Under the Cope of Heaven*, is headed in this direction. She claims that "evangelical Calvinism and religious rationalism did not carve separate channels but flowed as one stream toward the crisis of 1776" (p. 188). For a range of interpretations of the revolutionary period, including perspectives on religion, see *The American Revolution: Its Character and Limits*, ed. Jack P. Greene (New York: State Univ. of New York Press, 1987).

31. See again Diggins, *Lost Soul of American Politics*, and Heimert, *Religion and the American Mind*.

32. See esp. Lance Banning, "Republican Ideology and the Triumph of the Constitution, 1789 to 1793," *William and Mary Quarterly* 31 (Apr. 1974): 167–88; *The Jeffersonian Persuasion: Evolution of a Party Ideology* (Ithaca, N.Y.: Cornell Univ. Press, 1978); and "Jeffersonian Ideology Revisited: Liberal and Classical Ideas in the New American Republic," *William and Mary Quarterly*, 3d ser., 43 (Jan. 1986): 3–19.

33. See again Appleby, *Capitalism and a New Social Order*, and Pangle, *Spirit of Modern Republicanism*.

34. Bailyn, *Ideological Origins of the American Revolution*, pp. 37–40. Watts, of course, wrote a work in support of free choice, which Jonathan Edwards found lamentable. See Isaac Watts, *An Essay on the Freedom of Will in God and in Creatures*, in *The Works of . . . Isaac Watts*, ed. D. Jennings and P. Doddridge (London: T. T. Longman, 1853), 6:375–405.

35. Pocock's argument in *Machiavellian Moment* for a continuity of "Florentine political thought" in the "Atlantic republican tradition" behind the American revolution could be duplicated, and with more plausibility, through the history of Christian theology from Augustine to Grotius, and then on into the variety of "Protestant orthodox" theologies in the seventeenth and eighteenth centuries. At the least, the transformation of Western European Christendom into rationalized theological systems and the coincidence of this development with the rise of republics is suggestive.

36. In 1784 Dr. Benjamin Rush, founder of both the American Bible Society and the American Philosophical Society, described the United States as "the Kingdom of Christ and the empire of reason and science" (Rush to Charles Nisbit, 27 Apr. 1784, in *Letters of Benjamin Rush*, ed. L. H. Butterfield [Princeton: Princeton Univ. Press, 1951], cited by Michael Lienesch, *New Order of the Ages: Time, the Constitution, and the Making of Modern American Political Thought* [Princeton: Princeton Univ. Press, 1988], p. 21).

37. See, e.g., Isaac Kramnick, "Republican Revisionism Revisited," *American Historical Review* 87 (June 1982), who concludes that the founders "knew their Locke" (p. 664).

38. Pangle, *Spirit of Modern Republicanism*, notes this ambiguity in the liberal tradition without resolving it. "Americans reached out for harmonizing, compromising formulations that would enable them *to incorporate or exploit* the classical and biblical heritages as apparent precursors, or comfortable allies, of modern natural rights theory," he writes (p. 126). Pangle seems to favor the "exploitation" hypothesis, for he sees this as the basic Lockean move regarding religion. In my reading, the theologians were shrewder than that.

39. Nicholas Tyacke, "Puritanism, Arminianism and Counter-Revolution," in *The Origins of the English Civil War*, ed. Conrad Russel (London: Macmillan, 1973), pp. 119–43.

40. This is the implication at least of Harry S. Stout, "The Puritans and Edwards," in *Jonathan Edwards and the American Experience*, ed. Nathan O. Hatch and Harry S. Stout (New York: Oxford Univ. Press, 1988), pp. 142–59.

41. But see Gordon's telling critique of the "logical, if implausible, acceptance of colonial conspiracy theory" in "Crafting a Usable Past," p. 690. For the most recent updating of this theory, see Gordon S. Wood, "Conspiracy and the Paranoid Style: Causality and Deceit in the Eighteenth Century," *William and Mary Quarterly*, 3d ser., 39 (July 1982): 401–41.

42. Mark Valeri, "The New Divinity and the American Revolution," *William and Mary Quarterly*, 3d ser., 46 (Oct. 1989): 741–69, shows how this logic appeared among "New Divinity" students of Jonathan Edwards in the revolutionary era.

Lienesch, in *New Order of the Ages*, draws from a wider sample and simply labels the earliest origins of the republic as "The Paradoxical Past"; he then centers this portion of his argument around the topics of "sacred and secular history" and "decline and progress." Lienesch's argument is persuasive to me, although somewhat limited by his focus on concepts of time and millennialism. Still, his claim that "a politics of tension" (p. 13) marked the early republic seems to me accurate, as is his assertion that "many eighteenth-century Americans tended to combine the sacred and the secular" (p. 18).

43. See Wood, "Conspiracy and the Paranoid Style," who argues that "never before or since in Western history has man been held so directly and morally responsible for the events in the world," as a way to describe the significance of "the numerous controversies over free will that bedeviled the eighteenth century" (pp. 416–17). See also John Phillip Reid, *The Concept of Liberty in the Age of the American Revolution* (Chicago: Univ. of Chicago Press, 1988), on the understanding of "ordered liberty" that prevailed during these years and the resulting conceptions of the "opposites" of liberty—slavery or bondage (necessity) and arbitrary power (contingence or chance).

44. On the theme of center and periphery, see Jack P. Greene, *Peripheries and Center: Constitutional Development in the Extended Polities of the British Empire and the United States, 1607–1788* (Athens, Ga.: Univ. of Georgia Press, 1986), and Richard Vetterli and Gary Bryner, *In Search of the Republic: Public Virtue and the Roots of American Government* (Totowa, N.J.: Rowman & Littlefield, 1987).

45. For an argument along these lines, adding some contextual weight to the ideal types I assume here, see James H. Smylie, "Madison and Witherspoon: Theological Roots of American Political Thought," *Princeton University Library Chronicle* 22 (1960–61): 118–32. The documents of the ratification debate are conveniently collected in *The Documentary History of the Ratification of the Constitution*, ed. Merrill Jensen et al. (Madison: Univ. of Wisconsin Press, 1976–).

46. Morton White has made it one of his many scholarly aims to explain the "philosophy" behind American politics. White's analyses come to the edge of theology, but seldom delve into that field. See *The Philosophy of the American Revolution* (New York: Oxford Univ. Press, 1978), and *Philosophy, the Federalist and the Constitution* (New York: Oxford Univ. Press, 1987).

47. For the most successful of these monographs, see Robert N. Bellah, *The Broken Covenant: American Civil Religion in Time of Trial* (New York: Seabury, 1975), and William G. McLoughlin, *Revivals, Awakenings and Reform: An Essay on Religion and Social Change in America, 1607–1977*, ed. Martin E. Marty (Chicago: Univ. of Chicago Press, 1978). McLoughlin especially traces very nicely the role of "free will" as a guiding problem in American religion.

48. See esp. Nathan O. Hatch, *The Sacred Cause of Liberty: Republican Thought and the Millennium in Revolutionary New England* (New Haven: Yale Univ. Press, 1977); James West Davidson, *The Logic of Millennial Thought* (New Haven: Yale Univ. Press, 1977); and Ruth H. Bloch, *Visionary Republic: Millennial Themes in American Thought, 1756–1800* (Cambridge: Cambridge Univ. Press, 1985).

49. Bernard Bailyn especially has led the complaints against the tendency of followers of Alan Heimert to find "millennialism" behind the revolution. See for

his earliest broadside to this effect, "Religion and Revolution: Three Biographical Studies," *Perspectives in American History* 4 (1970): 85–172. Bailyn's argument here is particularly effective against the tendency to link religion and the revolution; it does not address the role of theology and the establishment of the republic.

50. Harry S. Stout, *The New England Soul: Preaching and Religious Culture in Colonial New England* (New York: Oxford Univ. Press, 1986), p. 8. Emphasis added. Stout still draws upon the "providential" themes, but he clearly wants to move historians toward a broader understanding of colonial religion.

51. Catherine L. Albanese, *Sons of the Fathers: The Civil Religion of the American Revolution* (Philadelphia: Temple Univ. Press, 1976), p. 80.

52. Sidney E. Mead, *The Lively Experiment: The Shaping of Christianity in America* (New York: Harper & Row, 1976), p. 61, cited by Albanese, *Sons of the Fathers,* p. 126.

53. Albanese especially employs the categories of Mircea Eliade to map out the patterns of belief and practice among the colonial revolutionaries. Interestingly, her work has been given relatively little attention by both secular and religious historians. The reasons for this may be complex, but I would suggest that the fundamental reason may reside in a "utopian" bias among historians of the American revolution and early republic. This is in contrast to the general trend of European religious studies (of which Eliade was of course a transplant), which has been, as Jonathan Z. Smith points out, "locative," focusing on continuities or patterns more than change. American historians have generally been fascinated by dislocations and change rather than relocations and continuity. The fixation of historians on millennialism in the American revolution is a perfect example. For the "locative"/ "utopian" distinction, see Jonathan Z. Smith, "The Influence of Symbols on Social Change," in *Map Is Not Territory* (Leiden: E. J. Brill, 1978), ch. 6.

54. Albanese's treatments of the "Jehovah, God of Battles" and "The Greatest Governor Governs Least," and of the theology of Christian orthodoxy and the Enlightenment, caricature somewhat the complexity of the doctrinal systems of the Calvinists and the Arminians respectively. Similarly, her focus on the documents of the republic as "covenants" nicely sketches the "sacred" character of the documents, while ignoring the texts, intentions, and ambiguities of the documents themselves. See *Sons of the Fathers,* Chs. 3, 4, 6.

55. To my mind, the term *civil religion* denotes a separate "religion," apart from both the churches and the republic, that serves to legitimate the state and demands loyalty from the people; the contention that any such thing existed would, however, have been as difficult to substantiate on the streets of 1760 Boston as in 1991 Chicago. *Public theology* better describes the way in which the religions of the churches, synagogues, and so on nevertheless contribute to defining a facet of the society—in fact, the deep symbolic dimension of the common life of the culture— while still maintaining the prospect of critical distance from the nation. Hence the preference. Essentially, my attempt in this work has been to revive Sidney E. Mead's effort to describe and provide a critique of the "theology of the republic," shorn of Mead's attempt to see this theology as "one big agreed upon thing" over and against schismatic, denominational religion. Mead's central concept of an enlightened "religion of the republic" based upon "synergistic cosmopolitanism" misses the signifi-

cance of the debates and conflicts between religious ideologies in the colonies. In fact, Mead's claim that "all streams of eighteenth-century thought" led to the assertion of human autonomy, or "free choice," actually undercuts his own limitation of the sources of this theology to "enlightened" sources. See Mead, *Lively Experiment,* and especially, *The Nation with the Soul of a Church* (New York: Harper & Row, 1975). For a critique of Mead's exclusion of the denominations from the "republican banquet," see Martin E. Marty, "Public Religion: The Republican Banquet," and "The Classic Public Theologian," in *Religion and Republic: The American Circumstance* (Boston: Beacon Press, 1987), pp. 53–76, 95–122. For a helpful revision of Mead along the lines of "debate," see Franklin I. Gamwell, "Religion and the Public Purpose," *Journal of Religion* 62 (Oct. 1982): 272–88. For the best summation of the results of a decade of work on "public religion," see John F. Wilson, *Public Religion in American Culture* (Philadelphia: Temple Univ. Press, 1979). Wilson is sanguine about any "theological model" of public religion, but his negative evaluation may well have been shaped by Mead's reductionist, Enlightenment approach (he rightly takes Mead to be the leading exponent of this model to date).

56. For an understanding of all theology as "public discourse," or discourse designed to "disclose meanings and truths which in principle can transform all human beings in some recognizable personal, social, political, ethical, cultural or religious manner," see David Tracy, *The Analogical Imagination* (New York: Crossroad, 1981), pp. 3, 55.

57. On the connections between the rhetoric of the Great Awakening and the revolution, see Donald Weber, *Rhetoric and History in Revolutionary New England* (New York: Oxford Univ. Press, 1988), who sees a "fragmentary mode of discourse," somewhat akin to the "rhetoric of fortune" behind both the Awakening and the revolution.

58. Thomas Jefferson, *A Summary View of the Rights of British America,* in *The Writings of Thomas Jefferson,* ed. Paul Leicester Ford (New York, 1892–99), 1:447, cited by Charles B. Sanford, *The Religious Life of Thomas Jefferson* (Charlottesville: Univ. Press of Virginia, 1984), p. 88.

59. As Lance Banning points out, "The quick apotheosis of the American Constitution was a phenomenon without parallel in the western world. Nowhere has fundamental constitutional change been accepted with so much ease" ("Republican Ideology and the Triumph of the Constitution," *William and Mary Quarterly,* 3d ser., 31 [Apr. 1974]: 167–88).

Index

Ability, 81, 113, 129. *See also* Democracy of law; Liberty, innate: ideology of

Absoluteness: of God's decree, 138; of existence, 154

Action, 24, 40, 45, 48, 91, 131. *See also* Morality; Virtue

Affections, 109, 204 n. 19

Africans, 12, 59–60

Albanese, Catherine, 174–75, 187 n. 6, 222 n. 53

Aldridge, Alfred Owen, 196 n. 25

Allen, James, 43, 44

Anabaptists, 36

Anarchy, 12, 176; and American Revolution, 173; Edwards opposes, 155; and King Philip's War, 50; Shepard opposes, 31–36. *See also* Chance; Chaos; Enthusiasm; Extreme(s); Indeterminism

Anaximander, 2

Andrews, Jedediah, 78

Anglicanism, 10, 194 n. 2; in American Arminian controversy, 119, 133–35, 141–44, 149; Checkley and, 64–67;

and democracy of law, 161; Franklin and, 71; growth in colonies, 63, 128; Keith and, 47; Mather opposes, 88; and morality, 160; political interests of, in colonies, 165–66. *See also* Arminianism; Church of England; Democracy of law; Establishment of mediation; Free choice, ideology of

Anti-Calvinism, 10, 82, 191 n. 1, 198 n. 1; Anglican, 63–67, 135–40; and Arminianism, 87; Calvinist response to, 85–86, 90–96, 116; Chauncy on, 115; of Franklin, 77–81; of Johnson, 139; of *New England Courant*, 71; Quaker, 60–62; of Wesley, 129–30. *See also* Arminianism; Democracy of law; Liberty, innate: ideology of

Anticlericalism, 10, 79. *See also* Elites

Anti-extremism, 7, 9–10, 13, 151, 161, 166; and indeterminism, 90, 165; *See also* Establishment of mediation; Extreme(s); Free choice, ideology of; Puritans

Anti-intellectualism, 174

ists charged with teaching, 55, 136–41; of Cotton, 23, 28–30; of Franklin, 72–77; as "heretical" extreme, 166–68; Mather on, 88; and moral life, 55, 129–32. *See also* Antinomianism; Determinism; Necessity; Predestination

Fiering, Norman, 190 n. 24, 213 n. 7

First Cause. *See* God: as creator

Fisher, Mary, 43

Force, 127, 139. *See also* Coercion; Politics

Foreknowledge, 5, 88, 131, 159

Fortune, 39, 95–96. *See also* Chance; Indeterminism; Rhetoric of fortune

France, 5, 172

Franklin, 7, 10, 69–82, 195 n. 6, 195–6 n. 11

Free choice, ideology of, 8, 12, 133–46; in Edwards, 151–61; in eighteenth-century politics, 12, 169–72. *See also* Republic of virtue

Freedom: of action, 48, 91; of agency, 48, 75–77, 130; of choice, 24, 75, 129–31; from coercion, 141, 151–52; of election, 64. *See also* Liberty

Free grace. *See* Grace

Free-thinkers, 124. *See also* Enlightenment, the

Free will, problem of: causes of colonial debate over, 2–6, 165–67; contours of colonial debate over, 12, 42, 82, 86, 116, 161, 191 n. 24; as cultural, 167–70; as political, 5–6, 12–13, 164–65, 170–76, 180 n. 31; as theological, 163–64, 173–76. *See also* Liberty; Public theology

Frontier, 165

Germany, 5

Girard, René, 180 n. 29, 186 n. 48

God, 3, 105–6, 164; and causality, 7–8, 22–23, 47–48, 137–41, 151–56; as creator, 91–92, 137–39, 154; Edwards on, 102–3, 108, 110–11, 147, 159; and fatalism, 72–74; foreknowledge of, 5, 88, 131; as giver of free will, 61, 77–79, 130–31, 176; and grace, 21, 44, 87–90, 97–98; incarnation of, 6, 167; as judge, 139; as moral example, 132; as moral governor, 135–36; omniscience of, 122, 141, 159, 167; power

of, 36, 143; and predestination, 4, 45–46, 64–65, 81, 126; providence of, 10, 39–40, 58–59, 74–76, 90–93; and salvation, 23–24, 26, 61, 123–24, 129; sovereignty of, 27, 139, 147; as Trinity, 17, 181 n. 2; and violence, 6, 11–12, 45, 167. *See also* Causality; Fate; Grace; Predestination; Providence; Theology

Gorton, Samuel, 183 n. 35

Government, 36, 98. *See also* God: as moral governor; Politics

Grace, 4, 12, 96–98, 101; common, 27, 44, 107–8, 113, 127–28, 139–41, 143–44; imputed, 21–25, 78; politics of, 171; special, 40, 122–25, 135–37, 145, 187 n. 8. *See also* Aristocracy of grace; Election; Providence; Salvation

Gravity (Earth's), 91–92

Great Awakening, the, 10, 11, 85–86, 116, 128, 202 n. 11, 203 n. 12; as Calvinist strategy, 123–28; Chauncy on, 104–6, 112–16; Edwards on, 94–97, 101–3, 106–12; and republicanism, 170. *See also* Conversion; Revivals

Greeks, 2–3

Habits, 24, 88, 157, 160. *See also* Morality; Virtue

Hall, David D., 179 n. 27, 181 n. 2

Halley, Edmond, 91–92

Happiness, 78, 144

Hartley, David, 74

Harvard College, 10, 46, 49, 125

Hatch, Nathan O., 191 n. 1, 205 n. 20

Hawley, Joseph, 150

Heathen, 40, 50

Heaven, 20, 100, 106, 113, 145. *See also* Grace

Hedonism, 197 n. 37. *See also* Morality

Hegemony, Calvinist, 11. *See also* Legitimation; Power

Hell, 106, 121, 143, 147. *See also* Reprobation

Hemphill, Samuel, 77–79

Hepburn, John, 60–61

Heresy, 77, 87, 125, 136; as extremes, 168. *See also* Extreme(s); Orthodoxy

Hick, John, 179 n. 28

Hierarchy, 58, 110

234

Books in the Series